Fractured Transitions From School To Work

Fractured Transitions From School To Work

Revisiting The Dropout Problem

Julian Tanner
Harvey Krahn
Timothy F. Hartnagel

Toronto New York Oxford
Oxford University Press
1995

Oxford University Press
70 Wynford Drive, Don Mills, Ontario M3C 1J9

Oxford New York
Athens Auckland Bangkok Bombay
Calcutta Cape Town Dar es Salaam Delhi
Florence Hong Kong Istanbul Karachi
Kuala Lumpur Madras Madrid Melbourne
Mexico City Nairobi Paris Singapore
Taipei Tokyo Toronto

and associated companies in
Berlin Ibadan

Oxford is a trademark of Oxford University Press

CANADIAN CATALOGUING IN PUBLICATION DATA

Tanner, Julian
Fractured transitions from school to work

Includes bibliographical references and index.
ISBN 0-19-541144-7

1. High school dropouts - Canada. 2. High school dropouts - United States. 3. High school dropouts - Employment - Canada. 4. High school dropouts - Employment - United States. I. Krahn, Harvey. II. Hartnagel, Timothy F. 1941- . III. Title.

LC146.8.C2T3 1995 373.12'913'0971 C95-930960-8

Cover photo by Carol Berry

This book is printed on permanent (acid-free) paper ♾ .

1 2 3 4 - 98 97 96 95

Printed in Canada

Contents

Acknowledgements

We gratefully acknowledge the information freely provided by the early school-leavers who participated in this study. Without their assistance, obviously this book could not have been written. We hope that our contribution to policy debates about the 'dropout problem' may, in part, serve to repay them. We also acknowledge the assistance in locating our subjects provided by high-school counsellors, personnel in training agencies, employers, social-service agency personnel, and a number of other Edmonton citizens.

Lawrence Walter completed the largest share of the interviews. His effort and insights added a great deal to the study. We wish to thank him and the other members of the interviewing team (Marie Carlson, Mary-Anne Hendrik, Della Letnes, Leslie Samuelson, and Alice Walter) for their able and essential contributions to this study. Useful library research assistance was provided by Marianne Neilson, Ahmet Oncu, and Lindsay Redpath. Equally important to the success of this study was the highly competent research assistance provided by personnel in the Population Research Laboratory, Department of Sociology, University of Alberta. Cliff Kinzel and David Odynak assisted with data processing, Kelly McGuirk looked after our many typing requests, and Lori Peredery cheerfully completed the huge task of transcribing 162 taped interviews.

Graham Lowe provided a great deal of assistance in planning the study and seeking funding for it. He also contributed useful comments on drafts of several chapters, as did Steve Baron. Ric Kitowski and Euan White from Oxford University Press were very helpful and accommodating throughout the process of producing this book. And Sally Livingston's editorial advice helped to improve the final manuscript.

The largest part of the funding for this study was provided by Alberta Manpower (now Alberta Advanced Education and Career Development), with additional contributions from the City of Edmonton, the University of Alberta, and Solicitor General Canada.

Some of the material discussed in this book has also appeared in Samuelson (1988) and Krahn and Tanner (1995), as well as in papers published in the *British Journal of Education and Work* (Tanner, 1993), the *Canadian Review of Sociology and Anthropology* (Tanner, 1990), the *Journal of Crime and Justice* (Samuelson et al., 1995), *Youth & Society* (Hartnagel and Krahn, 1989), and *Policy Options* (Krahn and Tanner, 1989).

Dedication

To our parents who taught
us the value of education.

JT, HK, TH

CHAPTER ONE

The High-School Dropout Phenomenon

INTRODUCTION

'Dropout disaster'. So read the front-page headline in the *Edmonton Sun* of 7 July 1991. The occasion was a speech on high-school dropouts delivered by the federal Youth Minister, Pierre Cadieux, to the Canadian School Boards' Association national convention in Edmonton. The *Edmonton Journal* reported the event under the headline 'Staggering waste linked to dropouts'. In his speech, Cadieux claimed that 300 Canadian students quit high school each day of the year, for a total of approximately 100,000 dropouts per year. He also stated that Canada's high-school dropout rate was about 30 per cent, making it one of the highest in the industrial world. This high rate, he argued, seriously affected Canada's ability to compete internationally, since the expected one million new dropouts over the next ten years would lack the basic skills needed to get a job in a new economy that demands more highly skilled and educated workers (*Edmonton Journal*, 7 July 1991). These dramatic stories were by no means unique. A week earlier, for example, the same paper had run a special report on the subject under the headline 'Dropout dilemma' (*Edmonton Journal*, 30 June 1991).

Nor were such concerns restricted to the summer of 1991. A year later (11 May 1992), the Youth Minister issued a press release to introduce a new study from the Conference Board of Canada (1992) entitled *Dropping Out: The Cost to Canada*. This report estimated that, with a current dropout rate of 34 per cent, the 137,000 early school-leavers of 1989 alone would cost Canada $4 billion in lost earnings, lost taxes, and additional social-service expenditures over the course of their working lives. In the spring of 1993, a three-day conference on dropouts in Edmonton attracted 1,200 high-school students and teachers from across the country. Reporting on the conference, the *Edmonton Journal* stated that 'studies show three out of 10 Canadian students never graduate from high school, a rate which is the highest in the industrialized world' (15 May 1993). The reporter went on to write that 'the current dropout rate will cost Canada more than $33 billion over the next 20 years in lost economic output and benefits for those who become unemployed'. Almost a year and a half later, in October 1994, another reporter for the same newspaper repeated the 30 per cent dropout figure and reported another frightening statistic: 'Canadian youths received more than $2 billion in social assistance in 1992' (*Edmonton Journal*, 27 October 1994).

These media accounts—and many more could be cited—reveal some of the depth of current public concerns about early school-leavers. A decade or two ago, when dropout rates were actually higher than they are now, educators and journalists alike were similarly worried about the 'dropout problem', disadvantaged youth, and the problems of delinquency. But today's expressions of concern have taken on a different tone, frequently pointing to lost productivity, reduced international competitiveness, and massive drains on the public purse. Today's news stories and research reports also demonstrate the appeal of dramatic statistics, despite obvious difficulties in measuring long-term social and economic costs—indeed, dropout rates themselves—and in making cross-national comparisons. But before looking more carefully at dropout statistics, we should address the basic question of why high-school dropouts cause us such concern.

PUBLIC CONCERNS ABOUT DROPOUTS

High-school dropouts attract media attention in much the same way as do juvenile crime rates and statistics on teenage pregnancies. Portrayed as social problems, as reflections of the failure of social institutions (the school, the corrections system, the family), these subjects make headlines and inspire editorials. But sometimes legitimate concerns grow into 'moral panics' as the media, social-science experts, and public policy-makers rattle statistics, trade adjectives, and point fingers at those groups or individuals who might be seen as responsible for the problem (Cohen, 1972:9).

Is the current dropout situation in Canada a serious social problem? Do current public concerns about high-school dropouts constitute a somewhat overblown moral panic? In our opinion, the answer to both questions is 'yes'. In the following discussion, we identify and assess some of the issues underlying public concerns about young people who leave the secondary-school system without graduating.

Among educators, concern about dropouts is certainly not a recent phenomenon. Charged with educating youth (and evaluated on the basis of standards such as graduation rates), and no doubt concerned about those young people who do not make their way through the school system, teachers and school administrators have long considered it essential to reduce the dropout rate. Recently, however, we have seen many more expressions of public concern, especially by the business community and various government bodies.

Most prominent in Canada has been the five-year, $300-million 'Stay-In-School Initiative' launched by the federal government in 1990. This project was intended to develop and expand labour-market programs and services for those young people most at risk of dropping out; to mobilize business, labour, educators, social workers, parents, and youth to find solutions to the dropout problem; and to increase public awareness of the consequences of dropping out and the realities of the labour market (Employment and Immigration Canada, 1990). For most Canadians, exposure to the Initiative has been limited to the television ad featuring a young male dropout making futile job-search calls from a telephone booth. Less obvious have been the many research projects (including the national School Leavers Survey of almost 10,000 18-to-20-year-old in 1991), conferences, policy analyses, and educational and training programs supported by these federal funds.

Provincial governments have also attempted to respond to the dropout problem. For example, in 1987 the government of Ontario commissioned a major study of high-school dropouts and the relevance of education in the emerging service economy (Radwanski, 1987). Broad reviews of the education system (including consideration of dropout concerns) have been initiated by the Ontario, British Columbia, and New Brunswick governments in the past several years (Ontario Premier's Council, 1990; British Columbia Royal Commission on Education, 1988; New Brunswick Commission on Excellence in Education, 1993). The Quebec and Saskatchewan governments have mounted major anti-dropout campaigns, urging youth to stay in school, and various provinces have undertaken their own analyses of provincial-level data from the 1991 national survey of early school-leavers (e.g., Alberta Advanced Education and Career Development, 1993).

The concerns of the business community have been voiced most clearly through critical assessments of Canada's education and training systems by a number of national 'think-tank', research, and lobbying organizations. In one of its last reports, *A Lot To Learn*, the Economic Council of Canada (1992b:1) elaborated on the connection between a poorly functioning education system (indicated by high dropout rates, among other things) and Canada's economic problems in the global economy:

> To improve productivity, trade performance, and innovation—to improve the overall competitiveness of a firm, an industry, or an entire economy—one of the critical factors is the enhancement of human skills. Indeed, individually and collectively Canadians face a painful choice: develop skills or accept low wages. But this begs the question: Do our systems of education and training enable Canadians to meet this challenge?

Similar comments are found in other recent Economic Council reports on labour-market polarization and Canada's productivity (Economic Council of Canada, 1990:19-20; 1992a:41).

The argument about the relationship between declining global competitiveness and indicators of a (presumed) faulty education system (dropout and illiteracy rates, for example) is echoed in *Reaching For Success* by the Conference Board of Canada (Bloom, 1990), in *Canada: Meeting the Challenge of Change* by the Canadian Labour Market and Productivity Centre (1993), and in *Canada at the Crossroads: The Reality of a New Competitive Environment*, prepared for the federal government by Michael Porter (1991) of Harvard University. Clearly, it was concerns like these that motivated the federal government to 'respond to the serious threat that the secondary school dropout rate poses to the future productivity of the Canadian economy' through its

Stay-in-School Initiative (Employment and Immigration Canada, 1990:14).

However, well before international competitiveness became a public concern in the late 1980s, educators, social workers, and social scientists were worrying about the individual and social consequences of dropping out (Rumberger, 1987; Wehlage and Rutter, 1986). As one literature review put it: 'By leaving high school prior to graduation, most dropouts have serious educational deficiencies that severely limit their economic and social well-being throughout their adult lives' (Rumberger, 1987:101).

Individual consequences of dropping out

In North America, acquiring a high-school diploma is an important rite of passage from adolescence to adulthood. It signifies a change in status and a public recognition of increased independence from parents. More important, the diploma has come to be seen as a ticket into either the adult labour market or institutions of higher learning, graduation from which allows access to higher-status positions in this adult labour market. Thus dropping out of high school disrupts the typical process of transition from school to work, and from adolescence to adulthood.

Accumulated research, much of it conducted in the United States, provides ample evidence of the labour-market disadvantages faced by dropouts, who, compared with graduates, have greater difficulty in finding and keeping jobs, have narrower and more limited job opportunities, are paid less, and earn less in the course of their working lives (Feldstein and Ellwood, 1982; Morgan, 1984; Rumberger, 1987; Lawton et al., 1988). For example, in the United States in the fall of 1982, dropouts from the previous school year had unemployment rates almost twice as high as those who had graduated (Rumberger, 1987). Dropouts who were able to secure year-round, full-time employment still earned from 12 to 18 per cent less than workers who had completed high school.

Ekstrom et al. (1986) used longitudinal data to show that, two years after leaving school, not even one in two dropouts was working either full- or part-time, and that almost one-third were looking for work. Inadequate educational qualifications result in even greater disadvantages over time, since dropouts are less likely than graduates to obtain the additional education and training needed to remain even relatively competitive in the job market. Almost a decade ago, Catterall (1985) estimated a lifetime cost to each dropout of as much as $200,000 in lost wages.

While less research has been conducted in Canada on the individual costs of dropping out, there is still clear evidence of a strong relationship between education and employment prospects. Figure 1.1 provides one indication, showing a consistent pattern over time whereby those young people (aged 15 to 24) with less education are much more likely to be unemployed.[1] In his study of Ontario dropouts, Radwanski (1987:22) cited survey data comparing the earning power of dropouts and high-school graduates that showed an

FIGURE 1.1: UNEMPLOYMENT RATES BY EDUCATIONAL ATTAINMENT, AGES 15 TO 24, CANADA, 1977–1992

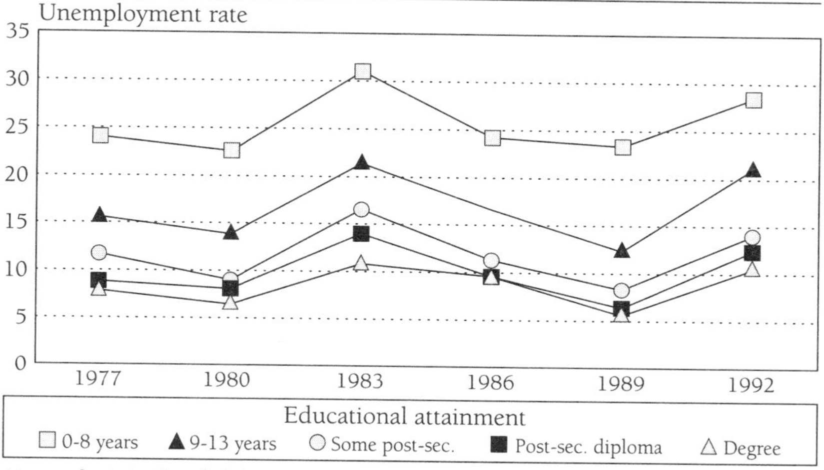

SOURCE: Statistics Canada Labour Force Surveys, annual averages.

average annual income advantage of $3770 for graduates. Dropouts were more likely than graduates to have been unemployed and to have received welfare or social assistance; they also tended to spend about twice as much time unemployed. The more recent national School Leavers Survey (conducted in 1991 and discussed in more detail below) replicated these findings, revealing higher rates of unemployment, lower incomes, and greater reliance on unemployment insurance and social assistance among Canadian youth who had not completed high school (Gilbert, 1993). Summarizing statistics such as these, the Conference Board of Canada (1992) estimated that dropouts lose about $70,000 in income over the course of their lives.

In short, dropouts from high school fare poorly in the labour market, are more likely to remain stuck in poor jobs, and contribute disproportionately to the youth unemployment problem. Unemployment, in turn, has been linked to a wide range of negative effects, including alcohol and drug use, crime and delinquency, and impaired physical and mental health (Brenner, 1976; Kelvin and Jarrett, 1985; Thornberry et al., 1985; Furnham and Lewis, 1986; Burman, 1988; Feather, 1990; Kirsh, 1992). Dropouts have also been shown to have lower cognitive development (Alexander et al., 1985), to experience substantially more personal and family problems, and to receive psychiatric treatment and various forms of public assistance more often than do graduates (Wagenaar, 1987). However, the causal impact of dropping out on subsequent experiences has not been adequately demonstrated. Most of the research has used either a cross-sectional or retrospective design, rather than a longitudinal one, making it difficult to determine whether the alleged effects of dropping out were present prior to that event (Wagenaar, 1987). Even so, it is clear that labour-market disadvantages do accumulate for those who leave school early.

Economic costs of high dropout rates

Over the past few decades, a number of studies have attached very large estimates of societal costs to the 'dropout problem'. Such economic concerns stem from the evidence that early school-leavers generally fare poorly in the labour market and often require some form of social assistance. For example, Levin (1972:ix) estimated a forgone lifetime income of $237 billion for a cohort (aged 25 to 34) of US male dropouts, which in turn would translate into forgone government revenues of $71 billion. Levin (1972:ix) went on to comment that related social-service and criminal-justice costs totalled roughly $6 billion per year. A decade later, Catterall (1985: Table 2) estimated forgone personal income of $228 billion and lost government revenues of $68 billion for female and male dropouts from the American high-school class of 1981.[2] Canadian commentators on the 'dropout problem' have also put forward very large estimates of its societal costs. Recently, for example, the Conference Board of Canada (1992) added up the costs of unemployment insurance and welfare payments, forgone taxes and UIC contributions, along with other social costs, to estimate that the single cohort of dropouts leaving school in 1989 would cost Canada approximately $4 billion over their working lifetime.

Nevertheless, while there are real and, no doubt, large economic costs associated with a high dropout rate, several critical comments about these high estimates are warranted. First, as indicated by the widely differing estimates, there does not appear to be a consensus on what should be counted among the 'costs' of dropping out. Individuals and groups wishing to dramatically highlight the 'dropout problem' can simply broaden their list of potential costs. Second, assuming a consensus on what to count, estimates of long-term societal costs are based on the assumption that dropout rates are accurately measured and that current cost estimates (for unemployment insurance payments, for example) can be projected into the future. Evidence (discussed in the next section) that dropout rates may be lower than we have come to believe; recent changes to Canadian unemployment insurance legislation, reducing payments and eligibility; and strong hints from governments at various levels that other forms of transfer payments may be eliminated to reduce deficits, all point to the shakiness of these assumptions.

Third, the largest share of these high cost estimates is typically attributed to reduced productivity and associated government revenues (mainly income taxes, but also unemployment insurance contributions) because of the high unemployment and underemployment rates found among early school-leavers. The key assumption here is that a high-school diploma would significantly improve employment prospects and income levels. In the past, this was typically true. However, economic restructuring over the past decade has sharply reduced the employment prospects for youth, not only for high-school dropouts but for graduates as well (Myles et al., 1988; Krahn and Lowe, 1990; Morissette et al., 1994). Consequently, while the prospect of reduced income-tax revenues is real enough, some of this forgone government revenue should probably be attributed to the country's 'economic problem' rather than its 'dropout problem'.

In fact, the apparent inflation in dropout cost estimates is probably a function of heightened concerns about Canada's global economic competitiveness and the role of the education system in enhancing productivity (Radwanski, 1987; Bloom, 1990; Economic Council of Canada, 1992b). In brief, the basic argument is that, in the new global economy, capital and technology can be quickly deployed anywhere. Hence the key competitive variable is the quality of the work force, and human-resource development must be a primary policy concern (Reich, 1991; Betcherman et al., 1994). If Canada's education system is inferior to that of other industrialized nations, our international competitiveness will suffer.

As we have already noted, several recent government and 'think-tank' reports have linked this thesis to concerns about high-school dropouts and widespread functional illiteracy in Canada. If the education system could be improved (as indicated by lower dropout and illiteracy rates), productivity would increase and Canada's position in the increasingly knowledge-driven international economy would improve. As the Conference Board of Canada (1992:3) concludes:

> Given the kind of future that is anticipated for Canada, one in which education will play an increasingly important role in emerging technologies, international competitiveness and economic production, action on the high school dropout problem is imperative.

However, such arguments tend to confuse potential long-term processes with more immediate cause-and-effect relationships. It is plausible enough to argue that present investments in education might, in time, translate into new jobs, economic growth, and increased international competitiveness. But to believe that graduating a larger proportion of Canadian youth from high school will quickly improve Canada's global economic position is to ignore two obvious facts: first, more than ten per cent of Canadians are currently out of work; and, second, almost one-quarter of those who are employed report themselves to be underemployed in terms of the skill requirements of their jobs (Krahn, 1992:110). In other words, reduced dropout rates do not automatically translate into increased job creation or an industrial structure with a higher proportion of highly-skilled jobs.[3]

So are current concerns about dropouts and their labour-market options unfounded? Obviously not, although these concerns may be misdirected.

While it is not as apparent as some might believe that lower dropout rates will quickly lead to higher productivity, it is very clear that in a more polarized labour market (Economic Council of Canada, 1990; Krahn, 1992; Morissette et al., 1994), individuals with limited education will be increasingly disadvantaged (Rumberger, 1987). Compared with the situation several decades ago, when a reasonable number of full-time, semi-skilled or skilled occupational positions were available to those with limited formal education, today's labour market is much less welcoming. Hence we believe that the increasingly difficult labour market faced by today's young dropouts constitutes a social problem of growing inequality more than an economic problem of low international competitiveness.

Other social implications of high dropout rates

From a somewhat different perspective, high dropout rates can also be viewed as a threat to the liberal principles on which the educational systems in Canada and the US are based. Equality of opportunity has been the great post-war rallying call for educational reformers (Richer, 1988) in a society where power and position have typically been seen as products of 'contested' upward mobility rather than inherited advantages (Turner, 1960). The goal has been to make 'it possible for anyone, regardless of sex, race, ethnicity, or social class background, to strive for the heights of the educational ladder, and from there to aim for the high status, highly rewarded positions in the occupational world' (Porter et al., 1982:8). Thus long-standing class, racial, and gender inequalities were to be reduced by the expansion of the public education system and by educational policies extending the same schooling opportunities to all children and youth.

However, high dropout rates undermine these policy objectives, particularly when dropouts from the school system share group characteristics such as race or social class. While the principle of equality of opportunity is not threatened by individual differences in educational achievement, group-based variations in educational outcomes are cause for serious concern. A long tradition of Canadian research on status attainment clearly shows that class background does affect educational attainment (Krahn and Lowe, 1993:118-23). Specifically, children from middle-class families are more likely than those from less-advantaged backgrounds to complete high school and to continue in the post-secondary education system.

Recent Canadian studies of dropouts have replicated the finding that lower-class youth (as indicated by parents' education and occupation) are more likely than others to leave school without a diploma (Radwanski, 1987:71; Economic Council of Canada, 1992b:5; Gilbert and Orok, 1993:4). Hence the concerns about dropouts expressed by some educational policy-makers may reflect their recognition of the failure of North American education systems to produce the equality of educational opportunity so central to post-war liberal ideology.

Some observers have taken an even broader perspective, viewing high dropout rates as a potential threat to democracy. Radwanski (1987), for example, argued that a knowledgeable and well-educated population is vital for the effective functioning of a democratic system of government. Over the years, public-policy issues have become increasingly complex. Citizens with insufficient background knowledge are ill-equipped to make informed choices. They tend to be indifferent to the political process or to simply follow those who are persuasive:

> But the workings of a liberal democracy can be well served neither by having an elite of the educated make all the decisions amid the apathy of the uninformed masses, nor by having great numbers of the uninformed steer the direction of society by the whim or emotion of the moment at the behest of various demagogues (Radwanski, 1987:21-2).

The research evidence that complete equality of educational opportunity has not been achieved (i.e., that dropouts are more likely to come from lower-class backgrounds) is clear and extensive. Yet there is little, if any, concrete evidence that dropouts are more politically apathetic than graduates, or more easily led by political 'demagogues'. Nevertheless, this untested hypothesis is both plausible and provocative, and—along with the other individual, economic, and social costs of dropping out discussed above—it could contribute to today's high public concern about the 'dropout problem'.

Summing up this preliminary discussion of why public concerns about dropouts have become more intense, we conclude that at least in one sense these heightened concerns do constitute a 'moral panic'. Stanley Cohen (1972:9) first defined this concept:

> Societies appear to be subject, every now and then, to periods of moral panic. A condition, episode, person or group of persons emerges to become defined as a threat to societal values and interests; its nature is presented in a stylized and stereotypical fashion by the mass media; the moral barricades are manned by editors, bishops, politicians and other right-thinking people; socially accredited experts pronounce their diagnoses and solutions; ways of coping are evolved or (more often) resorted to; the condition then disappears, submerges or deteriorates and becomes more visible. Sometimes the object of the panic is quite novel and at other times it is something which has been in existence long enough, but suddenly appears in the limelight.

As we shall see below, significant numbers of students have been dropping out of school for decades. The situation appears to be improving, however, as the dropout rate has been declining slowly. Educators have long been concerned about early school-leavers, but the issue became a public concern only a few years ago, when it was linked to serious concerns about Canada's faltering economy and its weak position internationally. It is here, in the belief that if dropout rates were reduced substantially Canada would quickly become more competitive in a high-technology, information-based global economy, that we see evidence of a 'moral panic'. Although investments in education and training, including efforts to reduce the dropout rate, would clearly be useful in the long term, it is equally clear that Canada's economic problems are much more complex than such a quick solution implies.

This observation notwithstanding, we still believe that large numbers of young people leaving school without completing even minimal secondary requirements constitute a serious problem. Research from an earlier era showed dropouts suffering more problems of social and psychological adjustment, frequently because of problems in finding satisfactory employment. In today's much more competitive labour market, the opportunities for young people without credentials are even more limited, and early school-leavers will be extremely disadvantaged. Furthermore, since children from less-advantaged families are more likely to drop out of school, a high dropout rate also reflects the reproduction, across generations, of patterns of social inequality. Thus, in our opinion, the 'dropout problem' is much more of a social problem, a problem of perpetuating inequality, than it is an economic problem. The following section will discuss the various attempts that have been made to measure the extent of this social problem.

MEASURING DROPOUT RATES

Although recent media accounts have differed slightly in their reports of the extent of the 'dropout problem' (some say 'three in ten' while others say 'one-third'), most have presented their statistics with the same level of confidence used in reporting unemployment rates, birth rates, and other official statistics. Few have acknowledged that the information on dropout rates in Canada has, until very recently, been no more credible than the American data (Natriello et al., 1986), which, as Rumberger (1987:103) notes, originates in a context where 'no one knows what the high school dropout rate really is'.[4] The data-credibility problem in both countries has resulted from disagreements about the definition of dropouts, differing methods of collecting information, and political pressures to report dropout rates either lower or higher than they really are (Anisef and Bellamy, 1993).

In many studies and school jurisdictions, dropouts are defined as individuals who leave school without obtaining a secondary-school diploma, although there is little consensus on the precise definition of leaving school (for a month? a year?). Even if these individuals later return to complete their high-school education, in a high school or some other post-secondary institution, they are still considered dropouts since, in fact, they have dropped out. Other studies and jurisdictions emphasize high-school completion rather than the act of dropping out, defining as dropouts those who have failed to finish high school. The critical question then becomes the cut-off age (by 18? by 20?). It could also be argued that completion of a college or trade-school training course is equivalent, in a general educational sense, to completing high school. However, credential equivalency seldom figures in discussions of the extent of the dropout problem.[5]

Given these definitional differences, it is not surprising that measurements of dropout rates differ widely across jurisdictions and studies. In some cases, these rates are calculated by dividing the number of students who leave school within a year by the number who began the term (typically, those who leave and return within the year would not be counted as dropouts). An extension of this annual rate calculation involves dividing the number of students within a cohort (of tenth-graders, for example) who leave school before graduation from grade twelve. As simple indices of attrition from specific schools, such measures might be reasonably adequate. But if these rates are meant to index the success of the school or the larger education system, they are less useful, since school records seldom show whether the 'dropout' reappeared in another school. Furthermore, since different school jurisdictions often use different recording methods (Hammack, 1986; Lawton et al., 1988), across-school comparisons can be hazardous.

A third approach, emphasizing completion status and focusing on some broader population (rather than a specific school or district), examines the proportion of a particular age cohort (20-year-olds, for example) who have dropped out at some time, or the proportion who have completed high school. In our opinion, the latter approach is the most useful for assessing the extent of the 'dropout problem': it provides an indication of how many young people eventually acquire minimal educational credentials; it includes as graduates those who drop back into the system and successfully complete high school; and it counts those who obtain their high-school credentials in a non-traditional institution, such as a community college.

Before examining some of the statistics generated by these differing definitions and measures, it is also important to note the political underpinnings of the problems of reliability and validity with regard to dropout rates. As Natriello et al. (1986: 435) state: 'it is often in someone's interest to minimize or exaggerate the dropout statistics, but seldom in anyone's interest to produce precise figures.' To the extent that school funding is influenced by attendance rates, there is clearly an incentive to use measures that show low dropout rates (Wagenaar, 1987).[6] Alternatively, demands for new program funding may occasionally be buttressed by evidence of severe dropout problems in a particular school or district. In short, the politics of the 'dropout problem' must be acknowledged when discussing measurement and definitional issues. As demands for greater accountability in the education system continue to grow (see, for example, Nikiforuk, 1993), we may expect to see more political 'spins' placed on dropout statistics.

Turning to the statistics themselves, we observe that 61 per cent of 15-to-19-year-olds in Canada were enrolled in elementary or secondary schools in 1990-91, an increase from 54 per cent a decade earlier (Figure 1.2). Disaggregating these broad statistics, we see 96 per cent of 16-year-olds,

FIGURE 1.2: ENROLMENT RATES IN ELEMENTARY/SECONDARY SCHOOLS, AGES 16 TO 19, CANADA, 1980–81 AND 1990–91

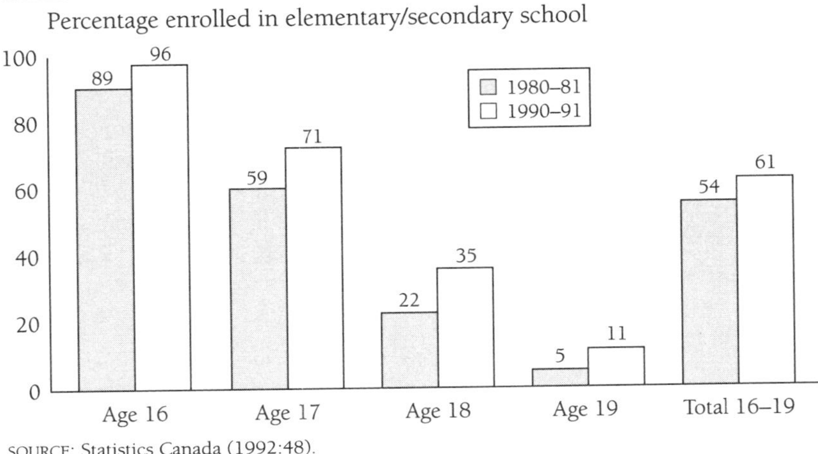

SOURCE: Statistics Canada (1992:48).

71 per cent of 17-year-olds, 35 per cent of 18-year-olds, and 11 per cent of 19-year-olds enrolled in elementary or secondary schools in 1991. For each age group, the percentage has increased since 1980-81 (Statistics Canada, 1992:39-40),[7] providing us with one indication that the Canadian dropout rate may have declined.

However, statistics such as these do not tell the whole story. For example, the 35 per cent of 18-year-olds attending elementary or secondary schools in 1991 appears to be a low figure until we realize that some 18-year-olds would already have graduated from high school. In fact, 24 per cent of that age cohort were enrolled full-time in post-secondary institutions in 1990-91 (Statistics Canada, 1992:130), and a smaller proportion would have been attending colleges, trade schools, and universities part-time. And the 1991 Canadian Census revealed that 80 per cent of 15-to-19-year-olds were attending school full-time (all forms of education), up from 66 per cent a decade earlier (Statistics Canada, 1993:1).[8] Consequently, other types of statistics are needed to give a more complete picture of the extent of early school-leaving in Canada.

Looking at Ontario data from the early 1980s, Radwanski (1987:68-70) estimated a dropout rate of 33 per cent, noting that only 67 per cent of the students who had entered grade nine in 1981 graduated four years later, in 1985. He arrived at a similar figure by multiplying by four the annual rate of students dropping out of high school (roughly 8 per cent), and noted as well that 31 per cent of 22-year-old Ontario residents identified in the 1981

Census had not completed grade twelve. His conclusion that the Ontario dropout rate was in the 31 to 33 per cent range is probably the source of most recent media reports of dropout rates.[9]

Denton and Hunter (1991) reported that the Ontario dropout rate had declined over the last 50 years,[10] but also suggested that it may have stabilized in the early 1980s and then increased slightly towards the end of the decade. Replicating Radwanski's (1987) 1985 finding, Denton and Hunter (1991) reported a 1987 retention rate of 68 per cent of the students who had enrolled in grade nine four years earlier. However, like Radwanski (1987:68), they also acknowledged that this approach probably overestimates the dropout rate, since it doesn't take into account those students who take more than four years to graduate, who leave and subsequently return, and who may be lost through death or migration.[11]

As we noted earlier, renewed concerns about the 'dropout problem' at the end of the 1980s prompted the federal government (Employment and Immigration Canada) to sponsor the 1991 School Leavers Survey (Statistics Canada, 1991). This study was designed to provide estimates of dropout rates as well as to collect information on the socio-demographic characteristics of dropouts, their reasons for leaving school, and their labour-market experiences. Instead of relying on administrative data from schools, this study surveyed a very large national sample of youth aged 18 to 20 about their educational experiences and attainment. Hence the estimates of dropout rates that it provides are probably closer to the real rates than are the earlier estimates discussed above.

To conduct the School Leavers Survey (SLS), Statistics Canada drew (from the Family Allowance File) a stratified random sample of 18-to-20-year-olds living across the country. A total of 9,460 young people were interviewed by telephone between April and June 1991 (see Gilbert et al., 1993, for additional details about the research design). Some of these individuals had graduated from high school (and some had gone on to further education), others were still attending (including some who had dropped out and returned), and others had dropped out (and not returned). The survey results clearly call into question the 'one-third of high school students drop out' generalization that has been part of most recent discussions of the 'dropout problem'.

Specifically, considering only 20-year-olds (who, compared with 18- and 19-year-olds, would presumably report the highest rate of 'ever dropping out'), 24 per cent stated that they had dropped out of school at some point in their past (28 per cent of males and 19 per cent of females). For the complete sample (all 18-to-20-year-olds), a total of 21 per cent had dropped out at some time. But not all of these individuals had stayed out of school. In fact, 47 per cent of these 'dropouts' (aged 18 to 20) had returned to school some time later. Of course not all of them had gone on to graduate. Nevertheless, 21 per cent of those who had 'dropped back in' had subsequently graduated, and another 27 per cent reported that they were still working towards obtaining a high-school diploma.[12]

In short, the 1991 SLS reveals that about one in four young Canadians *ever* drops out of school, and that not all of these individuals stay out. Fewer than one-fifth (18 per cent) actually fail to complete high school (Gilbert et al., 1993:16), rather than the one-third so frequently cited. The overestimates may have resulted from measurement strategies that overlooked the fact that many young people take an extra year to complete grade twelve, ignored those individuals who drop back into the education system, and could not track those who leave one school and enrol in another. Although the occasional newspaper headline has acknowledged that the 'School dropout rate [is] far less than 30 per cent' (*Edmonton Journal*, 30 May 1993), it is likely that the powerful 30 per cent figure will remain part of the 'dropout' discourse for some time to come.[13]

Because of its cross-sectional design, the 1991 SLS cannot tell us whether dropout rates are declining. But comparisons between the 1981 and 1991 Canadian Censuses reveal that the long-term trend towards higher graduation rates is continuing. In 1991, 18 per cent of Canadian 20-year-olds had not completed grade twelve and were not attending school (Gilbert et al., 1993:12), a figure that exactly matches the dropout rate estimated from the SLS of the same year. A decade earlier, the comparable figure was 29 per cent (Gilbert et al., 1993:13). Although there have been suggestions that in the mid- to late-1980s the dropout rate may have increased slightly (Denton and Hunter, 1991; Sunter, 1993:49), the severe recession that began in 1991 has probably again reversed the trend, encouraging more young people to stay in or return to school.[14]

To sum up, dropout rates have been notoriously difficult to estimate; different definitions, different measurement approaches, and political influences have all been partially responsible for this problem. However, the large national School Leavers Survey of 1991 appears more reliable than most. It suggests that the dropout rate may be considerably lower than the standard 30 to 33 per cent estimate, and demonstrates that, in many cases, dropping out is not an irreversible educational choice. Only about one in five fails to complete high school. This lower dropout rate also calls into question the huge estimates of long-term economic costs to society, suggesting that they also may be 50 per cent too high. However, even if the rates (and economic costs) are lower than we have been led to believe, current data still reveal that about one in five young Canadians enters the adult labour market with a severe educational handicap.

WHO IS MOST LIKELY TO DROP OUT?

What kinds of students are most likely to drop out of high school? Until recently, most research addressing this question, much of it from the United States, has focused largely on the personal characteristics of dropouts. While useful, such an approach can leave the impression that the roots of the dropout problem are primarily individually-based: that is, young people drop out because they are not motivated, are not committed, or do not have the required skills or career expectations. In other words, this approach can lead to 'blaming the victim' (Ryan, 1976), to the conclusion that dropouts themselves are largely at fault for not being sufficiently committed to education. Structural factors including characteristics of schools, curriculum content, and the changing character of the labour market may receive less attention. Hence it is important to balance the traditional focus on individually-based causes with a careful examination of structural causes.

Student and family characteristics

The accumulated research from both Canada (Radwanski, 1987; Denton and Hunter, 1991; Gilbert et al., 1993; Sunter, 1993) and the United States (Natriello et al., 1986; Wehlage and Rutter, 1986; Rumberger, 1987; Wagenaar, 1987) clearly demonstrates that certain background characteristics are associated with the probability of leaving school prior to graduation. Specifically, the students most likely to drop out are males, individuals from lower socio-economic backgrounds, those doing poorly in school, those in lower academic streams, those reporting themselves to be more alienated from school and less interested in education in general, those working an excessive number of hours while attending school, and those with single parents. Obviously, a number of these characteristics overlap. For example, students doing poorly in school may be working more hours than others, while individuals from lower socio-economic backgrounds tend to be placed in non-academic streams within their high schools.

Replicating a finding reported in most overviews of dropout statistics (e.g., Denton and Hunter, 1991; Rumberger, 1987; Wagenaar, 1987), the 1991 SLS revealed that among 18-to-20-year-old Canadians no longer attending school, 24 per cent of males had dropped out, compared with 16 per cent of females (Sunter, 1993:45).[15] Males are more likely to say that they have left school for work-related reasons (Gilbert and Orok, 1993:3), suggesting that they are more often enticed to leave by the possibility of earning more money and attaining adult status through a full-time job. However, one should not conclude from the higher male dropout rate that young women are necessarily more committed to formal education. Given gender differences in socialization and parental control, males alienated from the education system may be more likely to react by dropping out, while equally-alienated females may tend to stay enrolled in school but put little effort into their studies.

The relationship between social class and the probability of dropping out of high school is well-documented (Radwanski, 1987:71-4; Wagenaar, 1987). For example, Denton and Hunter (1991) reported that children of poorly-educated parents in unskilled or semi-skilled occupations were more likely than others to leave school before graduating. The 1991 SLS demonstrated that dropouts were more likely than graduates to have at least one parent with limited formal education, and to have parents in blue-collar occupations (Gilbert and Orok, 1993:4).

According to the 1991 survey, dropout rates tend to be higher in rural areas, and are particularly high among aboriginal youth (Gilbert et al., 1993:22-3). Along with the higher rate among aboriginal youth, Denton and Hunter (1991) reported higher dropout rates among those born outside Canada; this pattern was reversed in the 1991 SLS, which revealed lower rates among immigrant youth (Gilbert et al., 1993:23). Nevertheless, the general pattern of findings suggests that the effects of social class and minority status are probably intertwined (Wagenaar, 1987). On the other hand, several studies have suggested that social class is really the primary factor. Commenting on US statistics, Wehlage and Rutter (1986) reported that race is a poor predictor of dropping out, once the effects of socio-economic background are taken into account. Analyzing Ontario dropout data, Radwanski (1987) noted that racial differences disappeared when length of residence in Canada was statistically controlled. Immigrant groups typically have been able to better their socio-economic position within a few generations of arriving in Canada.

Although the relationship between socio-economic background and dropping out is clear enough, there has been little systematic research on the underlying processes that produce this pattern (Wehlage and Rutter, 1986; Rumberger et al., 1990). Like Wagenaar (1987), Radwanski (1987:73-4) speculates that children from less-well-off families have both fewer educational advantages and fewer role models who have gone on to higher education, and are responding to lower educational and occupational aspirations on the part of their parents. In other words, the same factors that lead larger proportions of children from more affluent families to go on to higher education (Krahn and Lowe, 1993:118-23) also account for the fact that more dropouts come from less-advantaged families. In the language of Pierre Bourdieu (1986), middle-class youth bring more 'cultural capital' to school: they are more likely to speak like their teachers, to be comfortable in a verbal and symbolic environment, to already know something about the subjects being taught, to have additional skills (e.g., music training), and to have access to educational resources in their homes (Teachman, 1987).

From this perspective, it also follows that differences in educational attitudes and performance (which are strongly associated with the chances of dropping out) have an underlying class basis. Among other findings, the 1991 SLS showed that 48 per cent of 18-to-20-year-old dropouts reported difficulty in mathematics, compared with 39 per cent of graduates. More than one-third (37 per cent) of dropouts had experienced difficulties in English (or French, if this was their first language), versus only 17 per cent of graduates. Only 8 per cent of graduates had failed a grade in elementary school, compared with 36 per cent of dropouts. And only 10 per cent of graduates reported that they did not enjoy school; the figure for dropouts was 41 per cent (Sunter, 1993:46). Most other studies of dropouts have revealed similar patterns (e.g. Wagenaar, 1987; Radwanski, 1987:78-81). For example, Denton and Hunter (1991:133) reported that Ontario students in the Basic and General streams were five times as likely to leave school before graduation as those in the Advanced academic stream.

A number of studies have linked part-time work and the probability of dropping out of school. Given that almost half of all Canadian high-school students work part-time while attending school (Cohen, 1989; Lowe and Krahn, 1992; Sunter, 1992, 1993), this is obviously not a sufficient cause. But working an excessive number of hours may increase the probability of dropping out. Radwanski (1987:81) suggested that more than fifteen hours per week of paid work is problematic, while some American studies have set the limit at twenty hours (D'Amico, 1984; Greenberger and Steinberg, 1986:117).

Using twenty hours as the cut-off and data from the 1991 SLS, Sunter (1993:48) showed that few hours of work were associated with a lower risk of dropping out, while excessive hours increased the chances of dropping out for males, but not for females.[16] Further research on these gender differences is warranted, as are studies on the cause-and-effect relationship underlying these statistical correlations. While excessive hours of work can clearly interfere with school performance (and so increase the chances of dropping out), it is also quite likely that young people with little interest in school are more likely to seek paid employment. In other words, it is difficult to tell which is the cause and which the effect.

There is a fairly consistent pattern whereby children from homes with two parents present are less likely to drop out. The 1991 SLS revealed that 83 per cent of graduates lived with both parents, compared with only 61 per cent of dropouts (Gilbert and Orok, 1993:4). One in four dropouts lived with a single parent, while 13 per cent lived with neither parent. Again, the underlying causal patterns are not all that clear. Since single parents typically have much lower incomes, socio-economic disadvantages may be part of the explanation. Single parents forced to maintain the family income while looking after all household and parenting responsibilities would quite likely also have less time to assist children with school work (Radwanski, 1987:74-6).

Finally, there are a number of individual (psychological) factors associated with dropping out (Rumberger, 1987). Dropouts appear to exhibit lower self-esteem and less sense of control over their lives. They expect lower levels of educational achievement and have lower occupational aspirations. However, as Wehlage and Rutter (1986) point out, there are not enough consistent measures of these concepts to allow strong generalizations. Furthermore, it is not clear if low educational/occupational aspirations, low self-esteem, negative school attitudes, and an external locus of control are brought to the school or are produced by negative school experiences. Socio-economic background could be part of the explanation, with young people from less-advantaged backgrounds exhibiting lower self-esteem and reporting lower educational and occupational aspirations. Thus, once again, the precise causal role of these psychological factors in the process of dropping out has not been demonstrated.

School characteristics

Given the large variations in dropout rates between schools and across school districts—differences that remain even after variations in student characteristics are taken into account—it seems improbable that the causes of dropping out reside only within individuals (Lawton et al., 1988). However, compared with research on individual characteristics of dropouts, relatively little attention has been paid to the influence of schools, their organization, leadership, teachers, and teaching methods (Rumberger, 1987).

It is unlikely that this research gap stems from a deliberate oversight on the part of educational researchers. Rather, the cost of conducting large-scale studies of schools—studies that compare schools in a variety of different settings, that look at both student and school characteristics, and that attempt to seriously examine phenomena as complex as 'leadership' and 'teaching method'—is probably the main reason why so few have been completed. Although recent studies such as the 1991 SLS have a national scope, they provide individual-level data that cannot be easily aggregated to describe specific schools. Similarly, the large national longitudinal studies conducted in the United States provide little information on school structure and educational processes (Natriello et al., 1986). Even if such studies ask about the school environment, as some do, the data still come from students' (or former students') observations and opinions, which would not be as reliable a source of data as systematic independent assessments of school organization and normative environment (Bryk and Thum, 1989).

However, intensive case studies of schools have shown that school organization does have a significant influence on learning (Chubb and Moe, 1990). Purkey and Smith's (1983) review of 'effective schools' research suggested that organizational variables such as clear school goals, rigorous academic standards, order and discipline, homework, strong leadership by the school principal, teacher participation in decision-making, parental support and co-operation, and high expectations for students were correlated with effective school performance. Furthermore, a second phase of the longitudinal High School and Beyond survey in the United States, which collected data describing school organization and environment from principals and teachers, basically replicated findings about the organizational features of effective schools and emphasized school autonomy, or freedom from bureaucratic controls as a critical prerequisite for the emergence of such schools (Chubb and Moe, 1990).

Thus the relationship between dropout rates and the institutional and normative character of schools is a critical research issue. In fact, some of the links between individual characteristics and dropping out (discussed above) may actually reflect the impact of structural factors. For example, Wagenaar

(1987) notes the obvious fact that wealthier families generally live in wealthier neighbourhoods, where more money is typically available for education. This, in turn, translates into better facilities and teaching resources, as well as more specialized services, and may also attract and retain more highly skilled and motivated teachers. In other words, a substantial part of the association between class background and dropping out might be traced to the difference in educational resources available in middle- and lower-class neighbourhoods.

Looking beyond differences in material resources to the school (and neighbourhood/community) social (and learning) environment, Lawton et al. (1988) analyzed questionnaire responses of administrators and teachers from 58 secondary schools in six Ontario school districts varying in student population, income level, and administrative structure. The study revealed that a positive image of the school in the community, a strong academic curriculum, high expectations by teachers for all students, high levels of collaboration among teachers, and time spent with students outside classes all were associated with lower dropout rates. Radwanski's (1987) prescriptions for reducing the dropout rate in Ontario schools showed a similar emphasis, stressing the importance of developing a school environment where personal relationships between students and teachers were encouraged.

In the United States, McDill et al. (1986) identified two general factors that appeared to describe schools with high dropout rates. The first was 'urban social disorganization': large schools, in large cities, with high proportions of students from minority groups, and located in communities with high unemployment, high crime, extensive poverty, and many single-parent families. The second key factor concerned school administrative problems and the social environment within schools, as indicated by poor teacher-administration co-operation, teachers who emphasized maintaining control over instructional objectives, students' perceptions that rules were not clear or fair, and large numbers of students with little commitment to conventional social rules.

McDill et al. (1986) concluded by emphasizing the importance of *school size*: smaller schools with low student-adult ratios typically have fewer problems because students are less anonymous, classes are smaller, schedules can be more flexible, and the student body is more homogeneous. Closely linked to school size as a critical variable was *curriculum structure and content:* an individualized curriculum and instructional approach are crucial for preventing the sense of academic failure and low self-esteem that are characteristic of dropouts. McDill et al. (1986) also highlighted three important components of *school climate*: governance, the system of academic rewards, and a normative emphasis on academic excellence by students, teachers, and administrators. Clear rules, consistently enforced are essential for maintaining an orderly environment, which in turn fosters academic achievement. The system of academic rewards must be attainable by potential dropouts and must be contingent on their effort and proficiency. A normative emphasis on academic excellence at both the school and classroom levels promotes student achievement and motivation, and so can influence dropout rates.[17]

Fine's (1986) ethnographic study of dropouts from a single comprehensive high school in New York City leads to similar conclusions about the effect of structural factors on dropout rates. The school she studied was overcrowded, which heightened student alienation and anonymity, and racial differences within the school were pronounced. The school also suffered from a district funding strategy that did not assist schools struggling with dropout problems but instead financially punished those schools performing poorly. In general, a profound sense of powerlessness was evident on the part of teachers, paraprofessionals, school aides, students, and parents alike.

In sum, the social organization of schools, school size and resources, and the social and educational climate within schools all appear to play powerful roles in influencing dropout rates. A clearer understanding of how school characteristics affect students can help to clarify some of the relationships between individual student characteristics and the probability of dropping out.

Until recently, research has tended to focus more on individual characteristics than on school-based factors. But with the growing number of commentaries on the link between dropout (and illiteracy) problems and economic competitiveness (reviewed earlier in this chapter), we have begun to see more criticisms of the education system itself. This shift in attention—away from dropouts, towards the institutions they have rejected—is probably useful, so long as the lessons of previous research are not lost. As the studies reviewed above have documented, a strong academic environment and high performance standards are important, but so too are sufficient resources and the fostering of strong, supportive relationships between students and their teachers. To some extent, recent criticisms have focused more on performance and standards, and less on providing the resources needed to develop an educational climate in which these standards can be met by a larger number of students.[18]

SELF-REPORTED REASONS FOR DROPPING OUT

In our discussion of the characteristics of students who are more likely to drop out, and of schools that tend to have higher dropout rates, we have tried to highlight some of the underlying causes of early school-leaving. But this picture is still incomplete: while individual and school characteristics may increase the probability of leaving school before graduation, they do not necessarily explain *why* a young student decides not to return to school. Hence it is useful to examine students' own reasons for dropping out. Their definition of the problem(s) that led to the decision to leave school—if in fact they saw the decision as a solution to a problem—can give us another valuable perspective on the dropout phenomenon.

Analysts of data collected from studies asking dropouts why they left school typically separate the answers to this question into three general categories: school-related, employment-related, and personal reasons. Like most other studies (Radwanski, 1987; Rumberger, 1983; Ekstrom et al., 1986), the 1991 SLS revealed school-related reasons to be most common (Gilbert et al., 1993:27). When asked to identify the most important factors in their decision to drop out, over 40 per cent of dropouts gave a school-related reason. Within the broad category of school-related reasons, boredom and hating school were mentioned more often than difficulty with school work or problems in getting along with teachers. Radwanski (1987:88) observed the same pattern in his Ontario study, noting that a general dislike of school, lack of interest in what was being taught, and boredom were mentioned more often than was difficulty with course material.

As Radwanski (1987:87) argues, school-related reasons are probably under-estimated in surveys such as this, since, when stating other reasons (taking a full-time job, for example), dropouts are frequently making an implicit comparison with school as a less attractive, important, or satisfying alternative. Radwanski also suggests that, along with boredom and a sense that course material is irrelevant, a crucial factor influencing the decision to drop out is the perception that the school system responds with indifference or hostility to weak performance. Potential dropouts may, on average, have greater difficulty with their studies, but 'a sense of having been rejected or ignored by the education system' (1987:89) is more often the critical factor.

Second in importance to negative feelings about schools, teachers, and course material are employment-related reasons for dropping out. Thirty per cent of the dropouts surveyed in the SLS left school to take a job, although only about one in four of these individuals stated that this choice was made out of financial necessity (Statistics Canada, 1991). As Radwanski (1987:96) observes, many young students are attracted to employment (as an alternative to school) not because they have to support themselves, but because a job represents adult status, money, and freedom, particularly if they feel rejected or frustrated by school. And, as was implied earlier, employment-related reasons for dropping out are not entirely distinct from school-related reasons: 'The strong drawing power of the work place is inversely proportional to the weak holding power of the high school as it currently functions' (Radwanski: 1987:98-9).

Personal reasons for leaving school—a broad category that includes problems at home, emotional difficulties, poor health, pregnancy, and marriage, among other reasons—were mentioned by about one in six (13 per cent) of the dropouts questioned in the 1991 SLS.[19] Problems at home, among the most frequently cited personal reasons, can upset or distract students, causing their school work to suffer, their self-esteem to drop, and their interest in school to decline (Radwanski, 1987). Excessive conflict within the home and abuse by parents or other family members may also force some students to leave home, which in turn may require them to seek employment and drop out of school.

While some earlier studies suggested that males were more likely than females to report school-related reasons for dropping out (Rumberger, 1983; Ekstrom et al. 1986), the 1991 SLS showed similar proportions of females and males giving this type of response (Gilbert et al., 1993:41). However, as in other studies, males were more likely to state employment-related reasons (38 per cent, compared with 16 per cent of females). On the other hand, 20 per cent of young women in this sample mentioned personal reasons, compared with only 6 per cent of males (Statistics Canada, 1991). Among the females listing personal reasons, almost half had left school because of pregnancy or in order to get married, a pattern also observed in the United States by Wehlage and Rutter (1986). Thus, as Wagenaar (1987) notes, some of the gender differences in reasons for dropping out reflect traditional gender-role socialization: males are more likely to leave school to work, while females are more likely to leave to take on a domestic role. In both cases, dropping out represents the replacement of a subservient student role by an independent adult role and status.

EXPLAINING THE PROCESS OF DROPPING OUT

Reviews of typical characteristics of dropouts and of schools with high dropout rates, and of self-reported reasons for leaving school before graduating, reveal the complexity of the dropout problem. In fact, the more closely one looks at such data, the more apparent it becomes that simple, single-factor explanations of how and why young people drop out of school are inadequate. As Mann (1986:7) concludes: 'The singular outcome—not finishing high school—is in fact a nest of problems.' Elaborating on this point, Wagenaar (1987:165) writes: 'The precursors to dropping out, the decision to drop out, the process of dropping out, the responses to dropping out, and the consequences of dropping out all result from a complex interplay of personal, social, situational, structural, and contextual factors.'

These comments suggest several basic strategies for developing a more complete understanding of the dropout phenomenon. First, instead of focusing immediately on one or two 'causes' of the dropout problem, we could learn more from a larger list of the many factors associated with variations in dropout rates, at the individual, family, school, community, labour-market, and government-policy levels. Following from this, it is essential to try to separate real 'causes' of dropping out from those factors that are better seen as symptoms of an underlying and more basic problem. Nevertheless, it is also important to recognize that, in some ways, the typical dropout may not be all that different from the typical graduate (Gilbert and Orok, 1993). Many students encounter difficulties in school, but only some drop out. Hence, rather than seek characteristics that set dropouts clearly apart, it may be more useful to think about the factors that increase the risk of leaving school before graduation. Finally, while it may be simpler to view dropping out as a single decisive act, it is probably more appropriate to see this act as only one event in a process of gradual disengagement from the education system, beginning long before the student finally fails to return to school.

In our discussion above, we have already begun to categorize the factors associated with dropping out, recognizing the need to look beyond individual causes towards a more comprehensive explanatory model (Rumberger, 1987; Rumberger et al., 1990). For example, Natriello et al. (1986:437) propose a reciprocal model of the relationship between the personal and socio-economic characteristics of students and their school environment. In such a model, background characteristics determine the kinds of schools and educational environments to which students have access. In turn, different types of schools tend to attract different types of students.[20]

Rumberger (1987) emphasizes the powerful cumulative influence that family background can have on school achievement through the kinds of schools attended, negative or positive attitudes about school, and the additional learning that takes place in the home. More recently, Rumberger et al. (1990) have suggested that the families of dropouts and the families of students who graduate exhibit at least three differences. First, dropouts are more likely to come from families with a permissive parenting style; consequently, they are more likely to make important decisions on their own. Second, parents of dropouts are more likely to use negative sanctions and emotions in response to their children's academic performance. Finally, parents of dropouts report that they were less involved with their children's schooling. Thus, from the perspective of the family, '[w]hat most distinguishes dropouts from other low-achieving students who stay in school is the higher levels of educational involvement by both the parents and the children who stay in school' (Rumberger et al., 1990:295).

Focusing more on school experiences, Radwanski (1987:89-94) describes how a feeling of rejection by schools and the education system develops over time. Looking back at their elementary-school years, three-quarters of the dropouts in an Ontario sample described this time as excellent or good. But fewer than half said the same thing about their time in high school. Radwanski attributes some of this dissatisfaction to the cumulative disadvantages encountered in high schools by students from lower socio-economic backgrounds who, typically arriving with more limited educational experiences, are soon 'streamed' into non-academic programs. The impersonal nature of many large high schools accents the emerging problem, as potential dropouts slowly lose interest in schooling and begin to withdraw from active participation in the educational system. LeCompte and Dworkin (1991) discuss similar processes, describing how some students begin to 'give up on school' when they recognize that it will probably not provide them with the life-style they expected.

Finn (1989) described two developmental models of withdrawing from school. The 'frustration-self-esteem' model identifies school failure as the starting point in a cycle that includes reduced self-esteem and may culminate in the student's rejecting, or being rejected by, the school. The 'participation-identification' model focuses on students' involvement in schooling, suggesting that participation in school activities leads to successful school performance, which in turn leads to an identification with school and a greater likelihood of successful completion. These are not alternative theoretical models so much as complementary pictures of how cumulative negative school experiences can increase the probability of dropping out. When we broaden our view to include the effects of socio-economic background and family structure and processes, we can begin to understand the complexity of the dropout phenomenon.

According to the 1991 SLS, 41 per cent of dropouts described most of their classes as 'not interesting', compared with 21 per cent of graduates (Sunter, 1993:46). Half of the dropouts in this large sample of 18-to-20-year-olds said they had not participated in extracurricular activities (versus 28 per cent of graduates), and 75 per cent admitted skipping classes in their final year (versus 59 per cent of graduates). Many dropouts just disappear over the summer, with 40 per cent reporting that they quit school in June (Statistics Canada, 1991). Almost half left without talking to anyone about the decision. Among those who did discuss it, most talked to parents; discussions with teachers or counsellors were conspicuously absent (Alberta Advanced Education and Career Development, 1993:46).

Thus it is apparent that negative attitudes toward school might be more usefully seen as symptoms of underlying problems rather than primary causes of dropping out (Rumberger, 1987; Lawton et al., 1988). Similarly, dropping out might be more accurately seen as a single, not necessarily decisive, act in a long-term process of gradual disengagement from school, a process that, as we noted earlier, sometimes involves quitting school, returning, and then dropping out again. Nevertheless, these statistics also remind us that, like potential dropouts, many graduates appear uninterested in school, and participate in only a cursory manner. It may not be helpful to overemphasize the factors that distinguish dropouts from graduates. In fact, the 1991 SLS also revealed that roughly half of the dropouts surveyed subsequently regretted their decision to leave school (Gilbert et al., 1993:33) because it had handicapped them in the labour market. Thus, while their interest in school was not strong enough to keep them there, many dropouts still appear to recognize the value of formal education.

ANOTHER STUDY OF DROPOUTS?

We began this introductory chapter by commenting on the high level of public concern about dropouts. Dropouts have been viewed as a social problem long before now, but there appears to be a new tone to the commentary today: specifically, a suggestion that by solving the dropout (and illiteracy) problem, Canada may be able to become more competitive in the global economy. We remain sceptical about this argument, not because we disagree about the long-term value of investments in human resources, but because we are also acutely aware of the high rates of unemployment and underemployment in Canada today. If a larger proportion of Canadian youth were to graduate from high school, the jobs they might desire would not necessarily materialize. In short, the Canadian labour market has become a more difficult place, particularly for those individuals with limited education. Hence, although we do view the dropout phenomenon as a social problem, we are especially concerned with the long-term implications for young people with few labour-market options. In addition, since young people from lower socio-economic backgrounds are more likely than others to leave school before graduating, we also view the dropout phenomenon as part of the process whereby social inequalities are perpetuated.

Our review of the research literature on high-school dropouts revealed, first, a lack of consensus about how to define dropouts and measure dropout rates. Obviously, different definitions are useful for different reasons, but it is important to be aware that not all school systems, and not all those who comment on the dropout problem, are using the same definition. It is equally important to recognize that the information base from which dropout rates are calculated is frequently less than satisfactory, and that the actual dropout rate may be considerably lower than the 30 per cent that appears to have become a social fact.

The literature review also identified the important individual, family, and school characteristics associated with high dropout rates, as well as the types of reasons dropouts tend to provide for their decision to quit school. Finally, it pointed to previous research findings showing that dropping out is typically only one event in a long process of withdrawal from the educational system. Why then, knowing so much about high-school dropouts, would we want to write about the results of another study?

There are a number of answers to this question. First, most of the research on high-school dropouts has been conducted in the United States. Our study is one of few recent in-depth Canadian studies addressing this issue.[21] Second, much of the research on high-school dropouts is somewhat dated. Industrial restructuring and workforce 'downsizing' in many organizations in the past few years have made the labour market even less hospitable to high-school dropouts. Hence a study examining the post-dropping-out experiences of a recent cohort of early school-leavers could be very useful. Moreover, the vast majority of dropout studies have focused on family backgrounds and personal characteristics of dropouts, on school experiences, and reasons for quitting; very few have looked in detail at the subsequent labour-market experiences of dropouts, their interactions with family and friends, their living arrangements and life-styles, and their goals and aspirations. Finally, to a large extent, previous research has focused on male dropouts, and we believe that a more gendered analysis of the phenomenon is needed.

Our study of dropouts was conducted in Edmonton, Alberta, in late 1984 and early 1985, a time of high unemployment in that city. By the late 1980s, unemployment rates had declined, and presumably the labour-market opportunities for dropouts improved somewhat. But in 1995 the unemployment rate is again up around 10 per cent, part-time and temporary jobs have become even more common, and, as was the case when our interviews were completed, young dropouts are among the most disadvantaged labour-market participants. Thus we believe that the employment situation for young people without secondary-school credentials is at least as difficult today as it was when we collected our data, if not more so.

As the next chapter will explain, we conducted semi-structured interviews with 162 young women and men who had left school before completing grade twelve. Some were still teenagers, others were young adults who had left school a number of years earlier. In our interviews, we built on previous research by asking about reasons for leaving school, parents' reactions to this decision, dropouts' current feelings about leaving school, and their attitudes and opinions regarding formal education. However, we also went well beyond this set of questions to enquire about labour-market experiences, including job-search behaviour, job satisfaction, and reactions to unemployment. In addition, we asked about current living arrangements and life-style, relationships with family and friends, opinions about youth unemployment, and personal goals and aspirations. In short, we tried to go beyond questions about *becoming a dropout* to address questions about *being a dropout.*

After elaborating on our research design, we begin our analysis with a discussion of the process of becoming a dropout, from the perspective of the dropouts themselves. The next three chapters address dropouts' labour-market experiences, commenting on job-search behaviours and experiences, reactions to jobs that typically offer few material and psychological rewards, and experiences of and reactions to unemployment. In Chapter 7 we shift our attention to questions about dropouts and delinquency, examining the illegal activities reported by some of the sample members. Chapter 8 delves deeper into the minds of our sample members by asking about their future goals and aspirations. Finally, we conclude by summarizing the more important findings from this study and commenting on some of their policy implications.

NOTES

[1]The unemployment rates in Figure 1.1 are annual averages, based on monthly estimates from Labour Force Surveys conducted by Statistics Canada. Obviously some of those in the 9-to-13-years-of-education group were still attending school. Their inclusion in these estimates probably makes unemployment rates lower than they would otherwise be.

[2]The estimates from Levin (1972) and Catterall (1985) are both cited by Rumberger (1987:115). For similar US estimates, see Wagenaar (1987:163).

[3]See Boothby (1993) for a similar critique of current concerns about the 'literacy problem' in Canada.

[4]For discussions of variations in dropout rates in the United States, see Rumberger (1987), Ekstrom et al. (1986), and Wagenaar (1987).

[5]Substantial numbers of students failing to complete programs of study in post-secondary institutions (colleges, trade schools, and universities) could also be viewed as a serious 'dropout' problem. However, this issue has received relatively little public attention.

[6]An extreme case of statistical distortion is reported by Hammack (1986) who describes an American school with a self-reported 'official dropout rate' of 1.9 per cent. The rate calculated by the central office was 58.3 per cent!

[7]The growing number of teenagers who take an extra year to complete grade twelve probably accounts for part of the increase in 18- and 19-year-olds enrolled in secondary schools.

[8]More than nine out of ten 15 year-olds (91.9 per cent), a similar proportion of 16-year-olds (90.2 per cent), 86.7 per cent of 17 year-olds, and 78.6 per cent of 18 year-olds were attending school either full- or part-time, according to the 1991 Census (Statistics Canada, 1993:144).

[9]See Lawton et al. (1988) for a critical assessment of Radwanski's analysis of dropout rates in Ontario.

[10]See Grant (1976) for a discussion of the long-term (1870 to 1970) increase in high-school graduation rates in the United States.

[11]Alternatively, this approach may be a slight underestimate, since it ignores students who drop out before grade nine. Denton and Hunter (1991:133) also discuss the annual 'retirement rate'—the percentage of students who leave the system each year without having graduated—noting that it increased from 11.8 per cent in 1981 to 13.3 per cent in 1987.

[12]These statistics are drawn from a number of different analyses of the 1991 School Leavers Survey including Gilbert et al. (1993), Gilbert (1993), Gilbert and Orok (1993), Statistics Canada (1991), Alberta Advanced Education and Career Development (1993), Anisef and Bellamy (1993), and Sunter (1993).

[13]For example, a 1994 compendium of 'background facts' on the Canadian social-security system reported that 'approximately 30% of students drop out of high school in Canada' (Human Resources Development Canada, 1994a:41).

[14]Sunter (1993:49) reports a decline in the dropout rate (estimated from school records) between 1990 and 1991, following an increase between 1983 and 1987. In 1992 the national youth labour-force participation rate declined to a 15-year low of 60.5 per cent, probably because large numbers of young people were returning to school to improve their labour-market options (Cross, 1993).

[15]When the analysis is restricted to 20-year-olds, the dropout rates are 22 per cent for males and 14 per cent for females (Gilbert and Orok, 1993:3).

[16]For males, the dropout rate for those with no job was 25 per cent, compared to 16

per cent for those working fewer than 20 hours per week, and 33 per cent for those working longer hours. For females, the equivalent figures were 22, 7, and 18 per cent, respectively (Sunter, 1993:48).

[17]Wehlage and Rutter (1986) reach similar conclusions, arguing that weak school authority, a climate of low expectations, large school size, and an absence of supportive relationships with teachers all lead to higher dropout rates. Bryk and Thum (1989) suggest that strong academic norms and an orderly school environment lead to reduced dropout rates, while an overly-diverse student body and too much differentiation in programs offered can have the opposite effect.

[18]For example, raising standards, increasing the mandatory time students must spend in school, introducing standardized testing, and other similar 'solutions' could increase the dropout rate, if the resources needed to assist students are not provided (McDill et al., 1985; Natriello et al., 1986).

[19]Fourteen per cent of the dropouts listed a wide variety of 'other' reasons in response to this question about the most important reason for leaving school prior to graduation.

[20]In the United States, Ekstrom et al. (1986) used data from the longitudinal High School and Beyond study to test a complex theoretical model relating demographic background of students, including race, family support for education, sophomore-year school ability and attitudes, and student behaviour at school to the decision to stay in or drop out of school.

[21]Radwanski's (1987) Ontario study and the 1991 national School Leavers Survey (Gilbert et al., 1993) are examples of recent Canadian studies of dropouts.

CHAPTER TWO

Research Design

INTRODUCTION

This study was undertaken in a time and setting in which young labour-force participants, particularly high-school dropouts, were encountering a very difficult labour market. Data were collected in late fall of 1984 and the first few months of 1985 in Edmonton, Alberta, a large western Canadian city with a population of around 600,000. During the 1970s and early 1980s, the local economy had expanded rapidly, largely because of increases in international oil prices. But heavy dependence on oil also meant that the recession of the early 1980s had a devastating effect on the local labour market.

Unemployment rates both in the province and in Edmonton, the capital city, had been as low as three or four per cent at the height of the economic boom, far below the national average. But the oil-driven provincial economy collapsed quickly, in classic boom-to-bust fashion. By 1984, the provincial (annual average) unemployment rate was 11.2 per cent; it dropped to 10.1 per cent in 1985.[1] In Edmonton (annual average) unemployment rates went even higher, to 14.1 per cent in 1984, before declining to 12.2 per cent in 1985.

Youth unemployment rates have typically been somewhat higher than adult rates, and this recession was no exception. The provincial annual average unemployment rate for teenagers (15 to 19 years old) was 18.2 per cent in 1984, compared with 15.4 per cent for young adults (20 to 24). But while the labour-market situation in Alberta had improved marginally for young adults by 1985 (their unemployment rate dropped to 12.9 per cent), the teenage unemployment rate actually rose to 19.6 per cent (1985 annual average). Estimates of unemployment among young dropouts in Edmonton during this period are not available, since Labour Force Survey estimates are not provided for such specific groups within a single local labour market. However, they were no doubt considerably higher than the overall averages, probably well above 20 per cent.

Thus both the setting and the timing of the study provided a useful opportunity to explore some of the critical questions about high-school dropouts, their early exit from the education system, and their experiences in the labour market. Is this group particularly vulnerable in times of recession and economic restructuring? How do they look for work, and what kinds of labour-market entry problems do they encounter? How do they cope with, at best, marginal jobs and frequent periods of unemployment? Do young people drop out of school because they see little connection between what they are learning and the demands and opportunities of a changing job market? Does the experience of unemployment lead dropouts to further devalue education? Does it dampen their ambitions, lead to alienation, or, perhaps, make them more critical of the ways in which the education system and society as a whole are organized? Is greater alcohol use associated with unemployment? Does joblessness lead to drug use, or other criminal activity? These and other questions are addressed in the following chapters.

SAMPLING

In 1980-81, the annual high-school dropout rate in Alberta was estimated to be about twelve per cent (Figure 2.1).[2] The rate dropped to 9.5 per cent for the 1981-82 school year, and then fluctuated between this level and 8.3 per cent for the next seven years. The 1989-90 annual dropout rate was estimated at 7.5 per cent, while the 1990-91 statistics showed a further decline to 6.3 per cent (Alberta Education, 1992:52). Recognizing the difficulties in trying to calculate and interpret dropout rates (see Chapter 1), it is still possible to conclude that dropout rates in the province appeared to decline in the early 1980s, perhaps because of the onset of the 1981-82 recession. The fact that jobs were much harder to get than they had been only a year or two earlier, when the provincial economy was booming, may have persuaded some potential dropouts to stay in school.[3]

FIGURE 2.1: ANNUAL DROPOUT RATES (STUDENTS AGED 14 TO 18) AND ANNUAL AVERAGE UNEMPLOYMENT RATES (AGES 15 TO 19), ALBERTA, 1981 TO 1991

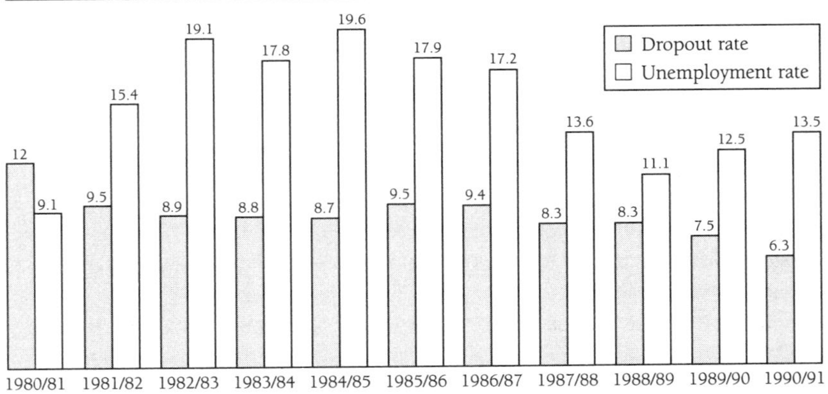

NOTE: Dropout rates are for the school year (e.g., 1980–81) while unemployment rates are for the calendar year (e.g. 1981).

SOURCES: Alberta Education (1992) and Statistics Canada Labour Force Surveys.

Many, but not all, of the young people interviewed in our study would have been among the dropouts whose decisions to leave school underlie these aggregate Alberta statistics. However, since we deliberately tried to include some older dropouts in our sample, a few respondents would have left high school prior to 1980. And because we did not restrict our interviews to young people who had begun high school in the province, our sample also included a few individuals who had moved to Alberta after dropping out of high school in another province.

While a random sample of dropouts would have been preferable, it was impossible to construct a sampling frame from which a random sample could be drawn. As we observed in the previous chapter, few high schools keep accurate records of students who have left, and any social-service agency that might work with dropouts would invariably be dealing with a non-representative group. Consequently, a non-random quota sampling technique was used to contact 168 individuals who had quit high school in the previous few years.

Gender and employment status are two important sources of variation in the experiences and coping responses of young dropouts. We attempted to balance female and male, as well as employed and unemployed, subjects in the sample. We also wanted to include both dropouts who had been in contact with social-service agencies and those who had not, suspecting that the intervention of social-service and job-placement agencies might shape the labour-market behaviours of sample members, as well as their interpretations of their circumstances.

Living arrangements were also of interest, since they reflect both the stage of transition from youth to independent adult status and the resources and support networks available to young dropouts. Hence we attempted to include some dropouts living with their parent(s), others living alone, with friends, or in a cohabitation or marriage relationship, and still others living in shelters or hostels. In addition, we deliberately set out to interview some dropouts who had returned to high school, recognizing that these individuals might have unique insights into the experience of dropping out and seeking employment.

Rather than rely entirely on a 'snowball' sampling technique to provide the respondent variation we sought, we constructed a sampling grid that identified a target sample of approximately two hundred young dropouts, spread across the various categories identified above. As the interviewing progressed, we monitored the characteristics of the emerging sample, attempting to fill the various cells in the sampling grid. The desired quota sample was constructed over a period of about four months, as we managed to contact and interview 168 dropouts (producing 162 usable interviews).

Our search for a diverse sample of dropouts took us in many directions. About one-quarter of the sample members were individuals contacted directly by members of the research team (Table 2.1). Some of these dropouts were identified as potential respondents by co-workers, friends, and neighbours of research-team members, while others were referred by dropouts already interviewed ('snowball' sampling). Still others were approached at their place of employment (restaurants, shops, and other workplaces where we thought dropouts might be employed).

TABLE 2.1. SAMPLE COMPOSITION BY SOURCE

	%	N
Personal contacts	27	43
High-school personnel	17	27
Job clubs/training programs	14	23
Educational institutions	13	22
Social-service agencies	11	17
Hostels/shelters	9	15
Correction centre/parole officer	9	15
Total	100	162

High-school personnel (principals and counsellors) in several schools provided lists of young people who had recently left their schools. In addition, interviews were conducted with a number of dropouts who had re-entered the educational system, either to complete high school in an alternative setting (Alberta Vocational Centre, Alberta College) or to pursue a trade (Northern Alberta Institute of Technology [NAIT]). Some dropouts were located in government-sponsored 'job clubs' and job-training programs, while others were found and interviewed in hostels or shelters. Social-service agencies provided some referrals, as did a probation officer, and a small number of dropouts were interviewed while serving time in the Belmont Correctional Centre.

INTERVIEWING

When first contacted, potential respondents were given a one-page summary that explained the study and invited the individual to participate. If willing, the subject would be interviewed (at the time, or at a later date) in a public place (usually libraries, restaurants, or shopping malls) or in the hostel, school, or agency where the initial contact had been made. Virtually all contacted individuals agreed to participate in the study. Members of the research team, along with half a dozen trained assistants (most of them graduate students in sociology), did the interviewing.

Semi-structured interviews were chosen as the primary method of data collection on the grounds that they could best illuminate the experiences and opinions of these young people. While there were clearly some central issues that the research team wished to address, semi-structured interviews could incorporate new themes and questions as this somewhat exploratory study proceeded. An interview guide containing lead questions and possible 'probes' was used to ensure that nine key topics were covered (see Appendix 1). While interviewers were instructed to address each of these areas, preferably in the order of their appearance in the guide, they were free to add questions, move away from sensitive areas, reorder and rephrase questions, and follow up new leads. Interviews ranged from around thirty minutes to over an hour in length.

After the interview, respondents were also asked to complete a short questionnaire including a limited number of demographic, labour-market, social-psychological, and deviant-behaviour measures (see Appendix 2). This self-report instrument provided a cross-check on some of the key information to be obtained through the interviews. It also allowed the inclusion of a few standardized attitudinal questions, and provided a more anonymous means of reporting alcohol and drug use, as well as criminal activities. All but five of the 162 dropouts who participated in the interviews also completed the questionnaire. Before beginning the study, both the interview guide and the questionnaire were examined and approved by a University of Alberta Research Ethics Review Committee.

In the event that interviewers might be asked for advice on obtaining social assistance, or finding a job or a place to live, or in case the discussion appeared to upset the respondent, interviewers were given an extensive list of counselling and social-service agencies to which they might refer respondents. However, use of this referral list was not required. Despite the inclusion of possibly sensitive questions about school and work problems, relationships with parents, and deviant behaviour, respondents appeared comfortable answering the questions or skipping those they did not wish to answer. To ensure anonymity, all identifying information about respondents was destroyed after the interviews were completed.

DATA ANALYSIS

The taped interviews were transcribed into computer files, providing the researchers with the option of analysis via micro-computer or on paper. In addition, a content analysis of the transcripts was undertaken, and a second quantitative data set was constructed from the textual data (see Krahn, 1990, for details). This data set was then merged with the already quantified data obtained from the self-report questionnaires. This approach allowed us to analyze the textual material in the traditional manner—that is, by reading the transcripts in a search for patterns—while also undertaking simple quantitative analyses of the interview and the questionnaire data.

By combining data from semi-structured interviews with quantitative survey data, we obtained a detailed and nuanced view of the experiences, behaviours, and opinions of dropouts. Nonetheless, some topics were not covered as comprehensively as others in each interview, since some respondents spoke at length on some subjects (e.g., reasons for leaving school) but were less forthcoming on others (e.g., their interactions with the criminal-justice system). Similarly, for some respondents, interviewers followed up 'leads' with additional questions, while in other cases little or no information was obtained on similar topics. Thus, while each of the nine key topic areas was addressed in each interview, there are variations in the sample size for specific questions included in the interview guide.

In the following chapters we will move back and forth between the self-report questionnaire data, the quantified textual material, and the verbatim transcripts. At times we rely heavily on the transcripts themselves: for example, when we discuss the complexities of dropouts' relationship with the educational system. Elsewhere we use selective quotations to highlight patterns observed in the questionnaire data. The discussion of psychological health in Chapter 6 and the analysis of deviant behaviour in Chapter 7 are two examples. Rather than restrict ourselves to a single method of data collection and analysis, we employ these multiple methods to improve our understanding of the dropout phenomenon.

SAMPLE CHARACTERISTICS

Just over half of the respondents were male (N = 82). The majority of these dropouts (85 per cent) were between the ages of 17 and 23 when interviewed. The youngest had just left school, at age 15; the oldest, at 26, had been out of school for almost a decade. On average, both females and males were 20 years old when interviewed and had been out of school for about three years.

Nine in ten sample members had completed grade nine and, 69 per cent had managed to finish grade ten, but only 36 per cent had stayed in school until the end of grade eleven. Female sample members were somewhat more likely to have stayed in school this long. As was noted in our discussion of sample composition, some of these young dropouts (N = 22) had made their way back into the education system by the time we interviewed them.

Over half of the sample (58 per cent of males; 52 per cent of females) were living with their parents when interviewed. One in ten (11 per cent) of the female respondents were living with other family members, compared with 6 per cent of the male sample members. Most of the others were living with friends (17 per cent of males; 11 per cent of females) or with their spouse/partner (16 per cent of the women; only 8 per cent of the men). Only a small minority of these dropouts were living alone (11 per cent of males; 10 per cent of females).

Most studies of dropouts reveal that teenagers from lower socio-economic backgrounds are less likely than others to finish high school (Rumberger, 1987:110; Radwanksi, 1987; Gilbert et al., 1993). It is not surprising, then, to find that many of these interviewees reported that their mothers (47 per cent) or fathers (50 per cent) had not finished high school. Only one in four respondents came from a family in which no one had been unemployed in the recent past. However, despite this over-representation of lower-status origins, 27 per cent reported a mother with a managerial or professional occupation, and 26 per cent had a managerial or professional father.

Since questions about unemployment were central to the design of this study, the sample was deliberately constructed to include equivalent numbers of employed (47 per cent) and unemployed dropouts (53 per cent). However, unintentional sampling outcomes resulted in a somewhat larger proportion of unemployed males.[4] Almost four in ten (37 per cent) of the 76 employed sample members were working part-time when interviewed.

While this sample of dropouts is relatively evenly balanced in terms of gender, and reflects considerable variation in age, employment status, living arrangements, and contact with employment or social-service agencies, it is still a non-random sample. There is no definitive way of determining whether it is really representative of the population of dropouts. Nevertheless, with respect to key socio-economic characteristics, our sample appears quite similar to Radwanski's (1987) Ontario sample and to the sample of dropouts interviewed in the 1991 national School Leavers Survey (Gilbert et al, 1993).[5] Thus while this study should not be used to generate precise estimates of, for example, the unemployment rate among dropouts, the size of the sample and the considerable variation within it makes it a very useful data source for examining the experiences, opinions, and behaviours of young dropouts in a difficult labour market.

NOTES

[1]Annual average unemployment rates are calculated from the Labour Force Surveys conducted every month by Statistics Canada and reported in Statistics Canada (1989).

[2]Alberta Education (1992:52) defines the *annual dropout rate* as the percentage of students aged 14 to 18 who begin a school term in September of a given year but are not enrolled the following September, excluding those who have successfully completed their program.

[3]The 1991 national School Leavers Survey reveals that only 14 per cent of 20-year-old Albertans had left school without completing grade twelve and not returned, compared to 16 per cent in British Columbia and Saskatchewan, 17 per cent in Ontario, and 19 per cent in Manitoba (Gilbert et al., 1993:16). Equivalent estimates for the remaining provinces were 20 per cent or higher. Since the 20-year-olds interviewed in 1991 would have begun high school about the time our data were collected (1984-85), these national statistics describe a somewhat more recent era. Nevertheless, they suggest that the incidence of dropping out of high school is somewhat lower in western Canada.

[4]Ten of the sample members (eight females) were referred from a 'job club' in which all participants had been helped to find a job. Another ten (seven males) were inmates in a youth correctional centre when interviewed, and so were classified as unemployed (even though, technically, they were out of the labour force). Thus, while the quota sampling technique produced a sample with almost equal numbers of males and females, and of employed and unemployed respondents, the inclusion of these two unusual groups led to the greater number of unemployed males.

[5]Unlike our study, which included some older (up to age 26) dropouts, the 1991 School Leavers Survey interviewed only 18-to-20-year-olds.

CHAPTER THREE

Becoming a Dropout

INTRODUCTION

As was noted in Chapter 1, many attempts to explain why some young people leave secondary school before graduating have focused on the personal or background characteristics of dropouts themselves. These explanations have frequently assumed that distinctive personality characteristics, or the social and cultural environments that dropouts come from, influence their ability to learn and their response to schooling. Thus the fact that dropouts disproportionately come from lower working-class homes or single-parent families has often led to the conclusion that these backgrounds are in some way responsible for the dropout phenomenon.

Characterized as a 'deficit model of educational failure' (Flude, 1974), this type of explanation has been criticized on several accounts. First, the nature of the deficits and the ways in which they might affect school achievement are seldom clearly specified. Do students drop out of high school because of an economically-deprived home environment, or because of a lack of cultural capital? In other words, is it the absence of material resources in the home that is primarily responsible, or are these young people mainly disadvantaged by the fact that they have not learned the language and values, and acquired the skills and behavioural repertoires, of middle-class teenagers? Second, and more important, the deficit model can quickly become an exercise in blaming the victim. From this perspective, students from lower-status families, and their parents, may be seen as personally responsible for the economic and culture deprivations and deficiencies that can lead to under-achievement in school.

Moreover, the concentration on students' backgrounds limits consideration of other critical factors affecting dropout behaviour—particularly the institutional structure of, social environment in, and curriculum offered by high schools. More recent research has somewhat reduced this imbalance by focusing in more detail on the school experiences and performance of dropouts. As a result, we are now able to identify a wide range of factors that are related to early school-leaving. We know, for example, that many dropouts leave school with poor grades as well as negative feelings about teachers and the curriculum, that they are less likely to have been enrolled in academic-stream programs, and that they tend to be frequent truants and holders of part-time jobs. We also have a somewhat better understanding of the types of school environment that appear to translate into higher dropout rates.

It is less clear, however, how these school-based factors actually influence the decision to drop out—or, indeed, whether they are primary causes or merely symptoms of some broader problem. For example, research demonstrating that school size, teaching resources, social climate within the school, and teachers' expectations of students are important correlates of dropout behaviour (see Chapter 1) may also reflect the indirect effects of social class, since teenagers from more-advantaged backgrounds typically attend better schools. Similarly, while a history of skipping classes often precedes the act of dropping out, and is therefore a useful predictor of that outcome, is it best seen as a cause, or simply as another indicator of estrangement from school culture? And do part-time jobs increase the chances of dropping out, or are they simply particularly attractive to those students who already have a weak attachment to schooling?

Whether the focus is on dropouts' social origins or the experience of high school, much of the research on dropouts also suffers from being descriptive rather than analytic. It is easier to describe the structure of educational inequality than to explain how these patterns emerge or are maintained over time. Recognition of this explanatory problem has encouraged research that concentrates on the process whereby adolescents from working-class backgrounds become more likely than middle-class adolescents to respond to schooling by leaving prematurely. Do working-class youth tend to drop out mainly because of cumulative disadvantages—that is, are they largely pushed out of an educational system weighted against them?—or do they perhaps actively participate by ultimately rejecting the values of this middle-class system?

In this regard, the writings of Paul Willis (1977) have been very influential. Willis investigated the process of school rejection by observing, and participating in, the activities of a small group of working-class adolescent males in the English Midlands. His goal was to discover why a working-class background predicts a working-class future, despite the intervention of an educational system whose manifest purpose is to break the connection between origins and destinations. While mass education is intended to provide the same educational opportunities to all young people, whatever their class background, the fact remains that teenagers from less-advantaged backgrounds are much more likely than their more-advantaged counterparts to leave school before graduating.

Although the connection between class background and early school-leaving may be more pronounced in Britain, above-average dropout rates among working-class youth have long been observed in North America as well (see Chapter 1). Hence Willis's concern with the process whereby 'working class kids get working class jobs' has been picked up by many researchers on this side of the Atlantic. For example, in his Willis-inspired ethnography, Jay MacLeod (1987) explored the different responses to schooling and the achievement ideology of black and white working-class males in a large eastern American city. A similar approach was used by Michelle Fine (1986) in her study of the process of dropping out in an American high school.

Thus, as we begin to examine dropouts' self-reported reasons for leaving school, one question underlying the analysis is whether, and to what extent, these young people have rejected the goals and values of the education system itself. At the same time, our analysis is influenced by the descriptive research literature discussed in Chapter 1, a literature that has typically separated dropouts' reasons for quitting school into school-based, work-related, and personal categories. Because our data were obtained from lengthy, in-depth, semi-structured interviews, the complexity and interrelatedness of these reasons quickly becomes apparent.

SELF-REPORTED REASONS FOR LEAVING SCHOOL

We began our interviews with questions about motivations for leaving school. Respondents were asked 'Why did you leave school?' and, depending on the direction the conversation took, a series of additional questions about the circumstances leading to the decision to drop out of school (see Appendix 1). As one might expect, the answers to these initial questions varied considerably, both in content and in length.

Some respondents offered no clear rationale for their decision to quit school, or emphasized the most immediate of motives. The following comment, from a young male dropout, is a good example:

> Well, actually I just left on a whim, I guess. I just never even thought of it before, about quitting school. I just went to school one day and I had lunch and then I came back to school and, uh, I went to my locker and I thought about, ah, maybe not going back to class that day. Then I just took off and never went back. I never opened my locker, left all the books there. . . [INT 029; male].

By contrast, other respondents offered many reasons for quitting, sometimes stressing how one factor (e.g., strained relationships with parents) led to another (poor marks in school), which ultimately caused them to quit:

> I left school when I was sixteen years old. I was experiencing a lot of personal problems in my home life, I had no father and problems with my mother. . . . I was failing because of my personal problems and I wasn't involved in school, and the counsellor at the school that I did decide to drop out of suggested that I should drop out rather than get kicked out. My attitude towards school wasn't good and my general conduct was lousy [INT 028; male].

> Well, mostly, I was pregnant, number one. I never really did like high school. Oh, I don't know, I just never did like the system, they made you feel like a kid and I was really rebellious [INT 035; female].

Although respondents typically discussed their interrelated reasons for quitting school without separating one from another, our reading of the transcripts suggested that 157 of the dropouts in the study identified at least one reason, 117 identified a second reason, and 68 mentioned a third. Table 3.1 lists these reasons for both female and male respondents, classifying them into three basic categories: school-based reasons, jobs/money-related reasons, and personal reasons.

TABLE 3.1. REASONS FOR DROPPING OUT OF SCHOOL BY GENDER

	Percentage		
Reason *	Male	Female	Total
School-based	61	58	60
Jobs/money-related	19	15	16
Personal reasons	21	28	24
Total	100	100	100
Total reasons	172	170	342
Total respondents	82	80	162

* Up to three reasons were coded for each sample member who answered the question. Most (N = 157) provided one answer, 117 gave a second answer, and 68 a third.

The first category, school-based reasons, included comments about basically disliking school (mentioned by 32 individuals), boredom (22 respondents), skipping too many classes (58 respondents), not getting along with teachers (18 mentions), and a variety of other, frequently negative, comments about schools, teachers, classes, and the school environment in general. Included in the second category (job/work-related reasons) were comments about wanting to find a job (27 in total), or wanting/needing to make some money (16 individuals). Six respondents mentioned that they had dropped out after finding a job.

'Personal reasons', the third category displayed in Table 3.1, were the most diverse in content. Thirty-five individuals mentioned problems in getting along with parents, including some who had been 'kicked out' of home. Ten individuals reported that their decisions to drop out had been influenced by friends' doing the same thing. A dozen respondents mentioned that they had been consuming too many drugs, or too much alcohol, or had found themselves in trouble with the law, and five young women stated that they had become pregnant.

The overall picture presented in Table 3.1 is certainly clear enough. From the perspective of dropouts themselves, the most common reasons for dropping out were related to experiences in high school. Neither gender nor class background (as indicated by parents' occupation and education) significantly modify the rank ordering of reasons. However, if we disaggregate the 'personal reasons' category, we do find that young women are more likely to report problems in getting along with family. In addition, 10 of the 12 individuals mentioning alcohol/drug use or problems with the law were males.

SCHOOL EXPERIENCES PRIOR TO DROPPING OUT

Allowing that school-based reasons are not necessarily independent of other types, it appeared useful to examine further our respondents' observations about the connection between their high-school experience and the decision to drop out. What was it about the school that made them quit?

The answer was 'a lot', although the specifics varied considerably. Respondents objected to particular teachers, teachers in general, specific subjects, or the presumed irrelevance of the curriculum as a whole. As one young man put it: 'I'm never going to go to Spain or use what I learned about Spain or Europe or nothin'. I'm never going to be there so why should I know about it?' [INT 041]. Some dropouts complained about childish and unfriendly peers; others reported poor grades and revealed learning difficulties.

Surprisingly, though, outright school failure was not a particularly significant determinant of dropping out. When asked how they had been doing in school, only one-third of the respondents answered that they had not been doing very well (female and male respondents answered similarly). In fact, almost one in four (24 per cent) remembered their school performance as being somewhat better than average. Respondents' willingness and ability to recall events that, on average, took place over two-and-a-half years prior to the interview require that we exercise some caution when interpreting this information. Nonetheless, these self-reports do challenge assumptions that all high-school dropouts are poor students.

On the other hand, repeated absence from school (skipping classes or extended periods of truancy) was a common step towards quitting school. The interview transcripts suggest that over half (56 per cent) of these young dropouts had been skipping a lot of classes before quitting school. About one in four (26 per cent) admitted that they had skipped some classes, and only 18 per cent stated that they had not been skipping. The following comments from two male respondents placed them into the 'skipping a lot' category:

> I don't know if you could call it skipping; I was sleeping in for afternoon classes [INT 002].

> Well, I skipped a grand total of two semesters, like the last half of '83 and the first half of '84. I skipped a grand total of four months out of that time. Like there was one time in a two-month period that I was there for two days straight [INT 049].

Skipping classes—especially frequent skipping—signifies at least a partial rejection of schooling. Carried out in conjunction with other students (which was often the case), it can provide associations that reinforce an anti-school identity. Skipping classes places students on a precipitous path that increases the likelihood of their ultimately dropping out of school. It is an activity that, once started, can develop a life of its own. One of our female respondents describes how she became progressively disengaged from school life:

> Why did I leave school? Um, I was going through a lot of trouble at home. My parents had split up, etc. etc. I was terribly, terribly, withdrawn. Half the time I couldn't face walking into the classroom, so I just skipped a class. . . . I don't remember making a conscious decision to leave school, maybe by the time it happened I really didn't consider myself part of the school system. [You] keep skipping until it reaches such a point that you're out of touch with it anyhow [INT 022].

TABLE 3.2. FREQUENCY OF SKIPPING SCHOOL/CLASS BY EMPLOYMENT STATUS AND GENDER

	Percentage					
	Employed			Unemployed		
	Male	Female	Total	Male	Female	Total
None	26	16	20	21	9	17
Some	30	26	27	28	22	25
A lot	44	58	53	51	69	58
Total	100	100	100	100	100	100
N	27	43	70	47	32	79

Table 3.2 reveals that girls (in both the employed and unemployed sub-samples) were more likely to report frequent skipping prior to dropping out of school. Why might skipping classes be more attractive for female students? While we did not address this question directly in our interviews, we may speculate that girls who do not like school are constrained by female gender-role socialization from adopting an active, aggressive anti-school

stance. Whereas boys might more quickly drop out of school, girls may skip classes to escape an unpleasant environment without inviting an immediate face-to-face confrontation with authority. This may also explain why female respondents had, on average, gone further in high school before quitting. Although 90 per cent of all sample members had completed grade nine, female respondents were more likely than males to have finished grade eleven.[1]

For some respondents, however, frequent skipping had a more direct impact on school-leaving. It could result in exclusion from classes, as this young woman recounted:

> I was basically bored with a lot of the classes, and because I was bored I wasn't going to some of them, and as a result I got kicked out of some of the classes [INT 136].

Or it might lead to outright expulsion from school:

> . . . that's how I got kicked out. . . . I got caught in the hallways [INT 035; female].[2]

> Well, in grade nine I got kicked out. . . . Actually, I didn't get kicked out but I kept on leaving the school for long periods of time and then finally I just got kicked out [INT 101; female].

Frequent skipping of classes brought students into contact with school counsellors who would then cast a critical eye over their attendance records. As one respondent explained:

> I missed 98 classes in two and a half months and they finally said, 'If you're not going to come then you might as well go home' [INT 021; male].

It is apparent that school counsellors can play an important role in 'creating' dropouts, since it is their responsibility to advise marginal students to either leave or stay. Advice of this sort led some interviewees to insist that their decision to leave school was not entirely voluntary, that they felt they had actually been pushed out:

> In a way I was sorta forced out of school. I had a lot of problems with the co-ordinator there. Nine of us in two weeks were released from [School X]. I asked him 'why?' and one of the reasons he gave was my attendance [INT 111; male].

In fact, it appears that there may have been a change in the truancy policy within the Edmonton school system sometime early in the 1980s, as one of our subjects noted when asked about his reasons for leaving school:

> Well, I was kinda forced out, like they have a new policy for absences and stuff and they gave me more absences than I had so they said I better leave [INT 103; male].

Likewise, although the next respondent claimed that the decision to leave school was his own, it is quite evident that he was strongly encouraged to quit:

> [I: How did you decide to quit, was it your own decision or someone else's?] It was my decision. [I: You didn't talk to a counsellor or anything about quitting?] Well, I talked to my co-ordinator about it and she and I never got along and she said 'Great, if you've been skipping you may as well leave for good' [INT 102; male].[3]

It cannot be assumed, therefore, that dropping out of school is always a truly voluntary decision. The choice involved is sometimes more illusory than real, and schools play a more active role in this outcome than is commonly recognized. Sometimes, as Radwanski (1987:90) notes, teachers and counsellors do little to encourage poorly performing students to stay in school. And, as several of our respondents reported, some counsellors encourage 'problem students' to leave.

But regardless of the weighting of suggestion and choice in the decision-making process, the fact remains that respondents' accounts of why they quit convey a message of generalized discontent with schooling. Negative encounters with teachers, the apparent irrelevance of the curriculum, and mind-numbing boredom are all indicative of a rejection of schooling. Something of this embryonic opposition to schooling is captured in the following exchanges:

> 'Cause I don't like, I didn't—it was getting to the point where I just wanted to go to work. I was tired—I was tired of going to school, I didn't like the teachers or nothin' so . . . I just quit [INT 044; female].

> Well, I—I had no interest eh? I just figured, uh, I know what I wanted to do and I figured school was just a waste of time [INT 121; male].

> It didn't interest me. I thought there was something else out there I was missing and I wanted to work. I've always felt that I was a little more mature than my peers [INT 129; male].

> I didn't really do that well in school. I really didn't care too much about school. I didn't want go to school, I just wanted to get out and work [INT 080; male].

> I got bored with it. I wanted to get out and work [INT 060; male].

> I found it very boring after a while. . . . I just wanted to go to work [INT 076; male].

DROPPING OUT TO TAKE A JOB

As these responses make clear, a general dislike of school can be associated with a desire for paid employment. Together, the prospective attractions of a job and the known drudgery of the classroom are clearly factors that could encourage early school-leaving. But, as Radwanski (1987:96) observed, it is not necessarily 'work' itself that is desirable so much as the adult status, income, and life-style that a paying job might provide. For that matter, only a minority of respondents gave work-related reasons for leaving school in the first place. As we observed in Table 3.1, school-based reasons for quitting greatly outnumbered job- or money-related reasons.

Thus we suspect that prior part-time employment plays a less important causal role in the dropping-out process than some researchers have assumed. Students who have already developed an aversion to formal schooling may be more likely to seek a part-time job, but, as we observed in Chapter 1, many continuing students also work part-time (Cohen, 1989; Sunter, 1992). Thus, in our opinion, holding a part-time job is seldom the ultimate cause of dropping out, or of negative attitudes towards school. It may, however, ease the transition into a labour-market role and become part of the justification for rejecting formal schooling.

Our interviews revealed that male dropouts were somewhat more likely to list job-related reasons for quitting, although the gender difference was really quite small (Table 3.1). In contrast, the 1991 School Leavers Survey showed considerably higher dropout rates for male high-school students reporting long hours of work (20 or more hours per week) while still in school: 33 per cent of these young men had quit school (at some time), compared with 18 per cent of young female students working long hours (Sunter, 1993:48). In other words, excessive paid employment appears to be more strongly associated with dropping out among males. Even so, this does not prove that long hours of work cause young men to quit school. As we argued with respect to gender differences in patterns of skipping school, males with little interest in schooling may tend to work more hours and then drop out of school. Equally uninterested females may also seek additional part-time work but be less likely to take the more aggressive step of quitting school.

However, there are two ways in which paid employment may be more directly linked to dropping-out. First, a small number of male respondents in our study said that they left school because of long-term ambitions to acquire a trade. At the time they quit (though not necessarily later on), they felt that high school was an obstacle to that goal:

> I had an opportunity to get into a trade I wanted to get into. . . . I wanted to get into it while I had the chance, 'cause I didn't know what it would be like INT 002; male].

Second, finding paid work became a priority for those respondents with the worst family situations. Life with one or both parents had become so intolerable for some that they left home and therefore needed a job to survive independently. It was at this point that they quit school:

> [I] couldn't keep up with the work 'cause I'm not living at home and I was trying to find a full-time job, so I'd have a place to live. . . . and I couldn't attend school because I needed cash [INT 010; female].

PROS AND CONS OF DROPPING OUT

The results so far clearly suggest that some of our respondents left school because they rejected its underlying value system. However, not all dropouts shared this motivation, even though they might use the same vocabulary when describing school and their reasons for quitting. Terms such as 'boredom' or 'dislike' can be short-hand expressions for deep-rooted and wide-ranging objections to the whole idea of schooling, but this is not necessarily the case. The same language was also frequently used to voice quite specific objections to school. Some respondents disliked the English teacher (but not the math teacher), while others hated math (but not English), and so on. In short, while some respondents quit because of an all-encompassing estrangement from school culture, others left for much more idiosyncratic reasons.

Thus, although school (rather than family or work) experiences provided the majority of our respondents with the motivation for dropping out, their antagonism to schooling was seldom well-developed or fully-articulated. In fact, what impressed us most about our respondents was not the magnitude of their opposition to or alienation from school, but the very opposite. Given that dropouts, by definition, are the educational system's most estranged clients, it was surprising to find how favourably they viewed this system, and how qualified and muted many of their criticisms really were.

Dropping out of high school was a fundamentally ambiguous experience for most respondents in this study. For example, only one-third disagreed with the statement 'Overall, I have enjoyed my time in school.' A larger proportion (44 per cent) agreed, and 23 per cent chose a neutral response on the five-point scale. After enquiring about their reasons for quitting school, we also asked sample members whether they felt, in retrospect, that leaving school had been a good or a bad thing. Equal proportions (36 per cent) answered that dropping out had been 'good' or 'bad', while the rest commented on both good and bad aspects. Class differences (as indicated by parents' education) in responses to this open-ended question did not form any systematic pattern; and, while male respondents were somewhat more likely to say that quitting school had been a bad thing (32 per cent, compared to 24 per cent of females), gender differences were also quite small.

On the one hand, then, some respondents viewed dropping out as a viable short-term solution to the various problems they had encountered in school. Indeed, some saw it as virtually the only option available to them, given their circumstances at the time. A few were even prepared to suggest that the decision to leave school qualified, at least in retrospect, as a cathartic experience.

On the other hand, respondents quickly became aware that dropping out had its costs. For one thing, it damaged (sometimes already poor) relationships with parents. Two-thirds (65 per cent) of the sample members reported that their parents had disapproved of their leaving school without graduating (24 per cent said their parents had been largely indifferent, while only 11 per cent reported parental approval). Some mentioned that dropping out of school had provoked parental ultimatums ('get a job or get back to school'), or that continuing to live at home was made conditional upon choosing one of these two options.

Spoiled domestic relationships were an early warning that the benefits of dropping out were likely to be short-lived. With time, respondents became increasingly aware that their early departure from high school would pose problems for them in the future. Their feelings about leaving school were, therefore, mixed—a dualistic response that can be summed up as short-term gain for long-term pain:

> Well, at first I thought it was a good thing because I was going to be moving onto something. Right now, I don't know [INT 014; male].

> I wouldn't say it was either good or bad. I would say that it was, ah, an experience that would have to be lived. I can't say that it's an enlightening experience neither. There was good and bad parts about it. I did have a good job, I was making money, but on the other hand, I missed being with my peers a lot, so I can't really say it was good or bad [INT 017; male].

> Well, it's got its pros and cons. If I would have stuck it out and got my diploma, I don't know what I might have done. I might have gone to university, but I don't know that I would have got high enough marks. The one benefit of leaving school was that it was kind of a learning experience 'cause I understand what it was like to go out into the workforce. And it turned out that I didn't like it that much. I couldn't picture myself doing that for the rest of my life—working at a blue-collar level [INT 020; male].

This last individual was not alone in feeling that his time as a dropout had taught him a few of the economic and social facts of life—not the least being the limited nature of unskilled blue-collar employment. Similar sentiments were expressed by another young dropout in his assessment of the early leaving experience:

> Well, it was bad because I lost some years. But it was good too because then I know exactly what education was and when I went out to fill out the applications for jobs, you know. Some jobs you have to have high school and you just don't find a good job without a high school diploma. . . . [I: So you feel that by quitting school you got to find out . . . what?] Yeah. I learned a few things. I learned about how hard work is, like a real tough job. Like I never really knew. I thought, you know, construction and stuff like that would be—wouldn't be too bad, but then it gets to you. It's hard [INT 026; male].

These specific comments about employment difficulties—a subject we shall return to in the next two chapters—reflect the general pattern of responses to the question about whether dropping out was a good or a bad thing. Only 29 per cent of the sample members who were unemployed when interviewed stated that dropping out had been a good thing, compared with 44 per cent of those holding jobs. Thus, although those fortunate enough to have a job when interviewed were somewhat less negative in their comments, difficult labour-market experiences after dropping out had generally forced a reassessment of the decision to leave school.

Results such as these leave little doubt that many respondents, male and female, from middle-class and working-class backgrounds, have retained at least a lingering commitment to an educational system that, on the face of it, they had rejected. We have already alluded to the job-related reasons for this ambivalence. First, most respondents clearly realized that completion of grade twelve would improve their chances in the labour market. Many felt that they had been exploited by employers who knew that they were in no position to challenge low wages or poor working conditions. Without a high-school diploma, these young workers were likely to be ghettoized in a very narrow range of low-paying, menial, and in many cases part-time jobs. As one middle-class male put it:

> There's not really anything out there other than working at something like McDonald's. . . . I don't like working for slave wages so that's why I won't work there [INT 038; male].[4]

Just as the labour market had tempted some subjects to quit school in the first place, it had also encouraged many more to contemplate returning. The recession was eliminating the sorts of unskilled or semi-skilled—but relatively well-paying—manual and white-collar jobs that have traditionally attracted those with few educational qualifications. Would-be apprentices, for example, realized that a recession was not the best time to be looking for a trade without a high-school diploma.

Second, many respondents now realized that completion of grade twelve signified to employers that a young person had, as one informant put it, 'staying power'. Regardless of what had (or had not) been learned in twelve years of schooling, a diploma was used by employers as a predictor of worker stability and reliability. 'If you go to a job and they see you don't have a diploma, they think you're a quitter' [INT 020; male]. In essence, their labour-market experiences forced these young people, often for the first time, to confront the stigma of being a 'dropout':

> When you're a high school dropout, a lot of the businesses really don't want to hire you 'cause they don't think you're intelligent enough the way you are. They don't realize that just because you've dropped out of school, it doesn't really mean that you're not capable of doing the job [INT 006; male].

Thus respondents' recognition of the likely career path for a high-school dropout led them to re-evaluate the merits of an educational system they had previously dismissed. Even though they might still not be convinced of the relevance of what school had been trying to teach them, increasingly they recognized the instrumental importance of schooling. Educational qualifications, beginning with a high-school diploma, were the means of escaping dead-end jobs and improving their own life-chances. As one male put it, 'a lot of jobs in the paper, if you got the trade, you get the job' [INT 050; male].

FUTURE EDUCATION PLANS AND GOALS

Given this broad acknowledgement of the power and value of educational credentials, it is not surprising to find that a large majority of respondents were still receptive to the idea of obtaining more education in the future. Since the possibility of returning to school was a central concern in this study, we addressed the issue three times, twice in the interview itself, and once again in the self-administered questionnaire. In each case, roughly two-thirds of the respondents answered positively; between 20 and 30 per cent answered that they might get some more education; and only a handful said 'no'.[5]

Gender differences were of little consequence for each question. Although dropouts whose own parents had gone further in school were slightly more likely to say they hoped to return to school themselves, these 'class' differences were small and not very systematic. However, for each of the three questions, respondents who were unemployed when interviewed were more likely than their employed counterparts to state that they would get some more education in the future. For example, in response to the question (in the self-administered questionnaire) 'Do you think you will ever get some more education (high school, Alberta College, NAIT, university, etc.)?', 73 per cent of the unemployed respondents answered 'yes', compared with 56 per cent of those with jobs. Individuals 20 years of age and older were also more likely to answer positively (72 per cent, versus 61 per cent of those under 20). Again, these results suggest that difficult labour-market experiences lead to a re-assessment of the value of formal education.

Answers to the open-ended question 'Would you go back to school?' indicate that, for some, the high school *as a particular type of educational institution* is perceived as a barrier to fulfilling educational aspirations. While 69 per cent answered 'yes', over half of these individuals (or 38 per cent of all sample members) qualified their answers by saying that they would not return to a high school to get additional education. Thus respondents appeared to be more hesitant about returning to the specific type of institution they had rejected than about acquiring more education. Male dropouts were more inclined to state that they would not return to high school, as were older respondents (Figure 3.1).

FIGURE 3.1: WOULD YOU GO BACK TO SCHOOL?* BY GENDER AND AGE

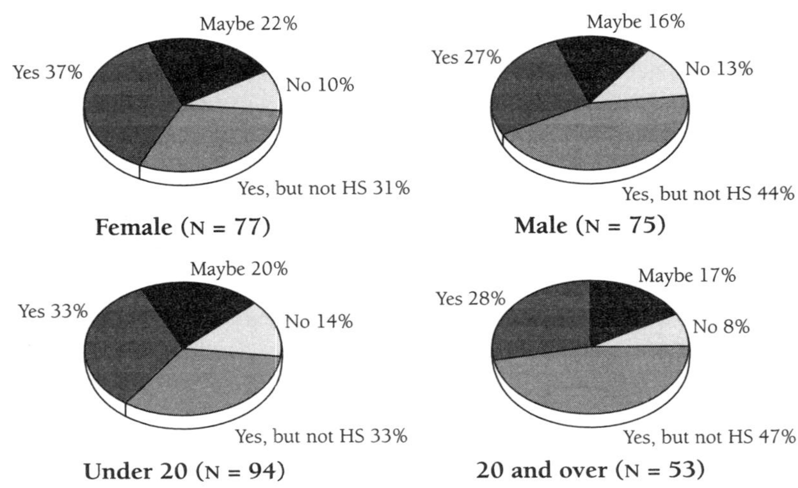

*Question asked after discussing reasons for leaving school.

Some of these respondents entertained ideas of attending university, while others were interested in trade-related or other types of vocational training. Some wanted to get their grade-twelve diploma through correspondence courses, and quite a few identified institutions such as Alberta Vocational College and Alberta College that offer high-school programs to adult students. These preferences provide further insight into the nature of young dropouts' antipathy to schooling. They suggest that the focus of discontent is often the institutional or social climate of the high school, rather than the learning experience itself.

In some instances, the reference point was the school's authoritarian atmosphere. Dropouts resented being treated like 'kids', denied the freedom and autonomy that they felt, as individuals on the brink of adulthood, they deserved.

> I just never did like the system, they make you feel like a kid and I was really rebellious [INT 035; female].

> I wasn't happy with school, I wasn't happy with the system, I wasn't a happy person. I had no interest in school at all, I thought it was garbage. . . [INT 105; female].

Complaints about the reluctance or inability of teachers to treat students as adults and about the 'phoniness' of high school imply a questioning of the school's moral authority. But respondents who spoke with bitterness about the quality of social relationships within the schools they had left were not commenting only on the adult authority structure or individual teachers: some were also referring to the prevailing peer-culture. In this regard, the major focus of complaint was the immaturity of fellow students:

> When you're eighteen years old and you're in a classroom of grade ten'ers you just can't handle the garbage that goes on in school. I couldn't handle being in a class with a bunch of immature people [INT 113; female].

Others highlighted the exclusionary nature of the dominant peer-groups. This is how one female respondent explained her decision to leave one of the more affluent and prestigious schools in Edmonton:

> Ah, 'cause I wasn't enjoying myself, I wasn't having fun there, I didn't really fit into that kind of group 'cause at [School X] people were one way or the other. The major people that I knew there were very rich and very full of themselves. If you weren't part of this group and didn't know these people, they wouldn't speak to you. They're all snobs, I was shocked because they were all so snotty. There's just no way you can get in with them unless all of a sudden you come into a lot of money. They judge you by what you wear and how you talk and what your parents do for a living and I felt I didn't have to justify anything. I didn't appreciate them at all [INT 082; female].

A male subject was even more specific when asked why he quit:

> Well, I was having a few problems with, uh, not only the teachers in the school, it was, eh, the kids in the school. Like I was brought up religiously; and, uh, kids were always, you know, 'Come on, let's go smoke dope' [INT 003; male].

Previous studies of high-school students involved in illegal or deviant activity have made much of the fact that involvement in informal peer cultures reinforces and supports the kind of anti-school attitudes and behaviours that culminate in dropping out (e.g., Willis, 1977; Corrigan, 1979). Given this emphasis, it is ironic to find some of our respondents explaining their decision to quit in terms of either their exclusion from the prevailing peer culture or their disapproval of its focal concerns. By their own accounts, a smaller number might have become dropouts had they been better integrated into both the formal and informal aspects of high-school culture.

DISCUSSION

Replicating previous research findings (see Chapter 1), we found school-based reasons for dropping out to be considerably more common than job/money-related or personal reasons. In fact, whereas the 1991 School Leavers Survey showed 40 per cent of dropouts identifying school-related reasons as most important (Gilbert et al., 1993:27), 60 per cent of the reasons provided by our respondents focused on the school in one way or another.[6] This relatively greater emphasis on school-based factors as pushing students out, rather than labour-market factors as enticing them to leave school, may reflect the difficult economic situation at the beginning of the 1980s, when most of these dropouts left school. But employment opportunities today, particularly for poorly educated youth, are equally, if not more, bleak. Hence a similar study today would probably generate a similar distribution of self-reported reasons for dropping out of school.

While school-based reasons were clearly most common, the interrelated motivations reported by our respondents highlighted the complexity of the process of becoming a dropout. For some, problematic family situations along with negative reactions to school led to the decision to quit. For others, the prospect of a job, especially the adult status and income it promised, made the decision to stop attending boring classes that much easier. Even so, the overall impression left by these interviews was that employment—either part-time jobs held before quitting or the prospect of a full-time job after leaving school—was seldom the root cause of dropping out.

Although the final outcome was the same, negative reactions to high school took many different forms. Some dropouts recalled specific incidents with particular teachers. Others discussed boring classes, the irrelevant (at least in their opinion) information they were forced to learn, peer groups from which they felt estranged, and rules and procedures that insulted their self-identity as young adults. With respect to this last complaint, a recent American study concludes that working-class youth are particularly sensitive to what they perceive as disrespectful treatment by teachers. This concern with self-respect and personal dignity manifests itself, as it does in our study, in the form of objections to being treated in a less than adult fashion (Schwartz, 1987).

Recognizing that some of our respondents might well have been behaving in a juvenile manner before dropping out, complaints about not being treated like adults are especially noteworthy with regard to how dropouts might be encouraged to return to school. When asked if they would ever return, almost four in ten respondents answered 'yes, but not to high school' (or words to that effect). Alternative educational institutions, within which dropouts can complete their high-school requirements while maintaining more of the 'adult' role they sought when they left school, are clearly part of the solution to the dropout problem (Krahn and Tanner, 1989).

Only a minority of subjects admitted that they had been doing poorly in school prior to quitting. Even though we have no way of confirming these self-reports, it is still important to note that dropouts are not drawn only from the ranks of poor students. Overstating differences in ability and interest in school between dropouts and those who graduate can easily lead to overlooking the many school-based factors—curriculum, rules, peer groups, teachers, and counsellors, to name the most obvious ones—that contribute to the dropout problem. But compared with those respondents who admitted they had not been doing well in school, many more reported skipping classes frequently. This suggests that dropping out of school is typically the last act in a long process of gradual disengagement from the education system.

In a number of cases, respondents recalled being advised to quit school by counsellors who were tired of dealing with truancy and behavioural problems. Previous research has shown how schools categorize and process students, thereby preparing them for different occupational futures. Frequently the focus of this research has been on the 'streaming' or 'tracking' system (Hargreaves, 1967; Polk and Schafer, 1972) that separates students into academic and non-academic programs on the basis of ability and interest in education. While, on the surface, streaming appears to be an efficient process, it has been justifiably criticized for permanently closing the door of educational opportunity on some students, since, once in a non-academic stream, a student will not complete the courses required for entry into post-secondary institutions. In addition, streaming is part of the process whereby class differences in educational attainment are reproduced, as students from less-advantaged families are more likely to be placed in non-academic programs (Denton and Hunter, 1991:129-31; Radwanski, 1987:192).

Looking at educational institutions from a similar perspective, Cicourcel and Kitsuse (1963) specifically examined the role of school counsellors. They investigated the ways in which counsellors construct categories of 'good' and 'bad' students and the consequences of the confirmation of those labels. We can extend this argument by suggesting that school counsellors may also help to filter weakly committed students out of the school system. Even though the majority of respondents in our study indicated that the decision to quit school was voluntary, some of their stories suggested that school officials had been influential in encouraging this decision.

Our respondents' negative reactions to various aspects of high school—whether the curriculum, the teachers, the rules, or fellow students—came through clearly enough in the interviews. Even so, we conclude that our findings are at odds with the assumption, popular among the ethnographers discussed at the beginning of this chapter, that most early school-leavers have completely rejected the values and goals of the formal education system. Willis (1977), for example, argued that English working-class males actively involve themselves in a school counter-culture that rejects higher education. By belittling book-learning and educational qualifications, by contemptuously dismissing all forms of mental labour, and by celebrating and anticipating the unskilled manual jobs that await them on leaving school, working-class males participate in the reproduction of class inequalities.

Since we interviewed only dropouts, we must rely on other research to document higher rates of early school-leaving among Canadian working-class youth (see Chapter 1). However, the majority of our respondents, whatever their class origins, continued to believe that more education was needed to get a decent job, to 'get ahead'. Roughly two-thirds stated that they would obtain more education at some time in the future. The fact that only a minority are likely to carry through with these promises (one of the findings from the 1991 SLS) does not negate the equally important fact that most dropouts continue to place considerable value on obtaining an education.[7]

Obviously, judging by their behaviour, dropouts are less satisfied with schooling than are those who graduate. But their grievances should not be allowed to obscure the fact that many quit school despite a continuing belief in the labour-market value of education. Even though, like the British Columbia youth interviewed by Jane Gaskell (1987:263-4), some of our respondents were critical of the (presumed) irrelevance of what they had been taught, their criticisms focused on what they were asked to learn, but seldom on the basic value of educational credentials. These dropouts were clearly still receptive to the instrumental, if not the moral, appeal of schools, and in this respect they bore little resemblance to the working-class rebels profiled by Willis (1977).[8]

In short, although they had quit school, most of these dropouts had not rejected the educational value system. This will become even more evident when we examine dropouts' experiences of work (Chapter 5), responses to unemployment (Chapter 6), and goals for the future (Chapter 8).

NOTES

[1]The 1991 School Leavers Survey did not reveal similar gender differences. In fact, although the differences were small, male dropouts in this national survey were somewhat more likely to admit that they had skipped classes during their last year in school (Sunter, 1993:46). Similarly, the national survey showed that, on average, male dropouts left school at a somewhat older age. An explanation for these different findings is not immediately apparent.

[2]In addition, a few (male) students who reported hitting teachers were expelled from school.

[3]This echoes a point made by Rosenbaum (1976), who found that guidance counsellors managed to direct students in such a way that both they and their parents felt they had exclusive responsibility for the educational choices made.

[4]The most negative comments about employers appeared to be reserved for the major fast-food chains, probably because respondents, particularly those who were somewhat older (see Chapter 5), did not regard such workplaces as part of a truly adult labour market. Working at a burger shop typically meant working at a non-adult job with non-adult co-workers for non-adult wages.

[5]The importance of examining respondents' answers in the context of the interview 'conversation' is highlighted by the somewhat different pattern of responses to these three questions. The subject of returning to school was first addressed after the respondent had been asked about reasons for leaving school. Eighteen individuals answered 'no'. The issue was then raised again following questions about labour-market experiences, causes of unemployment, and future occupational goals (see

Appendix 1); now, only 9 respondents said 'no'. When asked the question a third time, in the self-administered questionnaire (Appendix 2), only five people responded negatively.

[6]Results from the 1991 School Leavers Survey describe the proportion of dropouts who identified a particular type of reason as most important. Since we coded up to three reasons per respondent, our results describe the proportion of reasons listed. Hence direct comparisons of results from the two studies should be made cautiously.

[7]It could be argued that Edmonton dropouts are not representative of early school-leavers in other parts of the country, who might be much less likely to value higher education. While working-class male sub-cultures similar to those described by Willis (1977) may exist in some parts of Canada (e.g., Dunk, 1991), the similarities between the school experiences and attitudes reported by dropouts in our study and in the 1991 national School Leavers Survey (Gilbert et al., 1993) lead us to believe that our results are generalizable beyond Edmonton.

[8]See Tanner (1990:89-92) for a discussion of the generalizability of the Willis (1977) thesis to Canada and, for that matter, to the majority of British working-class youth. Weis (1990:21) also notes that almost all the white working-class American high-school students she studied saw 'some value for education, albeit in highly utilitarian terms'.

CHAPTER FOUR

Looking for Work

INTRODUCTION

While the recession of the early 1980s appeared to have ended in central Canada, the (annual average) unemployment rate in Alberta in the mid-1980s was still high: 11.2 per cent in 1984, dropping to 10.1 per cent in 1985. The provincial unemployment rates for teenagers (aged 15 to 19) were considerably higher at 18.2 per cent (1984) and 19.6 per cent (1985), while the comparable rates for young adults (aged 20 to 24) were somewhat lower (15.4 and 12.9 per cent). Edmonton unemployment rates (all ages combined) remained higher than the provincial rates, averaging 14.1 per cent in 1984 and 12.2 per cent in 1985. Thus the young dropouts we interviewed were looking for work in a very difficult labour market.

Since our non-random sampling procedure was designed to include roughly equal numbers of employed and unemployed high-school dropouts, we cannot use our sample to generalize about unemployment rates among Edmonton dropouts in the mid-1980s. Nevertheless, even with over half of these early school-leavers unemployed when interviewed, our sample may not have been particularly weighted towards the jobless. Given Edmonton's labour market in 1984-85, jobs were hard to come by, even for those with secondary and post-secondary credentials. Hence the statuses of 'employed' and 'unemployed' were far from stable among our respondents. Interviews with many of them suggested frequent movement in and out of jobs. The next chapter will discuss the types of jobs these dropouts managed to find, and their reactions to them. In this chapter, our emphasis is on how they looked for work.

The following discussion addresses four basic questions: (1) how do young high-school dropouts look for work? (2) what kinds of problems do they encounter while seeking work? (3) do young women and men, both handicapped by having not completed high school, use different methods of job search and encounter different types of labour-market entry problems? and (4) do employed dropouts report different job-search behaviours and experiences than those without a job when interviewed?

Implicit in these specific research questions are a number of broader questions that have important implications for our understanding of dropouts' situation in the labour market. For example, do the higher unemployment rates among high-school dropouts reflect their absent educational credentials, or their less well-developed job-search skills, or both? Does part of the problem lie in the reaction of employers to young people without a high-school diploma? Might it be, as we suggested in the previous chapter, that employers use high-school completion as an indicator of (potentially) superior job performance, even if the jobs in question do not require the skills acquired in high school?

Questions about gender differences are critical, given what we already know about the gender-based segregation of the labour market and the female-male wage gap (Gunderson et al., 1990; Krahn and Lowe, 1993:149-87). Are young women who have not completed high school doubly handicapped in their labour-market pursuits? Or does gender make little difference when competing for lower-tier service-sector jobs? Finally, will a comparison of the job-search experiences of employed and unemployed dropouts reveal some additional skills held by those who have been more successful in the labour market? Or are intermittent employment and unemployment generic experiences for all young people without a high-school diploma in a time of high unemployment? We shall return to these broader questions in the discussion at the end of this chapter.

LOOKING FOR WORK

Let us begin by examining dropouts' accounts of how they looked for work. While interviewers were permitted to skip questions and deviate from their sequence and wording, almost all asked respondents about their job-search methods, and about problems experienced while seeking work, usually in a fairly similar manner (see Appendix 1). Currently-employed sample members were asked two basic questions about their job-search activities (*How did you look for this job? Did you have any problems looking for work?*). Jobless respondents were first asked whether they were looking for a job. Twenty said 'no', including twelve who were in school when interviewed and seven who were in jail (in the discussion below, we classify these individuals as unemployed). This question was followed with several others about job-search tactics and experiences (*How do you look for work? How many jobs do you apply for in a week? What kinds? Any problems in looking for work?*). Respondents who were not currently looking for a job were asked about their previous job-search methods and problems.

Roughly half (27 of 55) of the unemployed respondents who were asked how many jobs they applied for answered that they typically applied for five or fewer per week, while about one in four (N = 13) stated that they applied for between six and ten. The rest of this sub-group (15 in all) said they were applying for over ten jobs per week, including four individuals who claimed to be applying for fifty or more. Examination of the interview transcripts for these few individuals suggests that these estimates were probably somewhat exaggerated. Taking these possible overestimates into account, we would still conclude that most of these young jobless dropouts were actively seeking work.

TABLE 4.1. JOB-SEARCH TECHNIQUES BY EMPLOYMENT STATUS AND GENDER

	Percentage					
	Unemployed			Employed		
Method *	Total	Female	Male	Total	Female	Male
Newspapers	24	22	25	13	14	12
Door-to-door	22	30	17	16	19	12
Phoning/Yellow Pages	12	9	13	4	-	9
Distributing résumés	6	3	7	2	2	3
Canada Employment Centres	8	8	8	1	2	-
Job clubs/referral agencies	6	3	7	20	21	17
Friends	12	14	11	21	10	24
Family contacts	6	6	8	18	19	27
Other methods	4	5	4	5	4	6
Total	100	100	100	100	100	100
Total number of methods	162	64	98	82	48	34
Total respondents	86	34	52	76	46	30
N reporting methods	79	31	48	70	42	28
Average no. of methods	2.1	2.1	2.0	1.2	1.1	1.2

* Up to three methods were coded for the unemployed, up to two for the currently employed; averages calculated for those reporting job-search methods.

Table 4.1 lists the types of answers these early school-leavers provided to the question about job-search techniques. When coding the transcript material, we recorded up to two answers for the employed, and up to three for the jobless. The latter tended to report more ways in which they were currently seeking work than did the employed, who were more likely to report only the successful method they had used to obtain their current position. Consequently, a direct comparison of the average number of methods reported by the unemployed (2.1) and the employed (1.2) is not appropriate.

However, comparisons of the percentages of each type of answer, by sub-group, are more useful (Table 4.1). The job-search techniques reported by sample members can be grouped into three basic types: *direct, impersonal, and relatively ad hoc approaches* (newspaper ads, going door-to-door, phoning possible employers located through the Yellow Pages, distributing résumés); *use of government-supported agencies* (Canada Employment Centres, 'job clubs'); and (c) *reliance on contacts* (friends or family).

Table 4.1 reveals that currently unemployed sample members were more likely than those with jobs to report 'ad hoc' methods of seeking work. Almost half (46 per cent) of the 162 methods mentioned by unemployed dropouts (N = 79) involved looking through the newspaper or going door-to-door asking about possible jobs. If we include phoning possible employers and distributing résumés in this category, we can account for almost two-thirds (64 per cent) of the job-search techniques used by the unemployed. Newspaper ads and door-to-door searches accounted for less than one-third (29 per cent) of the 82 methods reported by employed sample members (N = 70), with telephone searches and résumés bringing the total up to only 35 per cent.

Employed dropouts were most likely to state that they had obtained their job through a 'job club' (20 per cent) or family members or friends (39 per cent). The former is not surprising, since several 'job clubs' were included in our sampling frame, and a sizeable number of the respondents located in this manner were working in jobs they had found with advice or assistance from their 'job club' leaders. However, it is noteworthy that four in ten employed sample members had found work through informal networks of family and friends. Presumably the unemployed would also have turned first to family and friends. The fact that fewer jobless were seeking work via contacts may simply indicate that their social networks offered fewer job leads.

Few gender differences are observed in Table 4.1, except that a somewhat higher proportion of female respondents mentioned going door-to-door in their job search. This may reflect the types of work more often sought by young women; that is, it may be easier to go door-to-door in shopping malls seeking a sales-clerk position, a type of job perhaps more desirable to young women.

In short, these survey results suggest that use of contacts, followed by ad hoc searches (newspaper ads and door-to-door soliciting) and participation in 'job clubs', are the more successful types of job-search among young dropouts. Only one employed sample member mentioned obtaining a job through a Canada Employment Centre, and only 8 per cent of the methods mentioned by the unemployed fell into this category.

Relying on contacts

The interview transcripts provide a clearer picture of the variety of ways in which these young people looked for work. Contacts were indeed useful, although they certainly did not guarantee success in finding a job, as was noted by an unemployed male respondent:

> I look in the paper, that's for sure. Sometimes I go down to Manpower and sometimes I just talk to people. The only way to get into most businesses nowadays is if you know somebody. The odd time I do find a job by knowing people, like Northlands. A friend of mine worked there and he put in a good word for me and I filled out an application and that's how I got the job. Sometimes it works, sometimes it doesn't [INT 119].

Sometimes it was a family member who had provided the tip or introduction, sometimes a friend or distant acquaintance:

> Well, I curl at that rink, eh? I curl with the junior set and my mom curled with the boss's wife so they needed a new busboy so through connections I got the job [INT 103; employed male].

> The only way I got those two jobs was through friends. I had a friend who worked at Sears and needed help and at the other place, I knew a guy who worked the security there and that's how I got that job [INT 035; unemployed female].

> My sister's old boyfriend whose girlfriend works in the kitchen, she's one of the head chefs and they had a couple of openings so she phoned me up and said I should come down. I came down and they hired me [INT 092; employed female].

Some dropouts, such as this young man working as a janitor, had almost exhausted other methods, when a friend or family member helped to solve their unemployment problem:

> . . . So I just got the Yellow Pages out and looked at all the addresses for, uh, auto body repair companies. Shops, whatever. And I went around to most of them. When that didn't work I phoned every oil company and consultant, you name it. And that didn't work so I came over here, and I got a job. [I: How did you find this job?] A friend of mine was working as a security guard [INT 058].

A few younger sample members, however, appeared to be somewhat more willing to wait until a family member stepped in to help:

> Well I look up in the Yellow Pages and then I look at who's hiring and phone around. [I: How about looking in the newspaper?] Most of them are lost causes, you need a high-school education to do it, so I don't even bother. My dad's friend is a carpet-layer and he's going to hire me as soon as business picks up [INT 030; unemployed male].

> Um, my mom was working at the restaurant and so was my sister. . . . She got me a job making pizzas and I just got two or three jobs like that, I didn't quit, the owner just moved out. After a while my mom didn't find me a job so I just didn't bother working, I was just bumming around [INT 068; unemployed female].

Looking for work on your own

While reliance on contacts had a somewhat higher success rate, personal job search (newspaper ads, going door-to-door, looking through the Yellow Pages, or distributing résumés) was the most common method of seeking work among the unemployed sample members. A few had developed very systematic and well-organized approaches:

> . . . I spend my afternoons doing leads, follow-ups; you know, sitting with a newspaper, circling things, making phone calls, setting up appointments. . . . finding out if the job is suitable to me and vice versa. . . . Then, in the mornings, I go and take the ones that I have decided to apply for and the ones that you have to go in person [INT 005; unemployed female].

> Actually, I've got a really good technique. I get résumés made up and I sit down and go through the telephone book and write down all the names of companies I would like to work for and then I write a general covering letter and then send it away. I then follow it up with a phone call asking for an interview [INT 096; unemployed female].

But these two young women were exceptions. Much more often, these early school-leavers described an ad hoc, casual, and far from organized approach to seeking work:

> Fill out applications [I: Any other ways?] Well, through the newspaper, all that stuff. Any other possibilities, I'll listen around, like, if somebody comes up to me and says, hey, listen, these guys are hiring, like, I'm the first one down there [INT 013; unemployed male].

> Well, you look in the paper and you phone and when you go by places and that, you see Help Wanted signs, you go in and you fill out an application [INT 114; unemployed female].

Although their approach was not particularly well organized, some of the unemployed sample members reported putting a lot of effort into their search for employment:

> Um, well I just went up to Stony Plain Road and I started at the mall there and just put in applications everywhere and just went straight down Stony Plain and all the businesses and that, putting in applications anywhere they'd take them [INT 038; unemployed male].

> . . . I just walked downtown and if I liked what I saw I would think 'Ah, what the hell, let's go in and fill out an application.' One day I think I filled out about 40 or 45 applications and I still haven't received a phone call on one of them [INT 049; unemployed male].

But a few, answering surprisingly honestly, admitted to a rather easy-going approach to looking for work:

> [I: Are you looking for work?] Yeah, well, I guess sorta. I've been thinking

> about it but I haven't done anything yet. I've been looking through the paper and making a few phone calls but I'm not really doing anything [INT 001; unemployed female].

And, as this waitress recalled, some parents had participated rather actively in their child's job search:

> [I: How did you find this job?] Um, my mom actually. See, she was the one who started this 'You're going to get a job' and I'm going 'Yeah, yeah, yeah', you know and stuff, and I was sitting around and finally she found it in the paper, there was an ad. She drove me down there and I applied and they called me up and she drove me down there again and they just called and I just started to work [INT 118].

Quite a number of the currently employed sample members recalled that they had found their present job through a similar ad hoc job-search approach. The following three respondents, all working in the restaurant business, are typical examples:

> I was going to suntan and I saw a Help Wanted sign and I applied and they called me up [INT 108; waitress].

> An ad in the paper. Just went in and said 'I want this job, please', and she said 'Okay,' and that was all there was to it. I was really fortunate, I think, to be there at the right time [INT 088; waitress].

> Just saw an ad in the paper one day, went down and filled out an application and they called me up the next day [INT 041; busboy].

Employment Centres and 'job clubs'

As we noted in Table 4.1, only a handful of dropouts reported seeking work through Canada Employment Centres. The few respondents who mentioned them basically concluded that not many jobs were advertised in these centres, a fact that would have been difficult to dispute during the winter of 1984-85:

> [I: How do you look for work?] Go around and put in applications everywhere. [I: Any other methods?] Go to the unemployment centre and see what they had, usually garbage there [INT 021; unemployed male].

However, a number of subjects in this study had joined 'job clubs' while seeking work. Some were fortunate enough to have obtained a job as a result, while others were still looking (and hoping). In some cases, the young dropouts were given job-search advice, but had to look for a job on their own:

> Well, they give you leads on, you know, how to go about getting a job—filling out résumés, uh, questionnaires, and looking through the phone book to find employers. You call 'em up and give 'em a speech and that, and if they're interested they'll give you an interview, if not, they'll say no [INT 044; unemployed male].

Being in a program that provided wage subsidies to employers could be helpful:

> . . . I phoned Westown Ford and I got an interview and I got the job and [the government program] paid all my wages and then after that they got me on to—I forget the name of the other program—but I got on there which only paid half of my wages and Freedom Ford paid half but the government reimbursed them. After that I got on 'cause they were pretty well satisfied with my work [INT 066; employed male].

And a few lucky individuals had joined a 'job club' where the leaders first located the jobs and then placed the young dropouts in them:

> [I: How did you look for this job?] I didn't, I got it through Performance Plus. [I: How did you hear about Performance Plus?] I seen it on TV [INT 144; female employed in a drugstore warehouse].

PROBLEMS ENCOUNTERED WHILE LOOKING FOR WORK

Looking for work in a recession, without a high-school diploma, could be expected to be a trying experience. Even so, to avoid influencing respondents' answers, we began with a general question asking whether she or he had encountered any problems. If so, we then tried to continue the conversation on this topic. However, since the design of this study allowed interviewers to deviate from the planned list of questions, in about two dozen cases the discussion of job-search methods drifted into other topics. Among the remaining sample members, more than two-thirds (79 per cent of the unemployed and 65 per cent of the employed) reported some type of job-search problem.

Some of the subjects who stated that they had not experienced job-search problems appeared to recognize that they had indeed been fortunate:

> Problems? No. I've always managed to just find one. . . [INT 034; unemployed female].

Several pointed out that jobs were not all that hard to find, if one was willing to take whatever was available:

> No, I generally don't find I have any problems in getting a job. . . . like I don't think it's any problem getting a job that's medium or little pay, there's lots of jobs out there. It's a matter if they want to do them or not. Most people won't go for $3.75 an hour, they want $6. They'd rather wait seven months and find a $6 an hour job [INT 025; male employed in telephone sales].

In a handful of cases, youthful bravado, or perhaps a naïve self-confidence, appeared to underlie positive answers to the question about job-search problems:

> It mostly—mainly the problem is that, that I'm just plumb lazy. [I: (*laughing*) Is that right?] I'm sure, like, I've never been without a job for over two weeks. [I: Really?] This is just 'cause I'm lazy right now. But I can, I have no problems getting jobs, 'cause I know, I took Occupations in school and I know that, the good and the bad points about going to get a job [INT 003; unemployed male].

> No, as far as goes for looking for work, I'm a good hustler, I'm good at talking to people [INT 077; unemployed male].

> No, 'cause I know a lot of people in the restaurant business. [I: So you didn't have much trouble getting restaurant work?] No, that's why I'm waiting 'til I turn eighteen and I'll have a job, no problem [INT 074; 17-year-old busgirl].

However, as we have already noted, a substantial majority of the dropouts in this study did discuss problems they had encountered while seeking work. Because the unemployed tended to discuss more problems, up to three were coded from their interview transcripts, while a maximum of two problems were coded for the currently employed. Table 4.2 classifies the types of problems reported by both groups, in total and separately for female and male subjects.

For both the employed and the unemployed, a lack of experience (according to potential employers) was listed most often as a job-search problem (Table 4.2). Insufficient education and a perceived bias against young workers were also mentioned quite frequently. Together, these three types of response accounted for almost half of all the answers provided to the question about job-search problems.

About one in five answers identified a shortage of jobs (or of good jobs), while somewhat fewer addressed transportation difficulties (problems with getting to interviews or places of employment). Personal problems (e.g., anger, depression, giving up) accounted for 10 per cent of the difficulties mentioned by the unemployed, and slightly fewer of those remembered by those with jobs.

Table 4.2 reveals several gender differences worth noting. Young women, whether employed or unemployed, were considerably more likely than their male counterparts to identify a lack of experience, or youth, as handicaps when seeking work. By contrast, male subjects were more inclined to mention transportation problems. Both differences may reflect the types of work these young dropouts were typically seeking. To the extent that young women in the sample were applying for traditionally 'female' retail sales and clerical jobs, they may have been actively competing with somewhat older and more experienced women also seeking work in the same labour-market segment. Male dropouts were probably more often looking for manual labour and construction jobs farther away from home or off city bus routes.

The classification of job-search problems in Table 4.2 also shows that male

TABLE 4.2. JOB-SEARCH PROBLEMS BY EMPLOYMENT STATUS AND GENDER

	Percentage					
	Unemployed			Employed		
Problem *	Total	Female	Male	Total	Female	Male
More experience needed	27	35	21	24	32	15
More education needed	14	17	15	9	4	15
Too young	9	14	6	9	15	4
Gender/racial discrimination	2	3	1	2	4	-
Not enough jobs	16	17	16	19	19	19
Only low-level jobs	3	-	4	6	4	7
Transportation	12	3	16	7	7	7
Personal (give up/ angry/depressed/shy)	10	3	15	7	4	11
Other problems	7	8	6	17	11	22
Total	100	100	100	100	100	100
Total no. of problems	104	36	68	54	27	27
Total respondents	86	34	52	76	46	30
N reporting problems	57	20	37	40	22	18
Average no. of problems	1.8	1.8	1.8	1.4	1.3	1.5

* Up to three problems were coded for the unemployed, and up to two for the currently employed; averages were calculated for those reporting problems.

dropouts were more likely to mention personal reactions, such as anger, depression, or frustration. While our data do not allow us to directly test this hypothesis, it may be that young women were more likely to believe that they could rely on assistance from parents if they could not find a job, whereas young men felt more pressure to find work and support themselves.

Inexperience and youth

Inexperience was clearly the most common labour-market handicap for these young high-school dropouts (Table 4.2). Many were painfully aware of the irony that this barrier to employment could be eliminated only by finding employment:

> Yeah, if you don't have experience, nobody wants to hire you [INT 092; waitress].

> Not many people will hire you if you don't have any experience, and like how are you supposed to get any experience if no one will hire you? [INT 159; female bookstore clerk].

> I don't know, personally I go in and put an application in. A lot of times I find people look at the application and say 'Oh, not enough experience', and then again how do you get experience if no one will give you a chance? [INT 107; unemployed male].

> Yeah, nobody wants to hire me because I've got no experience in that field. And like you know, I had one guy that took an interview, he goes 'I'd hire you but you don't have no experience'. And I, like you know, before I walked out, I thought he was a nice guy, but 'I'd still like to say one thing to you. If you don't give me a chance how in the world am I going to get experience?' [INT 010; unemployed female].

The labels 'too young' and 'inexperienced' were often interchangeable in the rejection language of employers:

> Well, basically because of my age. Most people wanted someone a little older, 21, 25, something—you know. Since I'm only 19 it just, you know, they wanted someone more experienced [INT 043; unemployed male].

However, from the perspective of employers, the label 'youth' may have additional negative connotations such as immaturity, irresponsibility, and rebelliousness. While the interview transcripts did not include many references to employers' expressing such sentiments, a few subjects did appear to have picked up hints of such reactions:

> Um, my age, people would think that 'She's too young to work at this job' or maybe they didn't like my hairstyle and whatever [INT 055; employed female].

> Well, just the fact that they think I'm punk and that I'm going to rip them off. [I: Oh really? So there's a prejudice against the way you look?] Yeah, definitely. [I: I bet Le Chateau or one of the punkier places . . . ?] Yeah, but they always want a lot of experience [INT 128; unemployed female].

> There wasn't really anything for people that didn't have experience and I didn't really have much experience in anything but restaurant work. I looked for babysitting jobs but they were looking for older ladies [INT 157; female burger-shop employee].

Not enough education

As the analysis of job histories in the next chapter reveals, high educational qualifications were seldom required in the labour market occupied by these young dropouts. Most of the jobs sought, and held, by the subjects in this study were unskilled or, at best, semi-skilled. Nevertheless, a substantial proportion of the negative reactions that respondents reported receiving from potential employers fell into the 'not enough education' category (Table 4.2).

> Yeah, on the applications, like your work history, your education. With a work history you want to be impressive but unfortunately I can't be that impressive and that goes the same for my education [INT 062; unemployed male].

> . . . But then again, the goal I want to get at is way out of reach now because there's no way I'm gonna get on as a mechanic. I can do it, I can pull a motor apart and put it back together again, but I ain't got that piece of paper that says that [INT 013; unemployed male].

Recognizing that some of the jobs in question may have required a high-school diploma or additional qualifications, it is also likely that employers were using educational attainment as an indicator of suitability, dependability, and other generic personality traits. In a time of high unemployment, when dropouts, high-school graduates, and even college- and university-educated youth were competing for a limited number of jobs, employers could afford to be choosy. Even if the jobs they were offering did not require a high-school education, evidence of having completed high school might signal other desirable employee characteristics.

Not enough jobs

Some of the subjects in this study turned their attention away from their own personal liabilities to the labour market itself, pointing out the indisputable fact that unemployment rates were very high, or that only very low-level jobs were available:

> . . . just that nobody was really hiring [INT 031; unemployed male].

> Um, no, just nothing. Just like a dead end everytime you go someplace [INT 057; unemployed male].

> . . . Just the fact there's not really anything out there other than working at something like McDonald's. . . . I don't like working for slave wages so that's why I won't work there [INT 038; unemployed male].

Transportation difficulties

About one in ten of the job-search problems mentioned by unemployed dropouts involved transportation difficulties. Without money, or a car (which some advertised jobs requested), getting to work—or even to an interview—could be very difficult:

> Yup, it's a lot of trouble especially when like you're out of school and you

don't have a job and you don't have money to get around on the bus and that [INT 114; unemployed female].

Well, everything in the paper nowadays seems to call for either experience and grade twelve or a car and when you don't have any of them it's hard to find a job [INT 113; female data entry clerk].

Transportation. [I: You use the bus system?] Yeah, [I] got another impaired so I can't drive. Also, some people want grade twelve [INT 053; unemployed male].

As one might expect, a shortage of money and transportation difficulties can be particularly problematic for youth who are also inexperienced and uncertain of themselves:

Yeah, first of all I don't know how to do an interview but even if I do get an interview I don't know how to get to one. I don't have a car, it's hard to get around. I could probably use some different clothes, like you're supposed to dress up to go to an interview. I don't even know what I want so when I go for an interview I don't know what to say [INT 001; unemployed female].

Personal reactions to unsuccessful job-search

Only 11 per cent of the job-search problems mentioned by unemployed sample members addressed personal difficulties in dealing with a tough labour market. One should not conclude from this that only one in ten unemployed dropouts felt badly about their joblessness, since interviewers did not ask directly about this. However, additional analyses of more pointed questions about current mental health (see Chapter 6) do suggest that only a minority of the subjects in this study were deeply and continually depressed.

This does not, of course, indicate that the majority of young dropouts are doing well and feeling fine. Rather, such findings suggest that most of these young people cope as best they can with their marginal labour-market position, hoping that a good job-lead will soon appear. But at any point in time, a minority do feel very depressed about their lack of job-search success:

Everybody says that they're not hiring, I get tired of hearing that. [I: How does this make you feel?] Kinda down, some days I don't even want to get up and go look for work 'cause I feel like everybody is going to keep saying the same thing [INT 080; unemployed male].

. . . you get a lot of doors slammed in your face and then sometimes you just say 'to hell with it' and don't bother going out and looking for a couple of weeks or something [INT 115; unemployed male].

I'm not motivated anymore. I don't want to go and find a job because it's all going to be negative. It's not that I like to think negative, that's just what happens, you break your butt for what? [INT 047; unemployed male].

DISCUSSION

In our examination of the interview transcripts, we attempted to answer four basic questions: (1) how do young dropouts look for work? (2) what kinds of job-search problems do they encounter? (3) are there gender differences in job-search behaviour, and in the types of problems encountered while looking for work? and (4) do employed and unemployed dropouts report different types of job-search behaviour and different problems?

To sum up our findings, most of these early school-leavers appeared to be fairly active in their job search, although their accounts suggest that the search was often rather ad hoc and not well organized. Among the currently unemployed, looking through newspaper ads and going door-to-door enquiring about possible jobs were the most common methods. Quite a number of those with jobs also stated that they had found work in this manner, but a larger proportion reported that contacts (family or friends) had been instrumental in helping them find a job. Neither group appeared to make much use of Canada Employment Centres, but about one in five of those with jobs had obtained them through a 'job club' or referral agency dealing with unemployed youth.

Only a few gender differences surfaced in our analysis of job-search methods and problems. We observed that female respondents were somewhat more likely than males to report door-to-door job searches, and that they more often reported 'lack of experience' to be a significant problem when seeking work. Unemployed male subjects were more likely than their female counterparts to state that transportation problems made job-hunting difficult.

These differences probably reflect the different types of jobs sought by female and male sample members. Compared with male subjects, a significant number of whom were looking for manual-labour jobs to which transportation might be difficult, female subjects were more likely to be seeking clerical and sales positions, and doing so door-to-door in malls and other central locations. In the search for these jobs, young female dropouts might frequently be competing with older and more experienced women. Thus while male and female dropouts appeared to be working or seeking work in the same secondary labour market, and encountering an equal number of problems, gender-based occupational segregation was still very apparent.

The finding that almost half of the employed dropouts in this study had found their job through contacts is not unusual. Using data from the 1981 National Longitudinal Study (NLS), Holzer (1988) showed that the most common method of job search among American youth was checking with friends (85 per cent answered 'yes' to this question), followed by direct applications to employers (80 per cent). These were also the most productive methods in terms of time spent in the exercise. A large Scottish survey of young people leaving school in 1983 concluded that, in addition to age, qualifications, socio-economic background, and local labour-market conditions, all of which affected a young person's chances of finding work, access to informal social networks was also important. Just as many youth found employment through informal means as through formal approaches (Raffe, 1988:55).

Other studies, not restricted to youth, have also noted that many labour-market participants find their jobs via contacts (e.g., Anderson and Calzavara, 1986:318). Information from family and friends about available jobs can speed up the job-hunting process, since the unemployed individual can avoid wasting time approaching employers who are not hiring. Employers, particularly those seeking to fill low-skill jobs, may also prefer to rely on contacts. The costs of advertising are eliminated, while the (time) costs of interviewing may be reduced if the employer can rely on informal recommendations from the 'contact' about the job-seeker (Harris and Lee, 1988:184).

However, there do appear to be some important differences between the job-search behaviours of these young dropouts and the techniques employed by older, more experienced, and better-educated labour-market participants. Although different research methods make direct comparisons difficult, other studies have suggested that better-educated job-seekers employ a wider range of job-search techniques. An extensive analysis of the job-search behaviour reported by unemployed Canadians (interviewed in the Labour Force Survey) between 1977 and 1986 (Clemenson, 1987:113) reveals that those with more education tended to use a larger number of methods. A 1985 study of Ontario university graduates (Denton et al., 1987:172) reported that over half had written or telephoned employers, had used on-campus placement centres, had checked newspaper/media ads, and had contacted friends and/or relatives about possible jobs. About one-third mentioned checking with Canada Employment Centres and engaging in door-to-door job searches. Smaller proportions had talked to their teachers or professors (22 per cent), or had tried to obtain work while enrolled in a co-op program (10 per cent).

While highlighting the broader range of job-search approaches used by university graduates, this Ontario study also identified a number of methods not available to our respondents, precisely because of their dropout status. Having left school, these young people could not take advantage of school-based employment centres, could not seek work through enrolment in a co-op program, and could not (easily) turn to teachers for advice or 'leads' on available jobs. In addition, very few of the respondents in our study reported distributing résumés and applications widely, as better-educated job applicants often tend to do (see, for example, Burman, 1988:15-19). They were not applying for the types of middle-class, professional jobs where résumés are a standard part of the job-search process. Even if they had been, most would have had difficulty compiling a useful résumé because of their limited credentials, experience, and, in some cases, writing skills.

Clemenson's (1987) analysis of Labour Force Survey (LFS) data on the job-search activity of unemployed Canadians showed that contacting employers directly was the most common approach. In 1986, 70 per cent of the unemployed said they had used this technique. Almost half (46 per cent) reported examining job ads in the newspaper, and 40 per cent claimed to have checked with a government employment agency.[1] Again, different research methods make comparisons problematic (the LFS uses a checklist, and so may encourage a broader range of answers). Even so, it would appear that the unemployed dropouts in our sample were much less likely than a cross-section of the unemployed to take advantage of government employment centres.

So, can the higher rates of unemployment among dropouts be attributed to their more limited repertoire of job-search techniques? Perhaps, since comparisons with other studies do suggest that better-educated labour-market participants look for work in a wider variety of ways. However, a recent study of unemployed residents of Chicago (Kjos, 1988), which examined the success of various methods of job search (with a follow-up survey), concluded that the number and type of methods were not particularly important. Instead, job-seeking success was more often a function of the coherence of the job search. Individuals who sought work in a systematic and organized fashion were more likely to be successful.

Thus it may be that some of the job-search difficulties experienced by the young dropouts in our study can also be traced to their ad hoc and often disorganized methods of seeking work. Some of this may simply be attributed to youth and inexperience. However, a limited range of job-search techniques and an ad hoc approach are, no doubt, also products of insufficient education, as well as the many personal and family problems that originally contributed to the decision to drop out of school.

Yet to focus only on a lack of job-search skills among dropouts is to ignore the other half of the equation, the labour market itself. Unemployment rates in Edmonton were extremely high when this study was conducted. These young people were seeking work in a very difficult labour market, and were competing with others with considerably more education and experience. Thus, even if the types of jobs that most of these dropouts were seeking seldom required a great deal of education and experience, employers could use deficiencies in those areas to screen out job applicants.[2]

Our analysis of job-search problems reported by sample members clearly demonstrates that a lack of experience and educational credentials, along with employers' reluctance to hire young and presumably unreliable workers, were most often perceived to be the main problems.[3] These young dropouts typically found themselves at the end of a long queue of job-seekers, with more experienced and better-educated individuals in front of them. Their lack of money (for clothes and transportation) and the fact that they had fewer contacts (e.g., teachers) than would most high-school and university graduates, further complicated the problem. From this perspective, the very limited use of government employment agencies is perhaps a little more understandable. With few jobs advertised, and with better-qualified job-seekers more likely to be chosen for an interview, repeated visits to an employment centre might well appear pointless.

Thus both job-search skills (limited and poorly organized) and the labour market (difficult) seem to be part of the explanation of the labour-market problems of young high-school dropouts. But what about their work ethic? Perhaps, just as some of these young people left school because of a lack of motivation, or because of immaturity, they also failed to find employment because of motivational problems. A few of the interview excerpts presented above suggest that at least some of these early school-leavers were not all that anxious to find work. However, a careful reading of the transcripts suggests that these individuals were exceptions. Most of the sample members were concerned about finding or keeping jobs.

Included in the short questionnaire that all sample members completed was the statement 'I'd rather collect welfare than work at a job that I didn't like' (see Appendix 2). This statement obviously measures attitudes to welfare as much as willingness to work in a less-than-desirable job. Nevertheless, it may also tell us something, albeit indirectly, about the work ethic of the young dropouts in this study. Subjects were asked to respond on a scale of one (strongly disagree) to five (strongly agree). Nine in ten respondents (89 per cent) disagreed with this statement (scores of 1 and 2), with 78 per cent disagreeing strongly. Recognizing that this single indicator can only partially measure a complex concept, these one-sided results certainly force us to question the conclusion that these young high-school dropouts had a weak work ethic. Additional analyses revealed that female and male subjects were equally likely to disagree with this statement, as were employed and unemployed sample members.

A parallel survey of almost 1,000 Edmonton high-school seniors in May 1985 showed 77 per cent disagreeing with the same statement, with only 53 per cent disagreeing strongly (Krahn et al., 1985). The fact that a large majority disagreed with the statement in both studies implies that, in general, young people hold a negative view of welfare. Evidence that high-school dropouts were even more likely than twelfth-graders to disagree suggests that experience in a tough labour market makes welfare a less, not more, attractive option. To the extent that this statement also measures a desire to find employment (or the 'work ethic'), this comparison also helps to counter the argument that many high-school dropouts are unemployed because they lack the desire to work.

However, our analysis of the interview transcripts did reveal that, for some of the young dropouts in our study, a difficult job-search experience might lead to frustration, depression, and, in come cases, 'giving up' looking for work. Studies of the job-search experiences of older unemployed individuals have frequently identified this phenomenon (Hayes and Nutman, 1981:111).

In other words, motivational problems might result from job-search failure, rather than contribute to it. Furlong (1989:18) observed a similar phenomenon in his longitudinal study of young Scottish school-leavers' encounters with an inhospitable labour market:

> Unemployment is not a problem of 'attitude' as the unemployed are not characterized by low levels of commitment to work and experience of unemployment is not associated with a decline in employment-commitment. However, prolonged experience of unemployment leads to a reduction in job-search activity which in turn may reduce young people's chances of leaving the ranks of the unemployed.

In his study of unemployed residents of London, Ontario, Burman (1988:24) observed similar feelings of frustration, demoralization, and depression, but apparently much more frequently than we did in our sample of high-school dropouts. He also observed anger and cynicism on the part of the unemployed directed against employers who were seen as exploitative, cold, and uncaring (Burman, 1988:27-8).

A few of our respondents hinted at similar feelings, but such sentiments were not widespread. The difference may simply reflect the lower expectations of individuals who are highly aware of their handicap (an incomplete high-school education), and to youth—most of the subjects in our study were young, and still hopeful that their prospects would improve. Unlike Burman's subjects, many of whom had been employed full-time at some earlier point, very few of the high-school dropouts in our study had more positive previous labour-market experiences with which to compare their present situation. In the following chapter, where we discuss the reactions of these young dropouts to low-paying, insecure, and marginal employment, the same factors (youth and limited expectations) will again be shown to be important.

NOTES

[1]A more recent study of the job-search activities of unemployed Americans in 1992 also showed direct contact of potential employers to be the most common method (reported by 74 per cent), followed by placing or answering newspaper ads (42 per cent), checking with family or relatives (24 per cent), and use of public employment agencies (23 per cent). Compared to twenty years earlier, use of ads had increased considerably, while use of government employment agencies had declined (Ports, 1993).

[2]A number of studies of the criteria used by employers hiring for low-skill positions suggest that personal characteristics—the 'right attitude', a good 'work ethic', and (presumed) dependability and self-motivation—are typically seen as more important than specific skills (Environics, 1986; National Center on Education and the Economy, 1990:24). A high-school diploma could thus be viewed by employers as an indicator of these personality characteristics.

[3]Another study of unemployed youth completed several years earlier in Edmonton also showed that lack of work experience was a serious handicap for young people seeking work (Tanner et al., 1984).

CHAPTER FIVE

Coming to Terms with Marginal Work

INTRODUCTION

Our discussion of dropouts' job-search experiences has highlighted the precarious and disadvantaged labour-market position of young people without a high-school diploma. We shall explore this issue in more detail in this chapter by profiling the work histories of these young people and by describing the types of jobs they are able to obtain. In addition, we ask how young dropouts come to terms with their marginal labour-market position. How do they feel about jobs that most adults would reject if they could?

The career consequences of early exit from the school system are well known (see Chapter 1). Dropouts are more likely to be unemployed and, when employed, are over-represented in low-paying, insecure, and low-status jobs (Radwanski, 1987; Rumberger, 1987:112; Gilbert, 1993). The economic restructuring of the 1980s has simply amplified this pattern. While lower-tier service-sector jobs have increased (Myles et al., 1988; Krahn, 1992), we have seen a decline in the number of desirable entry-level positions offered by employers in the goods-producing sector and the upper-tier services. Consequently, many high-school graduates, and even some university graduates, are being forced to accept part-time, temporary, and lower-status jobs (Krahn and Lowe, 1990). Thus, as we observed in the previous chapter, finding a good job is difficult for high-school dropouts, who are always near the end of the job-seekers' queue. In fact, for some dropouts, obtaining even an unskilled and poorly-paid position is often difficult.

Leaving school and finding work is a critical step in the process of becoming an adult. These dropouts began this process much earlier than the majority of Canadian youth. They also made the transition from school to the labour force in a much more abrupt manner than do the larger proportion of young people, who often prolong this process for several years by mixing school and work in a variety of ways (Krahn and Lowe, 1991). Thus youth and labour-market inexperience may influence dropouts' feelings about employment, as well as unemployment.

On one hand, it is possible that marginal jobs and frequent spells of unemployment are easier to take when one is young and hopeful. Assuming that young dropouts are conscious of their educational handicap, they may also be relatively satisfied with jobs that better-educated youth would find unsatisfactory. On the other hand, for many of these young people, dropping out of school was a symbolic way of indicating their entry into an independent adult role. In this case, unemployment (which we shall discuss in more detail in the next chapter) and marginal jobs may be particularly distressing for them, psychologically.

DROPOUTS' WORK HISTORIES

As was noted in Chapter 2, our sample was deliberately constructed to include similar proportions of employed (47 per cent) and unemployed dropouts (53 per cent). Over one-third (37 per cent) of the 76 employed sample members were working part-time, reflecting the prominence of part-time jobs in the lower-tier service industries where most were employed. Female and male subjects were equally likely to be working part-time.

Over half (55 per cent) of the employed dropouts had held their jobs for less than six months, but a small minority reported several years in their current position. The average job tenure was 8.8 months. Only three of these young workers stated that this was their first job. Another handful reported six or more previous jobs, resulting in an average of 3.0 previous jobs for the whole group of currently employed respondents (or 4.0 jobs, including their current position). The unemployed members of the sample had held a similar average number of jobs in the past (3.8).

Unemployment figured prominently in the work histories of both the currently employed and the jobless sample members.The 86 unemployed dropouts had been without a job for 9.2 months on average. About three-quarters also reported earlier periods of unemployment. Including their current spell of joblessness, then, the unemployed dropouts in this sample had experienced a total of just over 12 months in this state, on average. A large majority (82 per cent) of the employed dropouts had been unemployed at some time in the past. A few had been without work for only a short time, but a larger number reported longer periods of joblessness: 9.4 months on average.

These summary statistics indicate few differences in labour-market experience between those dropouts who were working when interviewed and those who were not. The two groups reported a similar number of jobs held. The larger average number of months of unemployment reported by those currently without work may simply indicate that they were between jobs when interviewed. In short, the labour-market behaviour of the majority of these youth appeared to be rather unstable, with frequent movement between jobs and in and out of employment. While the following discussion focuses on the jobs held by the currently employed sample members, it is quite likely that similar stories would have been told by the currently jobless, had they been asked as many questions about their previous jobs.

While most of the employed respondents discussed their current jobs at length during the interview, a handful said very little, or were not asked all of the questions. Consequently, the following analysis of current jobs and work

TABLE 5.1. PRESENT JOB BY INDUSTRY AND GENDER

Present job	Female	Male
Restaurant manager	1	-
Chef	1	1
Hostess	2	-
Waitress	6	-
Bartender	1	-
Catering-truck driver	1	-
Kitchen assistant	1	1
Busboy	-	2
Fast food (burger shops, etc.)	4	1
Total food services	17 (40%)	5 (20%)
Sales manager	2	-
Sales clerk	11	3
Stockboy	-	2
Telephone sales	-	1
Total sales	13 (30%)	6 (24%)
Warehouse	3	2
Security services	-	2
Janitorial work	-	3
Car-rental assistant	1	-
Other personal services	2	1
Total other low-status services	6 (14%)	8 (32%)
Secretary	2	-
Data-entry clerk	1	-
Telephone operator	1	-
Bank teller	1	-
Physiotherapy aide	1	-
Daycare assistant	1	-
Youth-training project assistant	-	1
Total other mid-status services	7 (16%)	1 (4%)
Auto repair	-	1
Steel works/machine shop	-	2
Textile processing	-	1
Labourer (construction)	-	1
Total blue-collar industries	-	5 (20%)
TOTAL	43 (100%)	25 (100%)

histories is based on information provided by 68 dropouts (89 per cent of the employed sample members), while the information on job evaluations was provided by a slightly smaller sample of 62 individuals.

The distribution of jobs currently held by these 68 individuals (Table 5.1) demonstrates the limited range of work opportunities available to most young high-school dropouts. Only a handful had found work outside the service industries, and, with a few exceptions, the service-sector jobs obtained were of low status. Food-service positions were most common, especially waitress and fast-food jobs, followed by sales-clerk positions. Young dropouts were also employed in warehouse jobs, janitorial work, and a number of other low-skill positions.

However, Table 5.1 also reveals that a small number of high-school dropouts had managed to find somewhat better jobs. One woman was managing a restaurant, while two respondents were employed as chefs. Several of the waitresses in better restaurants reported reasonable incomes, with tips supplementing low hourly pay. In addition, seven of the female respondents were working in what could be described as 'mid-status' service jobs (as clerks or as assistants in the helping professions). By working many hours of overtime, the young man working in the steel mill was earning considerably more than most of the other respondents. And the machine-shop employee had begun an apprenticeship that might turn into a secure and well-paying job in the future.

These examples suggest that female dropouts may be somewhat more likely to find reasonable jobs. However, conclusions about gender advantages are probably premature, given our non-random sample and the fact that traditionally 'female' clerical jobs typically pay less and offer fewer career opportunities than do many 'male' white-collar jobs. But Table 5.1 does demonstrate that gender-based occupational segregation exists even at the bottom of the service industries. Food-service and sales positions were most common, but particularly among the female dropouts. On the other hand, none of the women in the sample were employed outside the service industries.

As was noted earlier, the employed dropouts in this study reported a total of four jobs, on average (including their current position). However, considering only different types of jobs (i.e., counting two jobs in the fast-food business as one type), these young workers had worked in an average of three types of job. Table 5.2 displays the cumulative work experience reported by these 68 individuals. Compared with Table 5.1, the occupational distributions reveal a somewhat larger number of specific jobs, but the percentages in the five job groupings are very similar.

In other words, with a few exceptions, these young workers were generally still employed in the same types of jobs in which they had begun their work careers (some after quitting school, some while still attending). The patterns of gender-based occupational segregation are also very similar. In a sense, the list of jobs in Table 5.2 describes the marginal work world within which young

TABLE 5.2. PRESENT/PAST JOBS BY INDUSTRY AND GENDER (CURRENTLY EMPLOYED ONLY)

Present/past job *	Female	Male
Restaurant manager/chef	2	1
Restaurant waitress/cashier/hostess	15	5
Baker/butcher/delicatessen	3	-
Catering-truck driver	1	-
Kitchen assistant/dishwasher/busboy	8	5
Burger chains/other fast-food	17	5
Total food services	46 (39%)	16 (21%)
Sales manager	2	-
Sales clerk	23	4
Cashier/stock (department store)	3	2
Telephone sales	4	3
Total sales	35 (30%)	9 (12%)
Warehouse	5	4
Security services	-	2
Courier/mail sorter	1	1
Janitorial work	-	4
Gasoline/car rental/oil change/car wash	1	7
Hotel/motel work	1	-
Theatre/bowling alley/amusement arcade	3	1
Hairdresser	1	-
Housekeeping/babysitting	5	-
Other personal services	2	1
Total other low-status services	19 (16%)	20 (27%)
Clerical/secretarial/data-entry/ bank teller/telephone operator	10	-
Daycare/nursing home/physiotherapy aide	4	1
Youth project assistant	-	1
Total other mid-status services	14 (12%)	2 (3%)
Plumbing/fitting/welding/machining	-	4
Heavy equipment operator	-	1
Oil rigs	-	4
Factory/packing plant/processing	-	6
Automobile repair	-	3
Labourer (construction)	3	8
Farm labourer	-	2
Total primary/secondary industries	3 (3%)	28 (37%)
Total jobs	117 (100%)	75 (100%)

* Jobs (including present job) held at least once by an employed respondent.

dropouts obtain their labour-market experience, and that many have trouble leaving (Radwanski, 1987; Rumberger, 1987:112; Gilbert, 1993).

The only noteworthy percentage shift between Tables 5.1 and 5.2 shows larger numbers of male dropouts employed in the primary and secondary industries in the second table. This probably reflects the depressed state of the Edmonton economy in 1984-85, when the interviews were conducted. A few years earlier, the oil and construction sectors were much stronger, and young male dropouts would have had a better chance of finding work in them. By mid-decade, some of these individuals had been forced into lower-paying service-sector jobs, like this 24-year-old who was now completing his high-school education at Alberta College and working part-time selling magazines over the telephone:

> I had a really good job in the oilfield business and I was making $2,200 a month on that, which is better than a lot of people do after seven years of education. I was happy with that. I was at that for five years. . . . the oil business went down three years ago when I got laid off [INT 025].

While a few of the older dropouts had been pushed back into the secondary labour market when the economy worsened, there were also some who had found their way into responsible and challenging positions within the service sector. Perhaps the best success story was the 23-year-old woman, a single parent, who was now managing a busy restaurant [INT 163]. She had begun work as a waitress eight years earlier, and had been with her present employer (a small chain of restaurants) for over three years, slowly working her way up to this managerial position. Similarly, a 23-year-old chef had begun with summer restaurant jobs and built his career from there [INT 086].

But these were exceptions. Most of these dropouts had experienced only horizontal job mobility, and a considerable amount of that. The work history of a 22-year-old woman currently driving a catering truck was not particularly unusual:

> . . . I worked in a butcher shop right after I quit for a year, and then I, after the butcher shop I worked for the Bay . . . in a self-serve restaurant, and then I went to work for Grandma Lee's as a baker. I worked [there] for a year and a half. It's early, early hours but it's all right. The pay was no good . . . you don't get paid anything. And after that I went to work for a delicatessen again. I worked there for seven months and then I went to the Renford Inn . . . for six months. [I: What did you do there?] I cooked. I learned how to fast-food cook and then I went back to Grandma Lee's again as a baker and I baked there for six months and then I got promoted to an assistant manager, and it's seven days a week any time they want you for a measly $1,100 a month . . . but then my boss told me not to bother his girls because he had them trained the way he wanted them. So I quit there and now I've got this job [INT 083].

Another 22-year-old woman working part-time as a bartender recalled a similarly irregular work history. As was the case for most of the other respondents, periods of unemployment figured prominently:

> . . . I was a general labourer. I cut brush and levelled cement and laid carpet and tile and sort of hammered. Well, we never actually built anything but we started to. And then . . . I moved to Edmonton because there's no work on Vancouver Island. I moved back here and I got a job as a mail clerk key-operator. Operating a Xerox machine and opening all the mail and running around and then I'd do some typing for other departments when I wasn't busy . . . And then with that company I got promoted to a data-entry clerk for the metals department. And I ran these reports for them and then I got laid off. And then I went on unemployment. . . . that was from . . . August 1981 to November 1982. . . . I didn't do too much. Well, I took a signing course for deaf people. . . . Then I started a computer programming course, nights at NAIT, and I was sort of looking for work and I didn't really find much and then I worked illegally for this flower cult for a while making corsages for mothers. . . . They paid me cash and they wrote it off as like flowers or something [INT 067].

Some of the causes of such irregular work histories can be traced back to the dropouts themselves. For some, quitting a job had been part of a plan (often unsuccessful) to return to school. For others, it reflected a youthful and impulsive response to a specific dissatisfaction at work. Living at home, as many of the younger dropouts were, made quitting easier. And in some situations it appeared that personality characteristics that might have been problematic in school also created problems on the job. One 19-year-old female, now working as a waitress, attributed her history of short-term jobs in fast-food restaurants to the fact that 'I was young and irresponsible for a couple of years' [INT 153]. A 21-year-old male working part-time as a janitor in a curling rink also seemed at least somewhat aware of his contribution to the problem:

> Well, the first job I got was at the Keg & Kleaver as a busboy. . . . I worked there for about eight months and then got into an argument with the boss over something he thought he heard but he didn't and then quit there. After that, I . . . just went to the farm for a week or two. . . . Then my brother got me a job at Jake's Potatoes and that was just basic labour, machine-runner and that. Then I got into an argument with him and I quit there. That lasted eleven months. Then I took another break for about four months and went to Mr Lube and that only lasted about four months too and then I quit 'cause I got into an argument with the boss over this and that. Then I went up north and worked for a construction company for two months and then I come back here because I was getting into too many fights that I shouldn't have been [INT 117].

Such examples notwithstanding, the interview transcripts also revealed that these irregular work histories could be blamed, in large part, on the nature of employment in the secondary labour market where dropouts are most likely to find jobs. Some of the jobs reported had been seasonal: working in construction, or at an outdoor ice-cream stand for the summer months, for example. Others, supported by government job-creation funds, had ended when the limited-term wage subsidies expired.

However, some respondents mentioned that the restaurants, shops, and other small businesses where they had worked had gone bankrupt, or laid off help to cut costs. As we have already noted, there were several examples of jobs lost in the struggling oilfield and construction industries. A 19-year-old male, now working part-time as a sales clerk in a sporting-goods store, remembered losing his last job in a grocery store:

> I was bitter. I suppose I saw it coming for quite a while because they had laid off quite a few people recently but I thought I would last at least until after Christmas. . . . when they laid me off I was bitter and angry. . . [INT 008].

In short, some of the labour-market difficulties experienced by this sample of dropouts were the result of the depressed economy during the first half of the 1980s. However, the recession merely aggravated a perennial problem for most young dropouts, inhabitants of a secondary labour market where employment is typically quite insecure.

JOB LIKES AND DISLIKES

Most studies of job satisfaction ask questions like 'All in all, how satisfied are you with your work?' (Krahn and Lowe, 1993:340-1). Such general measures typically reveal a large majority of satisfied employees, despite the evidence that many jobs pay little, require few skills, offer few personal satisfactions, and may be very insecure. This apparent contradiction is easier to understand when we recognize that many workers have little chance of obtaining a better job. Given few reasonable alternatives, most workers will report that they are relatively satisfied with their jobs (Kalleberg and Griffin, 1978:390; Rinehart, 1978:7). As Stewart and Blackburn (1975:503) put it: 'Satisfaction is expressed within a framework of what is possible, liking is expressed within a framework of what is desirable.'

This is an important theoretical distinction, particularly for a study of young dropouts in a restricted labour market. If, in fact, these young people see few alternatives to their present employment, most might be inclined to report satisfaction with their current job. The point is not to question such reports, but to move beyond them to discover individual likes and dislikes about a particular job.

Consequently, in this study interviewers were instructed to ask dropouts what they liked and disliked about their jobs, rather than if they were satisfied or dissatisfied with them. A detailed content analysis of answers to these questions led to the construction of a simple measure of job likes/dislikes. Employed respondents were categorized as generally liking, appearing ambivalent about, or generally disliking their jobs. A 17-year-old part-time hostess in a burger shop and a 20-year-old male stockboy in an automobile sales firm were among those classified as generally liking their jobs:

> I love everything about it. I always have. There really isn't anything I don't like [INT 154].

> I can't really say that there's too much that I don't like about it 'cause everybody seems to get along very well there, there's no hassles. What I like about it is I keep busy all the time, you don't sit around and twiddle your thumbs all day. It pays good . . . and I can get an apprenticeship out of the deal which I'm looking forward to [INT 066].

An 18-year-old part-time waitress was more ambivalent about her present job, replying that:

> The time goes quick and I like the paycheques [INT 091].

Another subject classified as ambivalent was this 24-year-old female secretary:

> . . . the hours are really good, the money isn't bad, the benefits are good, the work isn't hard. . . . Ah, it's boring, it's menial, it's got no challenge [INT 105].

Only four of the employed dropouts appeared to generally dislike their jobs. A 20-year-old male, working three hours a day as a paper shredder in a bank, gave the following answers to the interviewer's questions about job likes:

> Not too much at all. It just gives me enough money to keep my car running and have some social life [I: Is there anything you particularly dislike about it?] It's boring, tedious, no variety in it. It's the same thing every day [INT 007].

An 18-year-old male, working part-time as a security guard, stated:

> You can't go anywhere, the highest position you go to is supervisor and they get paid $4.25 an hour so it's a dead-end job. [I: Any likes at all?] You get to read a lot, that's about it [INT 112].

The other two respondents in the 'generally dislike' category were less descriptive but equally negative when asked what they liked:

> Not too much, just that I don't sit at home all day now [INT 108; 16-year-old waitress].

> The money. [I: What do you dislike?] The work [INT 151; 17-year-old female working nights, part-time, as a kitchen helper].

FIGURE 5.1: JOB EVALUATIONS BY AGE AND GENDER

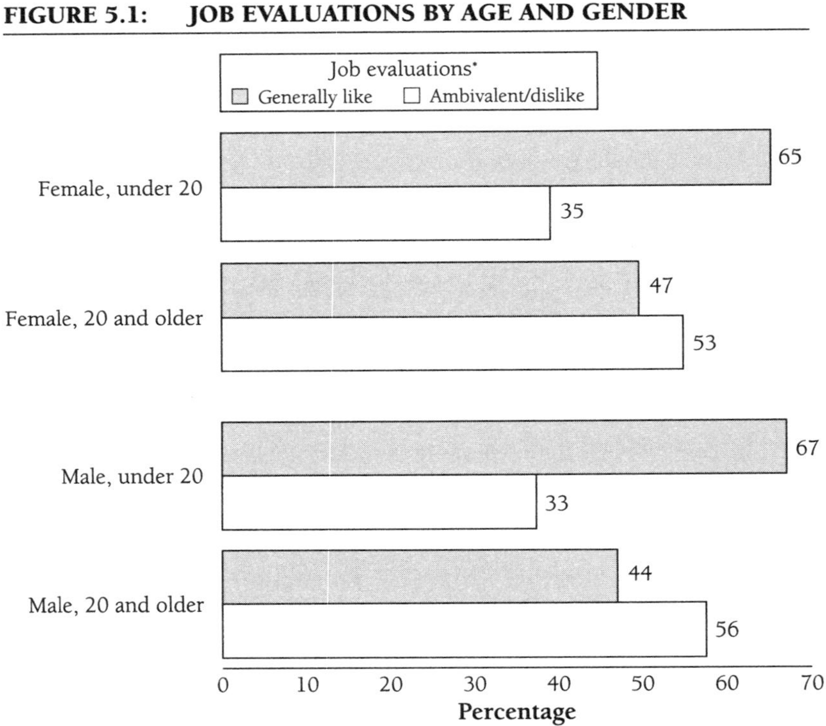

*Currently employed respondents' comments about their jobs were classified into two categories: generally like their job and ambivalent or generally dislike their job.

Only 7 per cent of the 62 dropouts who answered these questions were classified as disliking their jobs; a majority (57 per cent) were coded as generally liking their work, while the rest (36 per cent) were considered to be ambivalent.[1] Given the way in which general job-satisfaction questions tend to be answered, we would expect that, had they been asked, a somewhat larger majority would have reported themselves satisfied with their current jobs. In short, dissatisfaction was not particularly widespread, despite the fact that most of these dropouts were working in rather low-level service-sector jobs.

At the outset, we speculated that age might play a part in the job evaluations of recent dropouts. To examine this possibility, the 'ambivalent' and 'generally dislike' categories were combined (since only four respondents were included in the latter), and respondents were separated into two age categories (under 20 years; 20 and older). Two-thirds (66 per cent) of the younger dropouts appeared to generally like their jobs, compared with only

TABLE 5.3. WHAT RESPONDENTS LIKED ABOUT THEIR JOBS

	N	%
Meet/talk to nice/interesting people	18	
Nice/fun/interesting co-workers	14	30
Pay	12	
Promotion/advancement possibilities	5	
Hours (set your own/flexible/part-time suits family)	4	
Benefits	2	
Office environment	1	22
Interesting work/interested in the area	12	
Responsibility	7	
Variety in tasks	5	
Challenging	3	
In area of training	1	
Chance to get some training	1	27
No supervisor/work at your own pace	6	
Good management/expectations clearly defined	2	7
Keeps me busy/time goes quickly	7	
Easy work	2	
Gets me out of the house	1	9
Job is fine/I like everything/general answers	5	5
Total number of answers	108	100
Total number of respondents	61	

46 per cent of their somewhat older peers. Separate analyses of the job evaluations of currently employed female and male respondents revealed the same age differences for both groups (Figure 5.1). Thus these data suggest that job satisfaction was somewhat more common among younger dropouts.[2]

Positive job evaluations

Table 5.3 shows the job characteristics that respondents said they liked, while Table 5.4 (p. 89) classifies the features they disliked about their current positions. Positive evaluations were more common, as one would expect from a sample where a majority were coded as generally liking their jobs. The 61 dropouts who identified something they liked listed a total of 108 job characteristics. A smaller number (N = 49) reported something they disliked (62 answers in all).

The social aspects of the job—meeting interesting people and/or enjoying the company of co-workers—were identified most often (30 per cent of all positive comments) as good features of a job (Table 5.3):

> I like working with people and my boss, and the assistant manager, he's really easy to get along with, it's nice because you aren't just a number, you are somebody there. Everybody knows you and it's nice [INT 166; 18-year-old female working part-time as a cashier in a retail shop in West Edmonton Mall].

> . . . There isn't really anything I dislike about it. It's fun to work there, people are great to get along with [INT 092; 17-year-old waitress].

Extrinsic or material work rewards (e.g., pay, benefits, and promotion opportunities) were mentioned somewhat less often (22 per cent of all positive comments). While twelve respondents said something positive about their wages, not all of these individuals were that well-paid; one 17-year-old female was clearly impressed with the $5.00 an hour she was receiving. Another three mentioned pay in the 'at least I get paid' sense. Only two listed fringe benefits as an attraction, one of whom was pleased to be given paid holidays. Five of these dropouts spoke positively about the possibility of promotion, although it was by no means certain that they themselves would be so fortunate.

Intrinsic work rewards, or feelings of personal satisfaction resulting from performing the job itself, were evaluated positively somewhat more often (Table 5.3). A dozen respondents said they found their work interesting, including a physiotherapy aide, a secretary, several sales clerks, a young man employed as a cook in a fast-food restaurant, and a young woman working in a warehouse. About half a dozen mentioned responsibility, while a similar number liked the variety in their tasks, and three considered their work to be challenging:

> I like the responsibility, calling your own shots. . . . There's a lot of pressure, it's a lot of times when it gets really hairy, but you get used to it. It's always different, you can't blueprint your job [INT 086; 23-year-old male chef].

> Yeah, it's satisfying when you actually catch one [INT 137; 20-year-old male 'skip catch' for a collection agency].

A handful of respondents mentioned management practices as features they liked in their jobs, some noting that they were trusted to work unsupervised. But this category also included answers reflecting some antagonism to authority figures (e.g., 'no one tells you what to do'), a problem that might also have arisen earlier, while still in school. Finally, the positive answers provided by seven of these employed dropouts suggested that they had held previous jobs in which time dragged.

> Well, you're always busy and time goes by pretty fast, people are friendly [INT 144; 21-year-old female working in a drug company warehouse].

> . . . it's a great atmosphere to work in but. . . . the work is all right. I think what I like the most is that the work is fast-paced and the time just flies by [INT 153; 19-year-old female employed as cook/hostess in a restaurant].

Jobs in the secondary labour market are typically described as offering few intrinsic or extrinsic rewards (Krahn and Lowe, 1993:127-38). Although most of these recent dropouts were employed in this marginal work world, a few of the older sample members had managed to find somewhat better jobs. This probably explains why the older group provided four of the five positive comments about career-advancement possibilities. Some of the respondents also reported other intrinsic and material rewards from their work, but most did not. In general, then, these results reflect the negative characterization of the secondary labour market in which most young dropouts find employment.

More interesting, perhaps, is the value attached to workplace social relationships. A closer examination of the interview transcripts reveals that the younger employed dropouts were considerably more likely to mention nice/interesting customers and clients (13 times) than were the older respondents (only 5 mentions). Similarly, the younger interviewees said positive things about their co-workers more often (9 mentions versus 5 from the older sub-group).

It is unlikely that the customers and co-workers of the older dropouts were less pleasant than those of their younger peers. Instead, the greater emphasis on workplace social relationships among the younger sample members may reflect a different set of work orientations, or values, more preoccupation with fun and friends, and less concern about careers and personal self-fulfilment at work.

This interpretation suggests that young dropouts would not be aware, or would take little notice, of the general absence of intrinsic or extrinsic rewards in their jobs. For example, a 17-year-old male warehouse worker stated enthusiastically, 'Oh yeah, everything, everybody's just perfect' (INT 121), and later reported matter-of-factly that the job was temporary and would be ending in a week. For others, somewhat more aware of what they were missing, the emphasis on positive aspects of social interactions at work may have been a way of coping with, or compensating for, the absence of extrinsic or intrinsic work rewards:

> . . . It's not much, I don't get much money but at least it's, my mom's happy enough that I'm working. [I: What do you like about your job?] I like working with people. I always have. Like I have a tendency to get along with most people. . . . [I: So what do you do then, at the job?] I'm the counter person, I'm the one who serves you the food. . . . I don't make the food, thank God about that. I just serve it [INT 118; 17-year-old female working in a burger shop].

A similar argument has been used to explain why, in the labour force as a whole, instrumental work orientations (an emphasis on pay and material benefits) are relatively common. Individuals working in jobs with few intrinsic rewards will frequently stress the importance of good pay (Rinehart, 1978:7). Since the labour market inhabited by young dropouts is also short on well-paying jobs, positions where co-workers and customers are interesting and fun may come to be seen as 'better' jobs, particularly by the youngest dropouts.

Negative job evaluations

Inadequate extrinsic rewards were reported somewhat more often than other job dislikes. Low pay was mentioned most often (Table 5.4), and when it was, there was little doubt that the job in question did pay poorly.

> . . . I only bring home about $600 a month so that covers like all of our living expenses, our food and everything, but it doesn't cover the rent or nothing like that [INT 083; 22-year-old female driving a catering truck; living with her boyfriend].

> . . . Things are too expensive now, you can't support yourself on what you make these days. . . . $4.00 an hour, what is that, you know? Nothing. . . [INT 167; 18-year-old female holding two part-time sales jobs; living at home].

Several respondents disliked the long hours they were working, while a few were working part-time and wanting more hours. But complaints about irregular hours, shift work, or night work were more common. This 21-year-old woman was generally satisfied with her job as a telephone operator, having been recently promoted, but disliked the shift work required:

> . . . I don't work Monday to Friday, I work Saturday, Sunday, or midnights. I work many different hours of the day. So I don't, I can't—you know, I can't take a course in the evening and say that I'm going to be there every week because I don't know if I'm going to work or not. . . . They tell us two weeks of our schedule. . . . So I always know two weeks in advance. . . . I'm hired as a new operator, so the people who were hired before me, they'll get better shifts. . . . I'll get all the dirty shifts to begin with until some people are hired under me which will probably be a long time [INT 099].

Only a few of these dropouts commented on the absence of other extrinsic work rewards, such as promotion opportunities or fringe benefits. However, eight respondents mentioned hard-to-please customers as a dislike. This is not surprising, given the number employed in retail sales and food-service positions involving frequent contact with the public. Another five were irritated by lazy co-workers, while six commented negatively on their supervisor or manager. Having suggested earlier that some of these dropouts might have had problems in getting along with employers, one is tempted to interpret

TABLE 5.4. **WHAT RESPONDENTS DISLIKED ABOUT THEIR JOBS**

		N	%
Low pay		9	15
Hours:	too long	3	
	too few	3	
	irregular/nights/poor shifts	7	21
No promotion/advancement possibilities		3	
Unpleasant/unhealthy working conditions		2	
No benefits		1	10
Problems with customers/clients		8	
Unpleasant/lazy co-workers		5	21
Unpredictable/unpleasant management		6	
Having to supervise and be responsible		2	13
Boring/tedious work		6	
Lack of challenge/no variety		3	
Stressful work		2	16
Having to look busy		2	3
Transportation (to work) problems		1	1
Total number of answers		62	100
Total number of respondents		49	

these results in the same way. However, most of the examples point to management rather than employee problems, and this may reflect a fairly typical feature of employment at the lower end of the labour market.

For example, a 21-year-old male was being paid $5.50 an hour for silk-screening shirts, but was penalized the retail price of the shirt ($8.95) for any mistake he might make, despite a promise at the outset that he would be allowed three mistakes a day (INT 087). A 20-year-old waitress described her manager's expectations of her and other waitresses in the hotel dining-room:

> . . . I don't like working in the hotel that I'm working in now 'cause the management is just too much, but we all hope that that's going to change pretty soon. . . . [I: What sorts of things are they doing?] Oh, they're just

> really, really bad. . . . he treats us really bad but he expects a lot from us. He really gives us a hard time, he wants us all to come in with as little [on] as possible, and work in as little as possible, and take a lot of abuse that I won't take [INT 095].

Job dislikes focusing on the inadequacy of intrinsic work rewards were also noted by some of the respondents. One of the chefs found his supervisory position to be stressful, but his case was unusual. Respondents were more likely to complain about limited task-demands. Half a dozen respondents, in a range of different jobs, said they disliked the boring or tedious nature of their work. Two of these dropouts disliked having to look busy (in sales positions), and a handful found little challenge in their job:

> At the present moment I'm not exactly enthused about my job. I work a lot of hours, I work ten hours a day, six days a week. . . . our particular location doesn't have enough business to put more than one person in there. I really liked the job at first—well, it's still not bad—but it's becoming more routine [INT 158; 20-year-old female manager of a video shop].

> It's boring, it's menial, it's got no challenge [INT 105; 24-year-old female secretary who liked the pay, hours and benefits in her job].

Summing up, we find these dropouts identifying in their list of job dislikes some of the negative aspects of work often attributed to jobs in the secondary labour market (low pay, irregular hours, boring work, problematic management, and so on). No obvious age differences in the pattern of answers were observed. Younger and somewhat older respondents were equally likely to criticize these and a handful of other aspects of their jobs.

COMING TO TERMS WITH MARGINAL WORK

The interview data clearly show that a large majority of these young dropouts were employed in very marginal jobs. It is particularly noteworthy, then, that so few spoke negatively about low pay, few benefits, the absence of promotion chances, and boring, menial work. This lack of criticism does not mean that most dropouts were enjoying extensive work rewards. If they had been, they would presumably have said so when asked what they liked about their work (Table 5.3). But they did not. Rather, many appeared to like their work despite the deficiency of intrinsic and extrinsic rewards. We have already suggested that workplace social relationships may fill some of this gap, particularly for the youngest dropouts. But there are additional factors, some of them age-related, that help to account for these relatively positive job evaluations.

Limited occupational goals

When asked about their occupational goals, over half of the employed sample members reported either vague work-related ambitions or none at all.[3] It is impossible to tell whether the relative absence of occupational goals was a precipitating factor in dropping out of school, or whether the failure to finish high school meant that occupational goals did not develop. Whatever the causal direction, these interviews reveal substantial numbers of young dropouts with vague or unformed career goals.[4] Those under 20 were less likely to report specific occupational goals (61 per cent compared with 48 per cent of those aged 20 and older).

The absence of such goals was associated with positive job evaluations, probably because negative comparisons between a low-level job and personal ambitions would be less likely to emerge:

> As long as I'm working, I'm happy. [I: So you have no definite career goals?] No [INT 157; 17-year-old female generally liking her job at a burger shop].

> I'd like to be successful. I'd like to be happy always. Which I am right now, which is really nice. [I: What would success mean?] It would mean being happy at my job. Uh. . . . being financially stable at the time, and just enjoying life. [I: Do you have some long-range goals? . . .] Not as of yet. I haven't really decided. There's so many different types of jobs out there [INT 004; 19-year-old female generally liking her job in a car-rental firm].

The presence of occupational goals, however, increased the probability that the respondent would dislike his or her current job:

> Sure [I] would like to become a nurse but I don't think I ever will. [I: So you don't think you will be doing a job like that in five or ten years?] No, I don't. . . . I feel like I'm going to be stuck at that [video store] for the rest of my life sometimes [INT 158; 20-year-old woman managing a video shop and ambivalent about her current job].

Among the female respondents, reports of no clear occupational goals were frequently accompanied by comments about wanting to get married and/or have children. Alternative central life interests would obviously reduce the possibility of dissatisfaction with a low-level job. Eight of the women in the employed sample (20 per cent), including some of the older respondents, mentioned such traditional female goals when asked about jobs they would like to hold in the future:

> It doesn't matter as long as Mike is going to support me—he better! I want to be able to make enough money to have my own money but I want to be supported [INT 125; 19-year-old female generally liking her job as sales manager in a small gift shop].

> What are my major goals in life? I really don't have any right now. [I: What kind of job would you like to have in five or ten years?] I don't want to be working in five or ten years. I want to be at home having kids. . . [INT 083; 22-year-old female driving a catering truck; about to get married].

The comments of some sample members suggested that their occupational goals were only now beginning to take shape. In fact, in a number of cases it was clear that the goals reported were influenced by positive evaluations of the current job. In situations such as this there would obviously be little chance of a discrepancy between ambitions and the reality of one's job. Having left school without career ambitions, and having limited experience of the range of jobs available, a young dropout beginning to think more maturely about his or her occupational future could easily look first at the job he or she was already in:

> At first I wanted to be a vet but now I like clothing stores. You meet a lot of interesting people [INT 141; 17-year-old female sales clerk in a women's clothing store who generally likes her job].

> I'd like to be still working in shipping and receiving [INT 110; 20-year-old male in a warehouse job that he generally likes].

Finally, several of the sample members reported what might be considered unrealistic occupational goals. A few mentioned careers in popular music, even though none appeared to have the necessary skills. One wanted to be a psychologist, another a scientist, and one a lawyer. These individuals seemed aware of the education they would need in order to reach these goals, but reported them nevertheless. It is difficult to tell whether these really were occupational goals or just youthful daydreams. In either case, these 'goals' seemed too far removed from current labour-market realities to breed much dissatisfaction with more mundane current jobs:

> Well, I just want to finish high school and then I'll think about that later. I want to sing. I want to become a singer. [I: What kind of singer?] Soft rock and country. [I: Do you do any music right now?] I'm going to take guitar lessons. I've never taken singing lessons but . . . I sing pretty good [INT 100; 15-year-old female 'helping Dad with his books' part-time and generally liking her job].

> It's a long way down the road. I would like to be a lawyer in the Court of Queen's Bench. . . . [I: How likely is it that you will actually be able to achieve that sort of goal?] Very likely. I am good at debating and I have a very mean temper when it comes to arguments [INT 146; 17-year-old male labourer who generally likes his job].

Job hierarchies and opportunities for advancement

Although workplace social rewards played a central role in job evaluations for many of these young workers, others did comment on the presence or absence of intrinsic and extrinsic work rewards. For those in jobs with relatively few rewards, one way of coping was to point to other jobs that were even less desirable. There seemed to be some agreement among sample members about the hierarchy of jobs within the lower-level service industries.

Despite the good incomes and enjoyable jobs reported by several waitresses, two chefs, and a restaurant manager, white-collar jobs appeared to be more highly valued than restaurant jobs, at least according to several sales clerks who spoke disparagingly about their previous jobs in the food services. But it was unskilled work such as dishwashing and fast-food jobs that received the most criticism from those who had done better. As we noted in Chapter 3, fast-food jobs were frequently viewed as appropriate for adolescents, for student workers, not young adults who had left school behind them. A 20-year-old stockboy in a music store called them 'piddly jobs' (INT 089), while an 18-year-old male working in a steel mill further clarified the status distinctions:

> . . . I'll never work at a fast-food place. . . . it's the kind of job you grow out of, right? Once you get older you kind of—like I got out of Harvey's and I looked up to Zellers [a stock-boy position] and I figured well, there's a job. It gives me a buck fifty more an hour plus people don't laugh at you [INT 106].

A 19-year-old woman, ambivalent about her present temporary job as a data entry clerk, added telephone soliciting to the list of worst jobs:[5]

> I'm looking right now but there's not much out there except telephone soliciting. [I: You're not interested in that?] No, not really, I did it once before and I don't want to do it again. . . . If I get another dishwashing job, I better start thinking about the direction of my life. . . [INT 113].

Several other respondents made negative comments about telephone soliciting, but it was a 17-year-old female who pushed it to the bottom of the list, presumably below her own job at a burger shop:

> . . . one of my good friends right now is unemployed. . . . She tried a job as a telephone solicitor, I think everyone's done that at one time or another in their life and she hated it. . . [INT 118].

In fact, few of these dropouts had ever been forced to work in telephone sales (Table 5.2), and only one of the older male sample members (age 24) was currently employed in such a job. He was also attending school part-time, seeking to obtain his high-school diploma. His method of rationalizing a job at the bottom of the hierarchy, a job towards which he was somewhat ambivalent, was to identify further status distinctions:

> I'm not particularly fond of sales as a job, but the people don't slam the door in your face, they hang up on you. . . . Well, I feel the [magazine he is selling] is a pretty good product so I don't feel so bad about phoning people [INT 025].

Reminding oneself (and the interviewer) that there were even worse jobs was one way of maintaining face in this secondary labour market. Another was to point out the possibilities for advancement from the present position.

A number of the sample members had obtained their present jobs through participation in a 'job club'. Government job-training funds subsidized their salaries, but only for a limited time. Almost all these respondents were confident that the subsidized 'training' position would turn into a 'real job' when the program ended, a hope that was bound to be unrealized for some. Apprenticeships were relatively rare among these young workers, but one young man had been promised one, sometime:

> Eventually they're going to put me through on my apprenticeship and what they want to do is study my work habits to see if I'm a quitter or a self-starter. . . . [I: When will you start your apprenticeship?] Well, he said there's no guarantee but it could be anywhere from two days to two years. . . [INT 111; 18-year-old male generally liking his new job (6 weeks) in an automobile reconditioning shop].

Sales clerks were frequently told that they were starting low in the job hierarchy, but that there were opportunities to move into management or to become a 'buyer' for those who stuck with the job:

> . . . the position I am in work is probably the lowest you can go in that job, but there is room for advancement, and you can go different directions. You can either stay in the retail business or go into buying and executive positions if you stick with it long enough [INT 138; 20-year-old female, ambivalent about her job as a clerk in a clothing store].

And employees in fast-food restaurants were generally told how they could move up the ladder to better jobs:

> I'm a car host. I go out and take people's orders, and tell them to have a nice day and enjoy their food, and I have been training in the kitchen as well. I would like to train for supervisor, that's what I would like to do. They have been putting me in the kitchen and I have been cooking, and doing fries and things like that. . . [INT 154; 17-year-old female who clearly likes her job in a burger shop].

While this ladder had several rungs, a hard-working young person could climb it relatively quickly:

> . . . I started out car hopping, taking people's orders and cleaning and I was doing that for quite a while and then I started in the kitchen doing fries, onion rings, chicken and what not. I did front end, that's orders coming in, hand them to the waitresses, you don't take any orders. You handle the till. . . . and now I take care of the front end, I'm like an assistant supervisor, something like that. . . [INT 156; 18-year-old female, ambivalent about her burger-shop job, which she has held for seven months].

In a sense, these young dropouts were quite 'normal' in the way they rationalized their low labour-market position. Like older and better-educated workers, they looked down the job hierarchy for reassurance and up the promotion ladder for hope. But, unlike the more-advantaged workers in the primary labour market, they were much closer to the bottom of the occupational hierarchy and were also looking up a much shorter ladder.

Experiences of unemployment

Most of these young dropouts had been unemployed at some point, frequently for considerable lengths of time. For a few of the younger respondents, unemployment had not been all that stressful. Living at home reduced money problems, although it also meant putting up with concerned parents. But, as we shall note in the next chapter, most had found unemployment to be a relatively unpleasant experience. Depression and boredom were mentioned most often, along with difficulty in getting by on very little money. For some, living independently meant constant worries about paying bills. For those still living at home, the problem was more often one of embarrassment when friends with jobs had more money for leisure activities:

> . . . the first week and a half, I thought, right on, sleep till five in the afternoon. Then after a while, soaps, then I have no money, no cigarettes, stuff like this, or I wish I had this dress. I got really depressed [INT 154; 17-year-old female who generally likes her job in a burger shop].

> Times were really tough. You, you really had to save. . . . [I: How did you feel about yourself?] Really insecure. . . . 'cause at the time all my friends had jobs and they were always going out. . . . And you couldn't go out with them because you didn't have any money. . . [INT 004; 19-year-old female who likes her job as a car 'hiker'].

Compared with being unemployed, working in a marginal job might not seem that bad. Furthermore, since these dropouts tended to socialize with others who had failed to graduate from high school, their friends too were often unemployed, or working in similar types of jobs. And because, on average, these dropouts tended to come from lower socio-economic backgrounds, other family members might be employed in the same labour market. Thus comparisons with the jobs and work histories of friends and family members would not, in many cases, lead to negative assessments of an individual's own job:

> [I: How far did your mom go in school?] I think she got halfway through grade twelve. [I: And what does she do?] Right now, nothing, she was a waitress. . . . She's unemployed, last night she quit [INT 124; 17-year-old female who generally likes her job as a hostess in a restaurant].

> [I: What kinds of things does your boyfriend do?] He was a stockboy at K-Mart, he was a gas attendant, a cab driver, door-to-door salesman. [I: Is he working now?] No, it's always 'If we need you, we'll call you' [INT 113; 19-year-old female, ambivalent about her temporary job as a data-entry clerk].

In general, then, many of these young workers had only a limited understanding of employment alternatives. Most had never worked outside this lower level of the secondary labour market, and only a minority had friends or family members employed in primary labour-market positions. Furthermore, having vague or unformed career goals, many would not even imagine alternatives. As Blackburn (1988:232) notes in a discussion of the interactions between the structure of stratification and ideologies of work, 'those at the bottom of the stratification hierarchy not only have the least attractive jobs but also the most constrained experience.'

Education values and plans

It is quite possible that some of these young workers might not have considered the labour-market implications when they first dropped out of school. By now, however, even though their experience with employment alternatives was limited, most were beginning to realize that they were handicapped by not having a high-school diploma, a point we emphasized in Chapter 3. Comments such as these were not unusual:

> . . . I haven't had any problems with finding jobs, I've been working steady ever since. One thing about it is without the schooling, waitressing is about the only good job you can make money at. Every now and then I think that I would like to get a regular daytime job and I can't think of anything I can do without having more education than I do [INT 095; 20-year-old waitress ambivalent about her job].

> [I: Why do you think there's so much unemployment among young people?] . . . right now the job market is over-flooded and there are so many people, they're going to take the best, you know. If they have a choice between someone who dropped out of grade ten and really didn't do anything with their life for like two years, and someone who's graduated grade twelve, you know. . . [INT 118; 17-year-old female who generally likes her job in a burger shop].

In Chapter 3 we commented on the somewhat surprising finding that only a minority of the dropouts in this study appeared to have rejected the education system altogether. Most still placed considerable value on education, despite having chosen to quit high school. In fact, over two-thirds of the total sample stated, when asked, that they would like to get more education, sometime. Within this sub-sample of currently-employed dropouts, 56 per cent answered in the affirmative, 37 per cent thought that they might get some more education in the future, and only 7 per cent were certain that they would not.

Some of these dropouts would, no doubt, follow through on these promises; several had already returned to alternative schools to complete their high-school education. But for others such plans would probably not translate into future action. Nevertheless, they reveal a value system shared with the rest of society. Equally important, such public statements may have served an important function for young people beginning to recognize that they might be trapped in a marginal labour market. Like university students telling themselves that menial jobs are 'just for the summer', dropouts could promise themselves, and others, that their current labour-market situation was temporary. Once they returned to school and obtained their high-school diploma, new opportunities would open up. Thus maintenance of future education plans could be a means of coping with marginal work.

DISCUSSION

While studies of employment conditions in the lower-tier service industries are beginning to appear (e.g., Reiter, 1991; Yiannis, 1988; Krahn and Lowe, 1990; Krahn, 1992), the work experiences and job evaluations of young dropouts have received little attention. Our interview data clearly show that the majority of employed dropouts were working in the lower levels of the service sector. Their work histories were irregular, interspersed with frequent periods of unemployment, and had been accumulated primarily within the same secondary labour market.

But despite being employed in low-status, low-skill jobs, almost 60 per cent of this group appeared to generally like their work. Another 35 per cent seemed ambivalent in their job evaluations, but only a handful clearly disliked their jobs. Younger sample members tended to be more positive in their job evaluations.

More detailed analysis showed that social interactions at work, with co-workers and with the public, were most often listed as positive features of a job. Intrinsic satisfactions and extrinsic work rewards such as pay and promotions were mentioned infrequently, confirming the initial observation that most of these dropouts were employed in marginal jobs. Among aspects of their work that people disliked, the inadequacy of the extrinsic rewards was mentioned most often, although some respondents also stated that their jobs offered few intrinsic satisfactions.

The youngest dropouts were particularly likely to state that they liked the social aspects of their work, which suggests that, unlike older and better-educated workers, they might have been bringing different work orientations to their jobs. The central life interests of 16- and 17-year-old dropouts might still be 'pre-career', focusing on family, friends and fun. However, for some of these young workers, the prominent emphasis on workplace social relationships might also have been a way of coping with a job that offered very few other rewards.

A number of additional factors help to account for the generally positive evaluations of marginal jobs. First, vague, unformed, and, in some cases, unrealistic occupational goals were common, especially among the youngest sample members. It is quite likely that these vague or absent career goals reduced the possibility of dissatisfaction with relatively low-status, dead-end jobs. Second, although situated near the bottom of the occupational hierarchy and in a labour market where upward mobility was limited, many of these dropouts still managed to identify other jobs with even lower status, or to see some small chance of movement up and out of their current job.

Third, personal experience of unemployment could put the present job in a different light. Any job, no matter how lowly, was often seen as an improvement over no job at all. In addition, many of these dropouts had friends and family employed in the same secondary labour market. Hence negative evaluations of a job were unlikely to emerge from comparisons with the jobs held by others in a dropout's reference group. Finally, most of these young dropouts realized that educational credentials were needed to get ahead, and that the decision to quit high school had restricted their labour-market options. Thus many continued to promise that they might, someday, return to school. This commitment to future education could made current jobs appear less permanent, and probably helped these young people to cope with what might otherwise appear to be a dreary work future.

These interview results provide us with a much more detailed picture of the work experiences, job evaluations, and work values of young high-school dropouts. Within the huge research literature on the dropout phenomenon, the limited labour-market options of dropouts figure prominently, but the actual work experiences of dropouts have remained relatively unstudied.

The findings from this study are also noteworthy when compared with the equally large research literature on job satisfaction (Krahn and Lowe, 1993:338-70). First, our interviews clearly show older sample members describing their jobs more negatively, a reversal of the pattern typically observed in other studies (Kalleberg and Loscocco, 1983). Second, the strong emphasis on workplace social relationships as positive features of a job is uncommon. Employees generally emphasize some combination of intrinsic and extrinsic rewards, or, if the former are largely lacking, mainly material rewards such as pay and security.

One recent study of gender differences in job evaluations did, however, uncover a pattern similar to the one we observed (Mottaz, 1986). Women and men employed in primary labour-market positions tended to emphasize the importance of the same types of extrinsic and intrinsic job rewards. But in the secondary labour market, women were employed in poorer jobs and were more likely to say that they valued the social aspects of their jobs, whereas men working in the secondary labour market tended to emphasize extrinsic rewards. The author concluded that 'gender differences in work values found in lower-level occupations represent an accommodation on the part of women to an impoverished work situation' (Mottaz, 1986:372).

Beynon and Blackburn's (1972:66) earlier study of British factory workers also reported that (full-time) female employees emphasized the importance of friendly workmates, a feature largely ignored by male workers in the same firm. However, these authors explained the gender difference with reference to the differing work values of women and men: 'Clearly the different orientations of the women, as indicated by their priorities, reflect their roles in wider society. . . . less committed to work by economic necessity, with no interest in "getting on", they wanted to work with pleasant people in good conditions. . . ' (Beynon and Blackburn, 1972:84).[6]

These two studies highlight two basic explanations that might be put forward to account for employees who emphasize workplace social relationships as positive features of their jobs. On the one hand, such individuals might simply have different work values. On the other, their jobs might offer so few other rewards that friendly customers and co-workers are the only things that come to mind when they are asked what they like about their job. In this study, both explanations seem useful. The jobs held by these young dropouts, with some exceptions, offered few rewards, intrinsic or extrinsic. Hence the valuing of social aspects of the job might have been a form of compensation. However, for other sample members, especially the youngest, pre-career work orientations and absent occupational goals may also have played an important part.

This greater significance of work orientations is a third way in which these results differ from most findings on job satisfaction. Theoretical accounts of the sources of job satisfaction acknowledge that both work rewards (intrinsic and extrinsic) and work values (or orientations) are important explanatory factors. In fact, it is the match or balance between the two that ultimately influences an individual's subjective reaction to a specific job (Kalleberg, 1977). Typically, however, work orientations play a secondary role, while the presence or absence of work rewards has a larger impact on job evaluations (Kalleberg, 1977; Blackburn and Mann, 1979:167; Hall, 1986:95-9). For example, Miller's (1980:361) longitudinal study shows that 'job conditions are more strongly related to job satisfaction than are the social characteristics of the workers or predispositions they bring to the job'. In this study, particularly among the youngest dropouts who frequently reported considerable satisfaction with jobs that most workers would reject, individual predispositions to work appeared to have more impact.

These observations raise one final question, the answer to which lies beyond this study. What might we expect, in terms of job satisfaction, if we were to re-interview these early school-leavers today? As we have noted, previous research has typically revealed greater satisfaction among older workers, while our interviews showed the opposite. Older dropouts expressed more discontent with their jobs, and appeared to be having more difficulty in coming to terms with their marginal labour market position. Given that all our respondents were still relatively young, one might still predict that, in time, they would begin to express more job satisfaction, replicating the typical age-job-satisfaction relationship observed in other studies.

However, among the better explanations accounting for this frequently observed relationship is the simple observation that older workers have had time to move into better jobs (Hamilton and Wright, 1986:288). Hence a prediction that these dropouts would, in time, begin to view their jobs more positively presupposes that they would be able to slowly make their way up the job ladder into better positions. Unfortunately, the combination of their limited education and work experience with the emergence of a labour market in which higher educational credentials have become even more essential makes this an unlikely scenario.

Our data cannot tell us whether, in time, these dropouts will become more satisfied labour-force participants. Perhaps they will. However, our prediction would be that, unless they return to school and acquire additional credentials, most will be forced to continue to seek ways of coming to terms with marginal work.

NOTES

[1]Three of the four individuals coded as disliking their jobs were working part-time, but this did not appear to be the problem. The paper-shredder was also attending school at the time, which made part-time work necessary. The security guard disliked the hourly pay, but didn't mention a shortage of hours (as some other 'ambivalent' respondents did), and the kitchen helper actually said she liked 'the money' while disliking 'the work' itself.

[2]We chose 20 years of age as the cut-off point, since it produced two groups of roughly equal size. When 19, rather than 20, was used as the cut-off, similar results were obtained (64 per cent versus 52 per cent satisfied). When the cutting point was pushed up to 21, the percentage difference became smaller (59 per cent versus 50), but the direction of the relationship remained the same. An analysis based on only those employed full-time (using 20 as the age cut-off) revealed the same results (74 per cent of the youngest liking their job, compared to 53 per cent of the older dropouts).

[3]Included in the group reporting vague or no career goals were eleven individuals who were not asked this question directly by the interviewer.

[4]In a parallel survey of 665 Edmonton twelfth-graders (just prior to their graduation in 1985), only 13 per cent of the sample did not report a specific occupation to which they aspired in the future (Empson-Warner and Krahn, 1992).

[5]Burman (1988:38, 95) reports that unemployed individuals assessed dishwashing and telephone sales equally negatively. In a 1985 survey of twelfth-grade students in Edmonton, Toronto, and Sudbury, telephone sales jobs were ranked more negatively than a variety of other low-skill jobs, including work in fast-food restaurants (Lowe and Krahn, 1992).

[6]These data were collected over two decades ago (in 1966) and, no doubt, reflect the British situation at the time. However, such differences in the work values of men and women doing the same kind of work would be much less likely to be observed today.

CHAPTER SIX

Coping with Unemployment

INTRODUCTION

In the last chapter we examined how high-school dropouts come to terms with marginal employment. But menial jobs are not the only negative labour-market outcomes of early school-leaving. Dropouts must also contend with frequent periods of unemployment, particularly during periods of recession. Unemployment was an immediate concern for the half of our sample (53 per cent) who were without either full- or part-time work when they were interviewed. It had also been a prior concern of most of the currently employed dropouts, 82 per cent of whom reported having been unemployed at some time in the past.

This chapter examines dropouts' experiences with joblessness and their reactions to this situation. Our enquiry is guided by several general questions: (1) does unemployment negatively affect the psychological well-being of dropouts? (2) to the extent that unemployment leads to depression and other negative psychological states, precisely what causes these problems? (3) how serious are the negative psychological responses to unemployment? and (4) in addition to personal effects, does unemployment have discernible political/social effects among high-school dropouts?

THE PSYCHOLOGICAL EXPERIENCE OF UNEMPLOYMENT

We begin to address these issues by examining responses to a standard set of questions about psychological well-being included in the short questionnaire completed by all sample members (see Appendix 2). Respondents were asked *how often in the past few months they had felt depressed, felt lonely, felt like doing nothing at all, felt that people were unfriendly, and talked less than usual*. The possible response categories were 'never', 'rarely', 'sometimes', 'often', and 'almost always'.

First, among answers from the complete sample, 22 per cent stated that in the past few months they had felt depressed 'often' or 'almost always'; 19 per cent chose one of these responses when asked about feeling lonely; and 17 per cent answered in this way when asked about feeling like doing nothing at all. A smaller proportion (9 per cent) answered that they had often or almost always felt that people were unfriendly, while 14 per cent chose one of these answers in response to the question about talking less than usual in the past few months.[1] Thus, in general, these measures of psychological well-being do not indicate extensive feelings of depression or other negative psychological states within our sample of dropouts.[2]

TABLE 6.1. SELF-REPORTED PSYCHOLOGICAL WELL-BEING BY GENDER AND EMPLOYMENT STATUS

	Percentage			
	Female		Male	
	Employed	Unemployed	Employed	Unemployed
Felt depressed?				
Never/rarely	23	21	40	31
Sometimes	52	43	53	49
Often/always	25	36	7	20
Felt lonely?				
Never/rarely	49	48	60	51
Sometimes	38	25	27	27
Often/always	13	27	13	22
Felt like doing nothing at all?				
Never/rarely	47	27	47	23
Sometimes	44	55	50	36
Often/always	9	18	3	41
Felt people were unfriendly?				
Never/rarely	64	36	72	39
Sometimes	32	52	25	47
Often/always	4	12	3	14
Talked less than usual?				
Never/rarely	56	45	30	51
Sometimes	31	34	40	35
Often/always	13	21	30	14
N	45	33	30	49

Nevertheless, a comparison of unemployed and employed female and male dropouts reveals that, with only one exception (unemployed males were less likely than employed males to report talking less than usual), the unemployed were more likely to answer in a negative manner (Table 6.1).[3]

Evidence that greater psychological distress is correlated with unemployment does not necessarily mean that the latter causes the former. It is quite conceivable that the negative psychological feelings of unemployed dropouts pre-dated, and possibly hindered, their attempts to find work. In other words, instead of being a consequence of unemployment, feelings of depression and loneliness, for example, might actually decrease a young person's chances of finding work.

Because our cross-sectional research design examined the relationship between unemployment and mental health at one point in time, it cannot provide definitive answers about cause-and-effect patterns. However, the dropouts themselves had little difficulty in identifying joblessness as the source of their negative feelings:

> Physically the lack of work hasn't done anything, but mentally, it's kinda like a downer. You want a job, you don't know exactly what you're looking for. Once you find something that you do think you could handle, then for some stupid reason you are laid off or fired and that's kinda depressing 'cause kids want money [INT 049; unemployed male].

> I haven't had a steady job in over two years, and it's really depressing. You lack the cash, and [it] gets to the point where you sit around and you don't go out and look for a job 'cause it's hopeless [INT 047; unemployed male].

LOST FUNCTIONS OF WORK

Why do unemployed dropouts report more negative psychological states than do those with jobs? Finances play a large part in the answer. Predictably enough, unemployed dropouts have less money at their disposal, as the two quotations above indicate. Commenting about unemployment among adults in general, Jahoda (1982) observed that it is the loss of work's manifest function—the provision of an income—that is often a primary cause of distress for the unemployed.

In our short self-report questionnaire (Appendix 2) we asked *How would you describe your own financial situation?* Only a small proportion (7 per cent) of the dropouts interviewed answered 'I usually have more money than I need'; a large majority (65 per cent) answered 'I usually have enough money to get by'; while 28 per cent chose the third answer, 'I am usually short of money'. Table 6.2 cross-tabulates these answers by gender and employment status to give us another perspective on the financial deprivation felt by unemployed dropouts. Although the pattern is not particularly pronounced, unemployed dropouts (30 per cent of females and 43 per cent of males) were more likely to conclude that they were 'usually short of money' than were those with jobs (22 per cent of females and 14 per cent of males).

During the interviews, when describing income-related stresses associated with unemployment, some of the jobless dropouts discussed basic food, clothing, and shelter requirements. Some, for example, were not able to afford their own apartments, and so were forced to live at home with their parents longer than they (or perhaps their parents) preferred. Unemployment, in other words, frustrated their desires for domestic independence. Likewise, there was less money available for clothes. As one young woman put it: 'I look at my wardrobe every day and I get depressed' [INT 109].

TABLE 6.2. SELF-REPORTED FINANCIAL SITUATION BY GENDER AND EMPLOYMENT STATUS

	Percentage			
	Female		Male	
	Employed	Unemployed	Employed	Unemployed
More money than needed	11	-	10	4
Enough money to get by	67	70	76	53
Usually short of money	22	30	14	43
Total	100	100	100	100
N	45	33	29	49

Other dissatisfactions stemmed from the high priority that leisure has in the lives of young people. Without money, unemployed dropouts could not afford to regularly join friends in evenings at the movies or excursions to their favourite bar. A shortage of money could sometimes strain friendships, and frequently imposed an involuntary home-centredness upon their life and leisure activities:

> I found myself sitting at home a lot more than I would; or just going over to a girlfriend's place, like say, watching TV which, as opposed to—I used to love, I used to go out for supper and sit in cafés and, you know, go dancing and, and go to plays and go to the movies and go horseback riding and play racquetball and now I'm finding I can't afford these things. My self-esteem is

> getting really low right now as well. . . . because, you know, I don't have a job, I'm, I'm struggling now financially. I can't do the things I like to do. Somebody calls me up and now, 'I'm sorry, I can't go out, I'm broke' [INT 005; unemployed female].

> I felt like the world was spinning without me. A lot of the people I knew had jobs and they were going out and doing things and they had money [INT 104; female] .

> I'm kind of limited as to what I can do 'cause you can't do anything unless you have money. Yeah, I like to go out, got to a lounge, go to a movie, but you can't [INT 065; male].

> . . . I find when you've got money, you've got friends. When you don't have money, you don't have friends which really bothers me 'cause I don't really care what their clothes are like or anything like that. I find a lot of the people I know or have met, as long as I had the money they were there but once that stopped, they're just not there [INT 051; female].

Sports were another specific casualty of unemployment. Considerably fewer jobless dropouts (44 per cent of females, 55 per cent of males) than employed sample members (64 per cent of females, 67 per cent of males) regularly participated in sports. The explanation for this difference is not hard to find: maintaining an active sporting life can be an expensive proposition. As one unemployed male who had regularly played recreational hockey for about ten years put it: 'there's a lot of money involved in registration fees . . . which I just can't afford right now' [INT 056]. Similarly, another male said: 'being on unemployment, I didn't have the money to afford the five dollars a week to go bowling' [INT 002].

Although much of the psychological distress described by unemployed dropouts could be traced to the lack of an income, some of the negative feelings also stemmed from the absence of other beneficial functions of work. As other researchers (Jahoda, 1982; Burman, 1988) have argued, in addition to money, a job offers social-psychological benefits, the 'latent functions' of work. These include the fact that work structures time and demands regular activity, broadens contacts and experiences beyond the immediate family, provides a sense of purpose, and is a source of personal identity.

While it is difficult to distinguish the 'lost' manifest functions of employment from the 'lost' latent functions, it is the case that unemployed dropouts were by no means exclusively concerned with the economic costs of not having a job:

> I felt a lot better when I was working. . . . I felt better about myself in the sense that you'd come home and say 'Yeah, I did something today' and like now you come back and 'What did I really accomplish today?' [pause] 'Sweet bugger all' [INT 013; male].

> Ah, downhill both ways. I went downhill 'cause I wasn't doing anything physically, and downhill mentally 'cause I wasn't doing anything either. It was soap operas or. . . . I didn't even watch PBS. I was nothing. . . . I wasn't gaining any ground anywhere. . . [INT 020; previously unemployed male].

> . . . just sitting around knowing that you don't have a job, that I don't have to get up at six o'clock in the morning to go to a job, sitting around knowing that it's getting you nowhere, it's no good [INT 065; male] .

> Being employed? Ah, gee, that's a feeling I'll never forget. Like being employed and living on my own. Because um, well, pretty well you've got everything there for yourself and you—I don't know, I felt great when I was living on my own and employed and I just felt like I was getting up out there to the working world and I was making a lot of money and then when my cheque came in—this much goes to rent and this much goes to that and then I'd have money to spend—something that my friends didn't have and I felt good [INT 056; male].

> Yeah, it's changed, 'cause when I was first unemployed I had some money in the bank and something to back up on to, and I had money to spend so I was going out visiting friends and that. . . . now it's just a matter of sitting at home, wait until I get some money and, then, maybe go out [INT 002; male].

COPING WITH UNEMPLOYMENT

The evidence so far leaves little doubt that unemployment is disliked by dropouts, and that those with jobs report more positive feelings of psychological well-being. Thus, even though the jobs available to dropouts are typically marginal at best (see Chapter 5), even a poor job is better than no job. Nevertheless, we should still ask about the magnitude and intensity of negative psychological responses to unemployment among young dropouts. Just how damaging an experience is it for them?

Our answer to this question begins with the observation that, just as many dropouts have come to terms with marginal jobs (see Chapter 5), many may have learned to cope with unemployment, at least to some extent. While not enjoying the dropout 'life-style', they have not been completely destroyed by it either. The collective mood of our sample members was, arguably, best expressed by the young male who reported not liking unemployment, but whose experiences had not been 'depressing enough that I would kill myself' [INT 091].

This comment reflects the fact that, at the aggregate level, the self-reported psychological state of the young dropouts in our sample remained relatively positive. Comparisons with a large sample of Edmonton twelfth-graders revealed roughly similar proportions (approximately 15 to 25 per cent) in both studies reporting frequent feelings of depression, loneliness, and other negative psychological states.[4] We have, of course, documented more widespread negative feelings among unemployed dropouts, but even within this group only a minority reported feeling depressed, lonely, lethargic, and isolated 'often' or 'almost always' (see Table 6.1).

There are a number of factors that may explain how our respondents managed to reduce the psychological costs of unemployment. First, they were relatively young, and the optimism of youth is an indispensable resource when dealing with objective adversity. They could still look ahead to a better future, when their prospects might improve, when they had returned to school (as many promised themselves), and when the economy would be better. Unlike older unemployed workers looking back on a career and comparing past success with future uncertainty, these relatively young dropouts could still afford to be hopeful about the future.[5]

Second, many of these young dropouts may have been able to deal with negative feelings resulting from unemployment because they continued to enjoy the support of family and friends. These relationships, in turn, limited the financial and emotional costs of unemployment. For many, the problem of finding food and shelter was solved by living at home with one or both parents. Indeed, parental generosity was sometimes acknowledged to make the difference between surviving and not surviving. As one unemployed male explained, 'I'm getting by for the reason that my mom isn't charging me room and board right now' [INT 002]. Another unemployed male was even more emphatic: 'If I didn't have my family I'd probably be out on the streets sleeping in some gutter' [INT 109].

Of course, not all respondents were prepared to give such ringing endorsements of their parents. Quitting school and failing to find work was frequently a source of considerable conflict. Even so, many parents were still willing to provide some form of 'safety net' for their prodigal sons and daughters. Despite overwhelmingly negative reactions to the decision to quit school (over 80 per cent of respondents said that their parents disapproved) and frictions caused by subsequent unemployment, most respondents reported that they got along at least reasonably well with their parents.[6] Many could still rely on parents for sympathy, advice, and cheap (or free) accommodation. These domestic arrangements probably saved many dropouts from greater financial hardship.

In our interviews, when discussing current living and financial arrangements, we asked both employed and unemployed sample members the question *Have you had to cut back on anything?* About one in three said 'no', but, as we would expect, currently unemployed respondents were less likely to answer in this manner.[7] For both women and men, about 40 per cent of the employed reported no recent cutbacks, compared with about 24 per cent of the unemployed (Table 6.3).

However, Table 6.3 also indicates that the financial constraints forced on these young dropouts, both the unemployed and the employed, were more likely to focus on their leisure activities and non-essential consumption patterns. Cutbacks in entertainment and socializing with friends were most common, for both female and male respondents who reported having made cutbacks. But gender differences were also apparent, with young women mentioning cutbacks on clothes more often than male dropouts, who were somewhat more likely to mention entertainment, automobile, and tobacco/alcohol/drug expenditure cutbacks. Only a small minority mentioned recent cutbacks in food and shelter expenditures. While not having the discretionary income to go out with friends, buy clothes, put gas in the car, or participate in sports certainly makes life less pleasant (particularly when you are young), it is a manifestly less serious problem than being reduced to subsistence-level living.

TABLE 6.3 SELF-REPORTED CUTBACKS BY GENDER AND EMPLOYMENT STATUS

	Female		Male	
	Employed	Unemployed	Employed	Unemployed
% *not* reporting cutbacks	39	24	41	23
N reporting cutbacks	23	22	16	37
Total cutbacks reported	34	38	26	62
	(Percentage of total cutbacks reported)			
Food/shelter	15	18	8	5
Clothes	20	24	11	8
Entertainment	41	50	50	55
Car	6	-	8	8
Tobacco/drugs/alcohol	9	3	19	18
Other cutbacks	9	5	4	6

The pattern of answers to the question about cutbacks in expenditures suggests that, for some dropouts, a support network of family and friends was still providing assistance with basic living costs (and, of course, some sample members were obviously supporting themselves). These interview results also provide more evidence that curtailed leisure activities are an important social consequence of unemployment for many young dropouts (and, no doubt, unemployed graduates as well). But even here, cutbacks can be absorbed without great psychological cost, largely because dropouts can adapt to unemployment and fluctuating incomes by scaling their leisure activities up or down according to the resources available at the time.

To the question *How do you spend your time when you are not looking for work (or working)?* the most common answer (mentioned by about one in four respondents), regardless of employment status or gender, was visiting friends—an activity that can and does accompany a range of more or less expensive leisure pursuits. In bad times, when money is scarce, socializing is home-based and cheap (TV, cards, talk). In better times, it includes movies, bars, and meals out.

And while it is true that some respondents did complain of friendships that were lost because of unemployment, many more spoke of friends who helped, both financially and emotionally, when they were out of work. Furthermore, virtually all respondents (98 per cent, overall) said that they had someone to turn to when they had problems. The support person in question was most likely to be a parent or other family member (38 per cent of nominations), a close friend or friends (31 per cent) or a boy- or girlfriend (16 per cent). Neither the gender nor the employment status of the respondent modified this pattern. The importance of family and friends is perhaps best summed up by this unemployed woman who explained how she coped with unemployment:

> What really got me through was my friends, I think, and my family. It didn't matter how much I slacked off, but my mom and dad were always behind me. That's the important thing, as long as you've got support [INT 019].

In making the argument that family and friends can help poorly-qualified school leavers 'take the strain' (Hutson and Jenkins, 1989), it is important that we not overstate the case. The fact that the dropouts in our study adjusted to unemployment does not mean that they all did so equally easily. Those who lived alone in hostels or shelters had the poorest relationships with parents and the worst financial situations, and suffered more than other dropouts. There is little doubt that had more respondents faced this sort of adversity their aggregated experiences of unemployment would have been substantially worse.

A THREAT TO THE COMMUNITY?

To this point we have concentrated on the personal, largely psychological, effects of unemployment on high-school dropouts. However, an equally important aspect of the public's concern with unemployment, particularly among youth, is the threat that it is seen as posing to the broader community. Unemployment, it has been argued, endangers not only individual well-being but the wider social order as well.

TABLE 6.4. EXPLANATIONS OF YOUTH UNEMPLOYMENT IN CANADA BY EMPLOYMENT STATUS AND GENDER

	Percentage of all explanations provided			
	Employed		Unemployed	
	Female	Male	Female	Male
Individualistic explanations				
Young people are lazy/ have a poor attitude	44	46	30	22
Young people are not educated enough	12	7	9	4
Societal explanations				
Employers won't hire because of youth/ inexperience	21	21	19	22
Employers not hiring	7	14	2	6
Economy in general/ world economy/ changing technology	10	12	19	24
Government is not creating enough jobs	1	-	4	9
School preparation inadequate	1	-	2	5
Other explanations				
Fate/ 'I have no idea'	4	2	15	9
Total number of explanations	71	42	47	67

Fears about the political effects of unemployment are raised periodically by politicians and the mass media. Over a decade ago, Prime Minister Pierre Trudeau publicly worried that high unemployment 'is creating social discontent and many other uncertainties in the minds of young people' (*Globe and Mail*, 24 September 1983). The potential political costs of youth unemployment were also highlighted by Trudeau's Youth Minister who, a few months later, asserted that 'if we don't tackle the problem globally—by all of the partners in society—a generation will be sacrificed or a generation will revolt' (*Globe and Mail*, 30 January 1984). These anxieties were rekindled several years ago following Toronto's 'Yonge Street riots' in May 1992. And the media have regularly raised the spectre of the unemployed and underemployed youth of Canada (spearheaded by homeless drop-outs, or perhaps by a well-educated but underemployed Generation X?) as a mob ripe for collective disobedience.

But despite the intuitive plausibility (and media appeal) of such predictions, very little is actually known about how economically and socially marginal young people regard unemployment as a public issue, or how they might collectively react to this social and economic problem. One way to address this knowledge gap is to ask young people what they see as the causes of unemployment. On one hand, a widespread belief that unemployment is a product of individual shortcomings might encourage the unemployed to blame themselves and accept their situations (Shepelak, 1985; Lowe et al., 1988). However, to the extent that those without work see themselves sharing a problem in common with others, and place the blame for it on either or both government and industry, political action could result.

Guided by attribution theory (which, in its basic form, proposes that people blame their failures on factors external to themselves while crediting their success to internal factors), we were interested in the following questions: (1) to what extent do dropouts blame industry and government for their own failure to find work? (2) alternatively, do they tend to see unemployed people (and by extension, themselves) as responsible for high unemployment rates? (3) what solutions do young dropouts propose for the unemployment problem? and (4) are dropouts likely to react against a system that frequently denies them paid employment?

We invited our respondents' views on the causes of unemployment with a general question: *Why do you think there's so much unemployment among young people?* Since roughly half of the sample gave more than one answer, we coded up to two causes of unemployment for each person interviewed, grouping the answers in general categories as either 'individualistic', 'societal', or 'other'. Table 6.4 shows the types of answers provided by employed and unemployed female and male dropouts.

There were few noticeable gender differences in these explanations of youth unemployment (Table 6.4), but employed dropouts were somewhat more likely than those without jobs to lay the blame for high youth unemployment on the jobless themselves. Even so, about one in four comments received from unemployed sample members referred to young people as being lazy, having a poor work ethic, or expecting too much. In contrast, about 40 per cent of the answers from employed sample members had an individualistic tone, focusing on effort and/or attitude. Among both employed and unemployed respondents, individualistic answers citing inadequate educational credentials were much less common.

Within the societal category of answers, unemployed dropouts were somewhat more likely than those with jobs to blame the economy in general, or to attribute the problem to insufficient job creation by government. However, roughly equal proportions (approximately 20 per cent) of responses from employed and unemployed dropouts made reference to employers' reluctance to hire young, inexperienced applicants—a theme that surfaced in Chapter 4, in our discussion of the job-search problems encountered by dropouts.

Given the tight Edmonton labour market of the mid-1980s, in which employers could pick and choose whom to hire, it is not surprising that many dropouts saw themselves as victims of age-based discrimination:

> . . . everybody that's older got the experience. If I owned a business, and a guy came up to me and he was thirty and let's say he's been doing the job for fifteen years, and a seventeen-year-old came up to me to do the same job and he was only doing it for a few years, I would hire the thirty-year-old 'cause he's got the experience behind him [INT 023, unemployed male].

It is somewhat more surprising to see the large number of dropouts, particularly those without jobs themselves, who offered 'individualistic' answers, explaining youth unemployment in terms of the personal inadequacies and indulgences of people very much like themselves:

> I don't know. A lot of them, the way I see it, just want to go out and smoke drugs and get drunk and sleep, just be lazy bums [INT 130; unemployed female].

> . . . people ain't willing to do certain types of jobs because of the basic attitudes throughout society. You compare for instance Japan, Germany, people there are willing to do jobs, get paid less, their attitude toward work is different [INT 028; employed male].

> . . . a lot of it is skill, education. A lot of it is attitude. For a while there when the province was doing so well and everybody could work for $14 or $15 an hour, they got used to those big pay cheques and now they won't accept anything where they have to work for under $12, which I really think is terrible. . . . They should realize there's definitely work out there, you have to go out and find it and you have to accept a cut in your wage [INT 051; unemployed female].

As these quotations indicate, a popular theme among dropouts citing individualistic explanations of high youth unemployment was the absence of a strong work ethic among contemporary youth. As they described it, unemployment was a state that one entered almost voluntarily, a chosen life-style. One young man, without a job when we spoke to him, explained high youth unemployment in these terms:

> Responsibility. There's just some people that aren't responsible enough. . . .

> [I: Can you explain that a little bit?] Um, well young people right now, speaking for myself, like to be independent and they like to go out and do their own thing—whatever, if it's partying or getting drunk or whatever, getting loaded; they'll do that instead of going out and getting a job [INT 056].

After asking sample members for their explanations of high youth unemployment, we followed with another question: *Whose responsibility is it?* Although some had difficulty with this question, perhaps having never really thought in such terms before, almost all provided an answer. Similar proportions suggested that government should be doing something about youth unemployment (27 per cent) and that individual job-seekers were themselves responsible for dealing with their problem (26 per cent). Almost one in five (18 per cent) suggested that individuals and government should be responsible. About 12 per cent answered 'everyone', or something to that effect; 8 per cent took the opposite position, that 'no one is responsible'; and smaller proportions pointed to employers (3 per cent) or employers and government together (6 per cent).

Gender differences in responses to this question were of minor importance. As for differences between the currently employed and unemployed, the latter were somewhat more likely than the former (33 per cent versus 20 per cent) to give the responsibility for dealing with youth unemployment to the government, a pattern that would be predicted by attribution theory. Conversely, employed dropouts were somewhat more likely than their jobless counterparts (32 per cent, compared with 21 per cent) to leave the responsibility for youth unemployment with jobless youth themselves.

In short, the answers these young dropouts provided to our questions about the causes of and responsibility for youth unemployment tended to have an individualistic tone, even among a considerable number of unemployed sample members. The proposition that unemployed youth, at least those without high-school credentials, might begin to see unemployment as society's problem, and to react collectively against it, remains unsupported.

In fact, when we asked another follow-up question—*Is there anything young people can do about unemployment?*—the most common answer, provided by 37 per cent of those who answered, was 'nothing'. There appeared to be rather widespread pessimism about the value of any attempts to address directly the problem of unemployment among youth. Although about twenty sample members made some reference to writing letters, participating in demonstrations, or other acts of political lobbying, suggestions to return to school, start one's own business, or simply try harder to find work were much more common. As one employed male put it:

> They can look a bit harder, maybe apply themselves harder, and spend a little less time on the TV and more on their bikes looking for jobs [INT 146].

Political activism, while advocated by a small number of dropouts in this study, was more likely to be seen as a poor investment of time and effort:

> I think the only thing that you can do about unemployment is keep going to school until something happens. I would say just stay in school and find some career in computers or something and then when things start to open up, then away you go. As far as writing letters or protesting, that's not going to do a damn bit of good [INT 054; unemployed male].

We conclude, therefore, that fears about the political threat posed by unemployed dropouts are exaggerated. There was little conviction among our sample members that high youth unemployment should be blamed on either government or industry, or that much could be done to reduce unemployment. Political activism was not a high priority. Instead, there was a marked tendency to explain unemployment in terms of the failings of those directly affected, and to invoke personal solutions.

DISCUSSION

In this chapter we have examined how high-school dropouts respond to the experience of unemployment, which, along with marginal work, is a common consequence of early school-leaving. There is little doubt that unemployment has negative effects on psychological well-being. However, it is less clear that the psychological effects of unemployment are particularly severe and long-lasting for this group of young people. Certainly none of the dropouts in this study benefited from unemployment, but few were completely devastated either.

The interview data suggested, rather, that most of these young dropouts managed to cope with their marginal position in the labour market. They survived in good measure because the financial hardships they faced were irksome rather than traumatizing, and because they had access to supportive social networks. These are among the factors that underpin the argument that unemployment may be a less severe problem for youth than it is for older labour-force participants (Horwitz, 1984; Roberts, 1984; Breakwell, 1986; Warr, 1987). Young school-leavers rarely have extensive family responsibilities and may, in fact, be able to live relatively cheaply at home with parents. Without adult responsibilities, they may have a somewhat lower commitment to work. Nor are they as likely to have acquired an occupational identity, the loss of which is so destructive for older workers. Instead, they may be able to carry forward, for a while at least, a network of friends and leisure pursuits from their time in high school.

The ability to adjust to some of the pain of unemployment also has implications for its presumed political consequences. Much has been made in the media of the possibly negative consequences of unresolved youth unemployment. On the basis of our respondents' views regarding the politics of unemployment, it would appear unlikely that they will become part of any public campaign or social movement directed against the problem. From their perspective, unemployment often seemed to be a phenomenon rooted in individual inadequacies. And suggested solutions to youth unemployment were typically couched in terms of 'personal escapes' (Roberts, 1984). For most dropouts, therefore, unemployment was a private issue rather than a public problem (Mills, 1959).

Why does the personal take precedence over the political in dropouts' thinking about unemployment? First, the emphasis on the personal causes of unemployment may indicate the degree to which dropouts, along with other members of society, have been exposed, though the mass media and the educational system, to the ideology of individualism upon which capitalist society is based. Second, clinging to individualistic views about unemployment may also be a means of coping with the personal predicament of joblessness. Few of us understand the complex structural causes of unemployment, let alone have any influence on them. In the face of world-wide recession and inadequate or failed government policies, at least personal self-improvement and job-search efforts offer hope of changing one's situation. In this context, the emphasis on individual explanations and personal solutions may be a way of asserting control over one's life (Breakwell, 1985; Hutson and Jenkins, 1989). Following from this, personal efforts, although they cannot guarantee a job, may at least improve one's chances of finding one.

NOTES

[1]For each of these five questions, the 'often' response was chosen about five times as frequently as the 'almost always' one. Only five of the 162 dropouts in the sample did not answer these questions. Female dropouts were somewhat more likely to report frequent feelings of depression, while male dropouts were somewhat more likely to admit to feeling like doing nothing at all.

[2]A parallel survey of almost 1,000 Edmonton high-school seniors in May 1985 included the same questions. Within this sample, the percentages answering 'often' or 'almost always' were 22 per cent for feeling depressed, 21 per cent for feeling lonely, 26 per cent for feeling like doing nothing at all, 16 per cent for people appearing unfriendly, and 18 per cent for talking less than usual (Krahn et al., 1985). While the differences between the two studies do not allow strong conclusions, it is obvious that the dropout sample, as a whole, was not responding more negatively than the high-school graduate sample.

[3]Table 6.1 reveals one other interaction effect between gender and unemployment: unemployed males were twice as likely as unemployed females to state that they frequently felt like doing nothing at all.

[4]See note 2 above.

[5]This argument is similar to the earlier observation that age influences reactions to marginal employment. In Chapter 5 we showed that older dropouts were less likely to comment positively about their (generally low-paying and low-skill) jobs, and reasoned that with age comes the realization that such employment is not particularly rewarding. Following this line of reasoning, we checked to see whether older unemployed dropouts (20 and older) were more likely than younger ones to report frequent

feelings of depression, loneliness, and so on. The hypothesis was not supported. In fact, with the exception of feeling that people were unfriendly (older unemployed respondents were more likely to agree), younger unemployed dropouts were more likely to report frequent feelings of depression, loneliness, lethargy, and isolation.

[6]Verbal responses to a general question about *how you get along with your family* were placed into three categories: 'not very well' (17 per cent), 'OK' (40 per cent), and 'very well' (43 per cent). Female respondents were somewhat more likely to answer negatively, as were currently-unemployed members of the sample.

[7]Because of the semi-structured interviewing approach, some of the respondents (16 in total) were not asked this question. Percentages are calculated with these 16 individuals omitted.

CHAPTER SEVEN

Dropouts and Deviance

INTRODUCTION

In Chapter 1 we described the high level of public concern over school dropouts and how this issue has been seen as a social as well as an economic problem. The deviant behaviour of dropouts is an important aspect of the social problem, since research has documented a fairly consistent relationship between school difficulties and delinquency. Those who fail at school, particularly males, are more likely to engage in delinquent behaviour during their school years (Braithwaite, 1979; Schafer and Polk, 1967; West, 1984; Le Blanc et al., 1993).

The 1991 School Leavers Survey conducted by Statistics Canada showed that leavers were more likely than graduates to engage in a number of deviant activities during their last year in school (Gilbert et al., 1993). School-leavers were also more likely to be regular rather than occasional alcohol drinkers, and to use both soft and hard drugs more frequently. Compared with graduates, they reported four times as many convictions for criminal offences. In addition, the research literature suggests that poor school performance, lower academic ability and/or self-perception, boredom and lack of interest in school and school-based activities, and a general dislike for school increase the likelihood of rebellious and delinquent behaviour (Hartnagel and Tanner, 1982; Le Blanc et al., 1993).

What is less clear is the meaning and interpretation of this relationship between school failure and delinquency. For example, Farrington et al. (1986) suggest several plausible alternative hypotheses explaining why delinquents tend to do poorly in school. Some children are aggressive and antisocial before they come to school, and are hence predisposed to both fail in school and engage in more delinquency: the school itself does not cause their delinquency. Other children may find school work frustrating or boring (or both), become restless, and seek an outlet in various delinquent activities. It is also possible that children with mild behavioural problems get labelled as problem students, associate more frequently with other 'troublemakers', and find greater satisfaction in delinquency than do others.

Less research attention has been paid to the effects of dropping out of school on later, post-school delinquent or criminal behaviour. Official crime statistics reveal a correlation between educational attainment and crime: convicted offenders with less education generally have the highest crime rates

(Bell-Rowbotham and Boydell, 1972). Similar results have been obtained from samples of prison inmates, many of whom exhibit a history of poor school performance and are functionally illiterate (Harrell and Hartnagel, 1976). But disagreement characterizes the discussion of the specific relationship between dropping out of school and subsequent criminal behaviour. Some have claimed that dropping out does not increase delinquency (Farrington et al., 1986; Rand, 1987; Provonost and LeBlanc, 1980; LeBlanc et al., 1993) or is even followed by a reduction in delinquent behaviour (Elliott, 1966; Elliott and Voss, 1974). Other researchers have identified a positive correlation between dropping out and officially-recorded delinquency (Schafer and Polk, 1967; Schreiber, 1963; Simpson and Van Arsdol, 1967; Thornberry et al., 1985) as well as self-reported crime (Bachman et al., 1971; 1978). Moreover, while Thornberry et al. (1985) infer that dropping out is a cause of later crime, others have argued the reverse: namely, that delinquency causes adolescents to drop out of high school.

Of course, it is possible that different relationships between dropping out and delinquency are found within different categories of adolescents. For some, the school situation itself may be the cause or context of delinquency; in this case, leaving school would remove the stimulus for delinquency and thus lower its rate. In Chapter 3 we examined the reasons for leaving school given by our sample of dropouts, as well as the extent of their commitment to the education system. Perhaps these reasons and/or school commitment are related to criminal behaviour in the post-school years. Recent research (Jarjoura, 1993) has suggested that the effect of dropping out on later offending varies with the reasons given for dropping out. For example, dropping out because of dislike for school, or other unspecified reasons, was related to future delinquency. However, those who left school early because of problems at home did not report higher levels of offending. A continuing commitment to education may exert a controlling influence on the behaviour of dropouts, resulting in less delinquency (Hirschi, 1969).

Chapters 5 and 6 examined some of the labour-market, psychological, and social consequences of dropping out of school. For dropouts experiencing job-search difficulties, more frequent unemployment, boredom, insufficient financial resources, and low social support, there may be an increased risk of delinquency and crime. Even if, for some, delinquency declines after leaving school, it may again increase after encountering a difficult labour market. Thus the nature of the transition out of school, and the types and quality of later experiences, may be critical in explaining the relationship between dropping out and subsequent delinquency.

DROPOUTS AND POST-SCHOOL CRIME

A research emphasis on school experiences that motivate or control delinquent behaviour has meant a relative neglect of the diversity of dropouts' post-school experiences that might influence their criminal behaviour.

However, a few studies have examined the later criminal involvement of early school-leavers. Elliott and Voss (1974) recognized that the decline in delinquency following school-leaving was related to post-school factors such as marriage and employment. Dropping out should reduce the motivation for delinquency to the extent that dropouts make a satisfactory adjustment to the adult employment role. They hypothesized that employed, married dropouts would be less delinquent than unmarried, unemployed dropouts. Measuring delinquency by police contacts as well as by self-reports, they found unemployed males to be more delinquent than employed males, and unmarried dropouts to have a delinquency rate four times that of married dropouts (a large number of married, unemployed females had very limited contact with police). Marriage appeared to be more important than employment status in explaining post-school delinquency.

Bachman et al. (1978) examined the relationship between unemployment and delinquency across different levels of educational attainment. They found that it was among dropouts that the relationship between aggression and unemployment was particularly strong. Four years after the normal date for graduation from high school, unemployed dropouts reported aggression levels three times as high as employed dropouts. But similar relationships were not observed for theft, vandalism, or a composite measure of serious delinquency.

The positive correlation between dropping out of high school and later criminal behaviour reported by Thornberry et al. (1985) persisted despite statistical controls for age, marriage, and employment status. Thornberry and his colleagues also found that unemployment was positively related to crime regardless of education and marital status, but they did not examine the possible interaction between educational attainment and unemployment.

None of these three studies examined the variety of labour-market and economic-status variables that may influence criminal behaviour among dropouts. Criminologists have increasingly recognized that there is no simple link between employment status and crime. Various authors (Thornberry and Farnworth, 1982; Long and Witte, 1981) have suggested that job stability, as well as satisfying and rewarding work experience, is more important than simply finding employment. This suggests that those in secondary labour markets, which would include many young adults with low educational qualifications and job skills, would be more at risk for criminal conduct. But past research on dropouts and delinquency has been largely restricted to the single issue of employment status.

In addition, these studies of dropouts and delinquency are now dated, since they all rely on data collected prior to the mid-1970s. They are therefore less applicable to the changed social and economic context that has structured the transition out of school and the post-school experiences of more recent dropouts. The research reviewed in Chapter 1 has shown that high-school dropouts have more difficulty getting and keeping jobs, have more limited occupational choices, and earn less over their working lives

(Wagenaar, 1987; Rumberger, 1987; Feldstein and Ellwood, 1982; Morgan, 1984). Since a smooth transition from adolescence to adulthood is contingent upon successful integration into the adult world of work and marriage (Marini, 1987; Hogan and Astone, 1986), dropouts can be expected to have more transitional problems.

Successful integration into adult roles for dropouts has been made even more difficult in recent years because of changes in economic conditions. Young people have historically borne a disproportionate share of the burden of unemployment (Box, 1987; Employment and Immigration Canada, 1984). From 1966 to 1976—roughly the time period covered by the previous research—youth unemployment in the United States ranged from 7.7 to 14.8 per cent (Bureau of the Census, 1978). But it had climbed to 19.9 per cent in Canada by 1983. In 1984, when interviewing for this study began, the annual average unemployment rate for Canadian youth (aged 15 to 24) was 17.9 per cent, which dropped to 16.5 per cent in 1985 (Statistics Canada, 1983, 1984; 1985). Underemployment among youth has also been widespread. In 1984, 43 per cent of part-time workers in Canada were aged 15 to 24 (Statistics Canada, 1989:211).

Thus while recent economic conditions have made it increasingly difficult for young people in general to secure the jobs essential for gaining a social foothold on adulthood (Kraus, 1979), those with less than the minimum educational qualifications could be expected to experience even greater difficulty. This appears to be the case with respect to earnings and unemployment. Rumberger (1987) quotes a lifetime-earnings differential between male high-school dropouts and male high-school graduates of $260,000 in 1979, compared with $73,000 in 1968—a much greater increase than that in consumer prices over the same period. Similarly, unemployment rates for high-school dropouts were 20 per cent higher than overall unemployment rates in 1950, but 100 per cent higher in 1979. An Employment and Immigration Canada report (1984) on youth demonstrated an inverse relationship between educational attainment and unemployment: out-of-school youth aged 15 to 16 had unemployment rates of 40.5 per cent, while the rate was only 15.3 per cent for those with at least some post-secondary education.

Although the percentage of Canadian youth dropping out of school has been slowly declining (Gilbert et al., 1993) and participation in higher education has risen (Statistics Canada, 1992), research reviewed in Chapter 1 suggested that about 20 per cent of those starting high school still fail to graduate. Hence, as a larger proportion of young adults become 'credentialled', those who drop out can anticipate even greater difficulty in finding suitable and satisfying work. At the same time, new technologies have been eliminating many of the unskilled jobs traditionally filled by school dropouts. As a result, there is greater competition for marginal jobs (Krahn and Lowe, 1990) and the prospects for recent dropouts are worse.

Given these changes in the economy since much of the previous research was conducted, it is certainly possible that the nature of the relationship between dropping out and criminal behaviour may have changed. Dropouts of recent years, faced with a more difficult labour market, may be more likely to turn to crime and/or drug use than their counterparts in an earlier era. This may represent, in part, the effect of increased motivation for crime because of greater economic deprivation and/or frustration associated with labour-market difficulties. It may also reflect the lowering of the restraints or inhibitions on crime that may follow from a reduction in commitment to social norms. Weak integration into the labour market reduces these 'stakes in conformity' and lowers the costs of crime.

EXTENDING OUR KNOWLEDGE OF DROPOUTS AND CRIME

The present research focuses on a diverse sample of dropouts who had already left high school. Hence it does not share the in-school emphasis of the previous research. We are more interested in the question of why some dropouts engage in criminal behaviour while others do not. In this chapter, we begin by documenting the amount and type of post-school criminal behaviour reported by our sample of recent dropouts. We then examine a number of potential correlates of this criminal behaviour, focusing particularly on the reasons given for dropping out, labour-market difficulties, and other personal and social consequences of dropping out. We also consider a broad range of labour-market variables in addition to simple employment status, including the effects of length of unemployment, job instability, and financial deprivation.

Not a great deal is known about the consequences of dropping out of school, particularly from the point of view of dropouts themselves (Wagenaar, 1987). Although we have noted some of the objective transitional problems faced by recent dropouts, these do not necessarily translate into subjectively-felt distress and discontent. Chapter 6 revealed that, although our sample of dropouts experienced considerable unemployment and job instability, this experience had not generated a correspondingly high level of psychological distress or self-perceived social impairment. In Chapter 3 we observed that, despite dropping out of school, our dropouts had not rejected the dominant economic and normative order. They maintained surprisingly conventional goals, continued to believe in the ideology of achievement, and remained hopeful about the future.

In fact, it appears that the labour-market difficulties endured by dropouts may not lead directly to crime and drug use. Such behaviour may depend upon the individual's reaction to and interpretation of his or her labour-market problems (Box and Hale, 1985; Wright, 1981). If dropouts do not subjectively experience greater deprivation, and remain committed to occupational achievement, their labour-market problems may not increase their motivation to commit criminal acts. Thus we shall draw upon our interviews with dropouts to explore their own interpretations of the relationship between a difficult labour market and their own criminal behaviour.

Measurement

We used the self-report method of measuring criminal behaviour, as it is well known that the main alternative approach—relying on official statistics—measures only officially-known and recorded crime, thereby overlooking much of the deviant activity that is our focus.[1] In the self-administered questionnaire, respondents were asked to indicate how often, in the past year, they had been (a) questioned by the police as a suspect about some crime, and (b) convicted of some crime, other than traffic violations. In addition, questions asking for self-reports of nine specific violent and property crimes were included (see Appendix 2). In some of the following analyses we examine indices of total, violent, and property crime based on these self-reports.[2] Respondents were also asked to indicate how frequently they drank beer, wine, or other alcohol, smoked marijuana or hash, and used other non-prescription drugs. The response categories were 'every day', 'several times a week', 'once a week', 'once or twice a month', 'less than once a month', and 'never'.

Criminal activity and drug use

Thirty-one per cent of our sample reported having been questioned by the police, and 23 per cent said they had been convicted in court of a non-traffic crime in the past year. These rates are substantially higher than those for graduating high-school students (8 and 3 per cent) and university students (2 and 0.2 per cent) who took part in a parallel survey in Edmonton in 1985 (Hartnagel et al., 1986). As we would expect from previous research, dropouts are a more deviant group.

TABLE 7.1. PERCENTAGES ADMITTING CRIME IN PAST YEAR

Crime	%
Taken something from a store	26
Sold marijuana or other drugs	24
Got into a fight just for fun	21
Taken something worth less than $50	19
Damaged or destroyed property	16
Taken something worth more than $50	15
Attacked someone with a weapon	13
Broken into building or car	12
Used physical force to get money	7

Table 7.1 summarizes the frequency with which dropouts reported engaging in specific criminal acts. Between 7 and 26 per cent reported some specific criminal activity during the past year, depending on the type of crime in question. Generally, frequency of involvement varied inversely with the seriousness of the crime, a pattern typically found in self-reports of deviant conduct. So, for example, 26 per cent reported having taken something from a store without paying for it. Excluding this type of shoplifting, 15 per cent admitted having stolen something worth more than $50, while a slightly higher proportion (19 per cent) said they had taken something worth less than $50. But only 7 per cent reported using physical force to get money; 12 per cent had broken into a building or a car; and 16 per cent had damaged or destroyed property. While 13 per cent said they had attacked someone with a weapon, 21 per cent admitted getting into a fight just for fun. Finally, 24 per cent of the sample reported having sold marijuana or other drugs, the second most frequently-reported offence.

Also consistent with what we know from previous self-report research, few dropouts were repeatedly delinquent. For most offences, fewer than 8 per cent reported three or more illegal acts. The two exceptions were shoplifting, a fairly common offence among young people, and selling marijuana or other drugs, the two most frequently-admitted offences. Twelve per cent of the respondents admitted having taken something from a store three or more times, and 6 per cent said they had done so ten or more times during the previous year. A total of 17 per cent said they had sold drugs three or more times, and 11 per cent reported committing this crime ten or more times. It is possible that the high relative frequency of this offence may be related to economic circumstances among these dropouts: selling drugs may be one way for some dropouts to earn money to support themselves and/or their own drug habit.

We also asked our sample of dropouts to report their level of substance use. As can be seen in Table 7.2, alcohol is clearly the drug of choice: 64 per cent said they drank at least once a week. The reported frequency of smoking marijuana/hash and in particular, using other drugs, is much lower: 38 per cent said they smoked dope at least once a week, but only 5 per cent reported this level of use of other drugs.

Table 7.2 also compares dropouts' substance use with the levels of use reported by the samples of high-school and university graduates. Alcohol use is fairly similar across the three samples, although the university graduates and, particularly, the dropouts reported a somewhat higher frequency of drinking. The somewhat lower level of 'at least weekly' alcohol use (43 per cent) among the graduating high-school students probably reflects their youth: not all were of legal age when interviewed. 'At least weekly' marijuana use was much lower in the university (4 per cent) and high-school samples (10 per cent) than among the dropouts. About three-quarters of the graduate respondents had never smoked dope, compared with only about a third (32 per cent) of the dropouts. Use of other drugs was much less frequent in all three samples, but again the dropouts reported relatively higher levels of use. Thus it is quite clear that high-school dropouts are more deviant, in terms of substance use, than other categories of young adults.

TABLE 7.2. FREQUENCY OF ALCOHOL AND DRUG USE: EDMONTON DROPOUTS, HIGH-SCHOOL GRADUATES, AND UNIVERSITY GRADUATES

	High school*		University*		Dropouts	
Frequency	%	N	%	N	%	N
Alcohol (beer, wine, or other alcohol) consumption						
Every day	1	10	1	2	0.6	1
Several times/week	15	147	20	114	20	32
Once a week	27	261	33	195	43	67
Once/twice a month	23	219	25	146	22	35
< once a month	18	176	14	75	7	12
Never	15	147	8	48	6	10
Use of marijuana or hash						
Every day	2	14	0.2	1	7	10
Several times/week	5	43	2	9	21	33
Once a week	3	27	2	11	10	16
Once/twice a month	6	57	4	22	12	19
< once a month	12	115	17	97	18	27
Never	73	696	76	433	32	49
Use of other drugs						
Every day	0.3	3	-	-	0.6	1
Several times/week	0.4	4	-	-	1	2
Once a week	0.8	8	-	-	3	4
Once/twice a month	2	15	1	5	8	13
< once a month	6	59	4	20	22	35
Never	91	861	96	545	65	101

*See Hartnagel et al. (1986) for a discussion of the parallel studies of high-school and university graduates in Edmonton.

School experience and crime

The reasons respondents gave for dropping out of school were earlier categorized (in Chapter 3) as school-related, jobs/money-related, or personal. When these reasons were cross-tabulated with the total, violent-crime, and property-crime indices, as well as with the measures of alcohol and drug use, no systematic relationship was observed. This may be because, on average, members of our sample had been out of school for two-and-one-half years. While a relationship between reasons for leaving school and deviant behaviour might have been observed at the time they left school, these reasons would presumably have much less impact on their behaviour at the time of the interview.

We also examined the possibility of relationships between crime and drug use and measures of several other aspects of our respondents' school experiences—specifically, self-reported performance in school, enjoyment of time in school, and commitment to obtaining further education. Here again, no obvious patterns were observed, although other research has shown that school performance of students in general directly affects subsequent adult criminality (LeBlanc et al., 1993). Our results suggest that the school experiences of dropouts are not particularly relevant to their chances of involvement in post-school crime and drug use. Perhaps the labour-market difficulties they had experienced since then, especially in a depressed economy, had a more substantial impact.

Labour-market experience and crime

Information concerning sample members' current employment status was obtained from the self-administered questionnaire. Since fewer than 10 per cent reported never having been unemployed, we used current employment status (full-time, part-time, no job) as a general indicator of recent employment experience. In contrast to the case with school experiences, we found several significant relationships with the crime measures. Forty-two per cent of the dropouts with no job reported being questioned as a crime suspect, compared with only 19 per cent of those working part-time and 21 per cent of the full-time employed. Almost one-third (31 per cent) of those without a job said they had been convicted of a crime, compared with 19 per cent of the part-time and 11 per cent of the full-time employed. Thus lack of a job is associated with a greater likelihood of dropouts' reporting some involvement with the criminal-justice system.

We also examined the relationship between current employment status and the indices of self-reported violent and property crime. There was no difference by employment status in the index of self-reported violence. But employment status was significantly related to property crime. As Table 7.3 shows, 73 per cent of those without a job reported some criminal act, compared with 48 per cent and 45 per cent of those with a part-time or full-time job, respectively. Table 7.3 also indicates that a higher proportion (53 per cent) of the dropouts without a job reported having committed some property crime in the past year. Only 37 per cent of the part-time employed and 27 per cent of the full-time employed admitted to a property crime. More detailed analysis revealed only one particular property crime—taking something worth more than $50—that was significantly related to current employment status (22 per cent without a job, 11 per cent of the part-time employed, 4 per cent of those with a full-time job). Thus only in the case of more serious theft is the lack of a job related to a specific self-reported criminal act.

TABLE 7.3. TOTAL AND PROPERTY-CRIME INDICES BY EMPLOYMENT STATUS

Has respondent committed any crime?	No		Yes	
	%	N	%	N
Full-time job	55	24	45	20
Part-time job	52	13	48	12
No job	27	21	73	57
Has respondent committed a property crime?	No		Yes	
	%	N	%	N
Full-time job	73	33	27	12
Part-time job	63	17	37	10
No job	47	37	53	41

The potential relationship between employment status and substance use is also of interest. In fact, employment status appeared to be unrelated to frequent use of either alcohol or marijuana. However, dropouts without a job were significantly more likely to report the use of other drugs (43 per cent) than were those with a part-time (29 per cent) or full-time (26 per cent) job.

Currently-unemployed dropouts were categorized as either short-term (5 months or less) or long-term (6 months or more) unemployed. While small sub-sample sizes require cautious conclusions, the long-term unemployed appeared more likely to have sold drugs (38 per cent, compared with 14 per cent for the short-term unemployed), to have drunk alcohol much more frequently (79 per cent, compared with 47 per cent), to have smoked dope more frequently (53 per cent compared to 38 per cent), and to have used other drugs more often (57 per cent compared to 34 per cent for the short-term unemployed). But there were no significant differences between short-and long-term unemployed dropouts in the other types of criminal behaviour. Hence it would appear that lengthier unemployment is positively associated with dropouts' selling and using drugs and alcohol, but not with their committing other more acquisitive or violent types of crime.

Similarly, when all the dropouts who had ever been unemployed were categorized according to the total length of their unemployment, those who had a cumulative total of seven or more months of unemployment were significantly more likely to have smoked dope frequently (57 per cent, compared with 32 per cent of those who had experienced less unemployment) and to have used other drugs frequently (47 per cent, compared with 24 per cent). Using a different statistical technique (correlation analysis), we found significant relationships between months of unemployment and alcohol (r = .16), smoking dope (r = .177), and using other drugs (r = .175). However, cumulative unemployment was not associated with the commission of other (property or violent) crimes.

Episodes of unemployment are part of an unstable work history. Thus the number of jobs ever held by dropouts may be another dimension of labour-market experience related to criminal behaviour and substance use. Our study revealed that dropouts with more unstable work histories (three or more jobs) were more likely to report involvement in criminal conduct and drug use. Specifically, as Table 7.4 demonstrates, they were more likely to report having been a police suspect, having been convicted of a non-traffic crime, and having committed some property crime. Dropouts with unstable work histories also smoked dope and used other drugs more frequently. But only two crime measures—being questioned by the police (r = .203) and use of other non-prescription drugs (r = .223)—were significantly correlated with this measure of job instability. The results of these correlation analyses, and the small number of respondents in the cross-tabulations, suggest caution in drawing conclusions. Nevertheless, it appears that an unstable work history is associated with greater involvement in some crime and drug use.

TABLE 7.4. SELF-REPORTED CRIME BY WORK HISTORY

	Percentage reporting									
Work History	Police suspect %	N	Con-viction %	N	Property crime %	N	B & E %	N	Theft over $50 %	N
Stable	21	13	15	9	26	16	3	2	7	4
Unstable	42	32	30	23	49	36	20	15	22	17

Consistent with previous research (see Hartnagel, 1992), male dropouts reported more criminal behaviour than did the females in our sample. There were no gender differences in alcohol or drug use. However, additional analysis (see Hartnagel and Krahn, 1989) revealed that the combination of being male and unemployed was particularly related to crime and drug use.

As was mentioned above, financial need or economic deprivation may be another aspect of dropouts' labour-market situation that is related to crime and drug use. In fact, dropouts who described themselves as usually short of money did not report significantly more criminal behaviour, involvement with the criminal justice system, or alcohol use. However, respondents who are usually short of money did report that they smoked dope more frequently (52 per cent) than did those with enough money (32 per cent). They were also more likely to report greater use of other drugs (48 per cent) than dropouts who said they had enough money (31 per cent). Similar results were observed when dropouts were asked whether they had cut back on any expenses or activities, a second measure of financial need. When correlations were calculated, we observed statistically significant but weak relationships between a shortage of money and the number of property crimes ($r = -.178$), use of marijuana ($r = -.140$), and use of other drugs ($r = -.168$).

We also examined the relationship between dropouts' current living arrangements and their self-reported crime, expecting that those living with parents, other family members, or a spouse/partner would be subject to greater informal social control, and hence less likely to engage in criminal behaviour. However, this hypothesis was supported only for the property-crime index; 62 per cent of those living alone or with friends reported some property crime, compared with 35 per cent of those living with their family or spouse/partner. But dropouts' perceptions of how well they got along with members of their family were not related to criminal behaviour or drug/alcohol use.

Dropouts' opinions on labour-market difficulties and criminal behaviour

We suggested earlier that subjectively-experienced effects of labour-market difficulties might help us to interpret the relationship between such difficulties and crime and/or drug use. As part of this analysis, respondents were categorized on the basis of their sense of job entitlement (whether or not they thought everyone has a right to a job) and self-perceived likelihood of getting the kind of job they would like in five to ten years. But neither of these subjective measures was related to self-reported crime or substance use.

Dropouts' explanations of their own criminal acts, and their opinions about the link between labour-market problems and criminal behaviour, are also of interest. The interviewers had been given a set of optional questions about criminal behaviour to be asked at the end of the semi-structured interview. These questions focused on types of criminal activity, how the respondent had become involved, and his or her opinion about whether unemployment had been a contributing factor. Given the potential sensitivity of these topics, and the fact that the interviews were recorded, interviewers were instructed to ask about crime only if they felt that sufficient rapport with the respondent had been developed. In some cases, however, the topic of crime had already emerged earlier in the interview. These optional questions were introduced with 80 per cent of the sample, and thirty-three of the dropouts went on to discuss this topic at length.

The generalizability of the conclusions that can be drawn from these conversations is certainly limited by the non-random nature of the sample, as well as by the fact that not all dropouts were asked or responded to these questions. Nevertheless, these subjective self-assessments of the link between employment difficulties and crime are informative. When asked directly—*Do you think that being unemployed had anything to do with the charges that were laid against you?*—one of the female subjects answered:

> Yes. . . .because if I had've been working and had the money, then I could've went out and bought whatever it was that I wasn't paying for with the money I had [INT 055].

However, this comment was an exception. Examination of the interview transcripts reinforces our earlier conclusion that a shortage of money is seldom the direct cause of criminal behaviour. Even this subject went on to explain that

> . . . when I first started ripping off things it was the people pressuring me into it and then like I couldn't say no, and then finally just the hell with it.

The few other subjects who did mention money tended to do so along with other rationalizations of their behaviour. One male subject began by commenting on a shortage of money, but concluded with reference to the excitement of shop-lifting (and with a reminder that age is a critical correlate of crime):

> Well when I was sixteen I got busted in Edmonton, when I first came here, for stealing a pair of jeans from Eatons 'cause I didn't have any clothes and I didn't have a job to buy anything. . . . [I: Were you stealing primarily because you didn't have a job?] Yeah, like if I had a job. . . . like I don't steal anymore. I guess stealing was a game for me when I was younger and I guess I've just gotten tired of the game, the same with drugs. . . [INT 062].

Another subject, describing how he had been caught stealing a large amount of food from a restaurant freezer, attributed the act to being 'really broke and we didn't have much for food' [INT 065]. Filling in the details, he explained how 'partying with a bunch of guys', being out at night, and stumbling across an open door culminated in the theft. Although he stuck to the economic explanation of his own behaviour, he concluded with a different interpretation of why other unemployed youth commit crimes: 'Yeah, all young unemployed kids do is drink, get high, and that just leads into troubles. . . .'

Multiple explanations of the link between unemployment and criminal behaviour were the norm among the sample members willing to talk about this subject, as these examples demonstrate. Drugs and alcohol were mentioned frequently, as were free time and boredom leading to deviant behaviour. One male respondent who had been heavily involved in the drug subculture, and who had been charged with possession of both marijuana and chemical drugs, described the process:

> . . . when you're unemployed you drink, right? Or I did. I did a lot of extra drinking. A lot of people get into trouble when they drink and I got into trouble. . . . you get bored and you see a little chance for a little excitement and stuff like that, you know. . . . get roaring drunk. . . [INT 032].

Another dropout described how he had become involved in drugs:

> I don't know. . . . I wouldn't blame it on peer pressure 'cause maybe my friends pushed me but I pushed them just as hard. We kind of got each other into trouble constantly, and it started out as experimentation, more or less out of curiosity, when you're that young, you don't know any better. [I: Do you think when you're unemployed, do you think that had any effect on your illegal activities?] Well, I increased the amount of drugs and booze 'cause I was bored and I think that had a great effect, the psychological instability it created later on, maybe, and the fact that I was dormant upstairs [INT 020].

This oblique reference to anxiety about joblessness as leading to drug use was one of very few comments that could be taken as evidence that such stress is an intervening variable. Boredom and a youthful quest for excitement were mentioned much more frequently, as were the effects of 'hanging around' with others in the same situation. A female respondent admitted she was 'really lucky' not to be caught:

> . . . 'cause I wasn't going to school at the time and I was hanging out with the wrong people and they were trying to get me to do the wrong thing [INT 101].

Another male subject who had been involved in car theft and burglary listed all the typical ingredients:

> Um, I guess my friends asked me if I wanted to do it and I was drinking at the time and there was nothing to do so I thought I may as well try 'cause we never did it before [INT 073].

Anecdotes that would support a control-theory explanation (i.e., having a job reduces criminal behaviour because of the greater commitment to and involvement in conventional activity) are somewhat harder to find, although this may reflect the way the questions were asked.[3] One subject commented wryly, in response to a question about whether unemployment had led to his breaking-and-entering escapades: 'Oh yeah, if I had been working I wouldn't have been up that time in the morning' [INT 076]. A search for several elements of social control revealed that highly criminal dropouts, particularly males, were much less likely than non-criminal dropouts to report the presence of such controls (Samuelson et al., 1995). Most often, though, reminiscences about past criminal activities highlighted the interacting effects of free time, boredom, youthfulness, drug and alcohol use, and peer-group pressure. Having dropped out of the conventional activities of school, and failing to become fully integrated into the conventional world of work, these young people were living in, or had lived in, a somewhat unique subculture. Their descriptions of this social milieu do not identify a single explanation of the link between unemployment and crime, but they certainly shed light on some of the more critical factors.

DISCUSSION

The self-reports of this sample of dropouts show them to be a considerably more deviant group than high-school and university graduates. A majority of dropouts admitted committing some criminal act in the previous year. Compared with graduates, they were also more frequent drug-users. While this post-school crime was not associated with the previous school experiences of dropouts, we did observe relationships between labour-market experiences and deviant behaviour.

Exactly how do labour-market experiences during a period of relatively high youth unemployment affect criminal behaviour among school dropouts? Our statistical analysis and our examination of respondents' own views on the subject reveal a complex and incomplete answer. This study clearly demonstrates the existence of links between the labour market and crime, but it also highlights the importance of distinguishing among types of labour-market experiences. Current unemployment, particularly for males, is related to most of our measures of crime and drug use. Similarly, an unstable work history is related to several of the dependent variables. However, none of the labour-market variables is related to violent crime. Furthermore, current financial status and cumulative unemployment appear unrelated to the crime measures, although both are related to drug use.

The absence of a relationship between financial status and property crime casts doubt upon both 'economic hardship' and 'strain' (i.e., the lack of legitimate means to achieve material success creates pressure to use illegitimate means) as explanations of property crime, at least for high-school dropouts. The interview data reinforce the conclusion that the crimes these dropouts committed were not primarily motivated by economic considerations. Perhaps enough money could be obtained from other family members, or through social assistance, to reduce the economic pressures leading towards crime. The lack of a relationship between months unemployed and property crime further weakens the economic-deprivation explanation.

Interestingly, however, the longer dropouts were unemployed, the more frequent their use of drugs was. This pattern may represent another form of the general proposition that unemployment is more likely to lead to passive forms of withdrawal from society than to active confrontation with it (Tanner et al., 1984). In other words, our subjects' tendency to retreat into frequent use of drugs with lengthier exposure to unemployment suggests a parallel with findings from other studies which have suggested that unemployment is more likely to lead to depression and lowered self-esteem than to active expressions of discontent.

Among these dropouts, the combination of being male and unemployed was particularly related to being stopped and questioned by the police, to more frequent smoking of dope and, generally, to more involvement in crime. The interview data suggest that this may all be part of a generally deviant lifestyle. Bored, unemployed males with time on their hands hang out together, engage in certain types of deviance that promise some 'action', and present a visible target for the police. Increased involvement in deviant behaviour for unemployed dropout males may thus be a normal part of a somewhat marginalized world where the social controls of a job are absent, where peer-group influences are strong, and where free time and boredom combine to increase the opportunities for and the temptations to engage in deviant behaviour.

The relations between dropouts' labour-market experiences and deviant behaviour, then, are complex and multi-faceted. Consequently, answers to questions about causality (Does a difficult labour market lead to more post-school crime among dropouts? Does a predisposition towards deviance handicap dropouts in the labour market?) are incomplete, since causes, effects, and intervening variables are intertwined, cumulative, and likely reciprocal in nature. Obviously, to return to a central theme running through our analysis of the lives of these early school-leavers, the higher rates of deviant behaviour among dropouts are a serious social problem. Higher crime rates are problematic not only for society as a whole, but for the dropouts themselves, as their deviant behaviour can only exacerbate their already marginal status in society. Drug use and criminal behaviour further limit employment options already reduced by a lack of credentials, and may also reduce the possibility of returning to school. In brief, crime and drug use appear to be central elements in the lives of many dropouts, along with a marginal labour-market status. And, whether as a cause or an effect of labour-market difficulties, such deviant behaviour serves to limit their life-chances even further.

NOTES

[1]Of course, the self-report method is not free of measurement problems; for a discussion and evaluation of these, see Elliott and Huisinga (1989).

[2]These indices were created by summing the number of self-reported specific crimes. The total crime index was composed of all nine items (see Appendix 2, Question 10, items C through K). The property-crime index was constructed from items C, D, J, and K. The violent-crime index was created from items F through I.

[3]Respondents were asked whether unemployment had influenced their criminal activity, but not if having a job had reduced this activity.

CHAPTER EIGHT

Looking to the Future

INTRODUCTION

In the previous chapters we have commented primarily on the past and present experiences of high-school dropouts. We have documented their ambiguous feelings about schooling, their relationships with their families, their job-search experiences, their methods of coping with marginal work and frequent unemployment and, finally, for some, their deviant activities. To round out our study of the social world of young high-school dropouts, we now turn our attention to their future aspirations.

Previous research has shown that Canadian youth generally report very high occupational aspirations, expressing a distinct preference for managerial and professional careers (Empson-Warner and Krahn, 1992). However, such studies survey students who are still in school, who expect to graduate, and who have little or no experience of finding jobs to match their ambitions. Under such circumstances, high occupational aspirations are not particularly surprising, particularly within an education system that encourages all students to work towards common goals (Turner, 1960) and in a society that awards low prestige to skilled manual occupations.

High-school dropouts find themselves in a somewhat different situation. Although they began in the same education system from which their peers graduated, most have already encountered a less-than-hospitable labour market (see chapters 4 through 6) and hence may have lowered their career aspirations. Perhaps some opt out of the competition for good jobs completely, and in so doing minimize the importance of paid employment and career success in their own hopes for the future. We might also hypothesize that some dropouts, perhaps more often young women, substitute marriage and parenthood goals for career goals when they confront the realities of the labour market. Alternatively, the absence of good career opportunities might lead some dropouts to postpone marriage and family formation.

MAJOR GOALS IN LIFE

To address these and related questions, we invited our respondents to discuss their future ambitions, asking *What are your major goals in life?* Some of the answers we received were as general as our question (e.g., 'to be happy'; 'to get a good job'). In fact, it was apparent that some respondents had given very little thought to their goals in life:

> Good question. I don't have any right now [INT 152; female].
>
> To be successful. . . . Right now, I have no idea [INT 133; female].
>
> I haven't even thought about that. . . . I just want to do something that I enjoy [INT 082; female].

But other sample members were quite specific about their future goals (e.g., 'to become a nurse'). Many described several different goals (e.g., 'to make a lot of money and to travel'). When quantifying the interview data, therefore, we coded up to three different types of major goals. Table 8.1 profiles the several hundred major life-goals listed by the 147 dropouts who answered this question.[1]

TABLE 8.1. MAJOR GOALS IN LIFE BY GENDER

	Percentage		
Type of goal	Female	Male	Total
Specific occupational goal	24	25	25
Work (to get a job/a good job)	15	17	16
Education/skills/training for a trade	16	16	16
Money/material possessions/success	11	15	13
Family (get married/have family)	18	10	14
Happiness (in general)	8	6	7
Travel	4	4	4
To help others	2	4	3
Other	2	3	2
Total	100	100	100
Total number of goals	130	140	271

One-quarter of all the answers identified a specific occupation as a major goal in life. About one in six (16 per cent) were comments about finding a job or a 'good job', and an equal proportion mentioned getting more education or specific training for a trade. Thirteen per cent of the answers simply mentioned getting a lot of money, being successful, or acquiring material possessions. Thus, in total, 70 per cent of all responses to the question about future goals addressed employment, education, income, and material success, a checklist of aspirations not unlike what one might obtain in any survey of young people. As the analysts of the 1991 School Leavers Survey have noted (Gilbert and Orok, 1993), in many ways young high-school dropouts are not all that unusual.

Gender differences in self-reported major goals were of little consequence, with the exception that a higher proportion of answers from female respondents (18 per cent, versus 10 per cent of answers provided by males) mentioned family and marriage goals, a subject to which we shall return later in this chapter. Table 8.1 also shows a small minority of dropouts, both female and male, discussing more intrinsic personal goals including 'happiness' in general, the chance to travel, and opportunities to help others. However, extrinsic life-goals focusing on employment, education and material success were much more common.

OCCUPATIONAL GOALS

Following the general question about major life-goals, we asked *What kind of job would you like to have in five or ten years?* As was noted in Chapter 5, about half of the young dropouts in this study reported vague or no occupational goals or work-related ambitions. A few entertained what could best be described as fantasy aspirations, including the young woman who wanted to be a talk-show host [INT 098]. One male respondent wanted to become a lawyer, reasoning that he was already 'good at debating and I have a very mean temper when it comes to arguments' [INT 146]. Another male hoped to become an architect because 'I took a lot of it in school and I can draw pretty good' [INT 119; male]. However, if we use broad categories and overlook the vagueness (and perhaps wishful thinking) in some of the employment goals reported, we can crudely classify the occupational goals of almost 90 per cent of our sample members (Figure 8.1).

The gendered nature of dropouts' occupational goals is perhaps the most obvious pattern in Figure 8.1. Four in ten female respondents aspired to professional occupations (nursing and teaching were typical occupational goals), compared with 22 per cent of male sample members. And 30 per cent of female dropouts mentioned some other kind of white-collar occupation (e.g., secretarial or sales work, or a managerial position), along with one in ten males. But a much higher proportion of male respondents (39 per cent) stated that they would like to be working in a skilled trade in five or ten years, as did 12 per cent of female sample members. Thus, with respect to the traditionally 'female' and 'male' flavour of their occupational aspirations, these young high-school dropouts were rather conventional.

Various observers (e.g., Economic Council of Canada, 1992b) have commented on the fact that Canadian youth tend to ignore the skilled trades in favour of presumably higher-status managerial and professional careers. When asked about their occupational goals, Canadian teenagers are more likely to mention white-collar than blue-collar or technical occupations.

FIGURE 8.1: OCCUPATIONAL GOALS BY GENDER

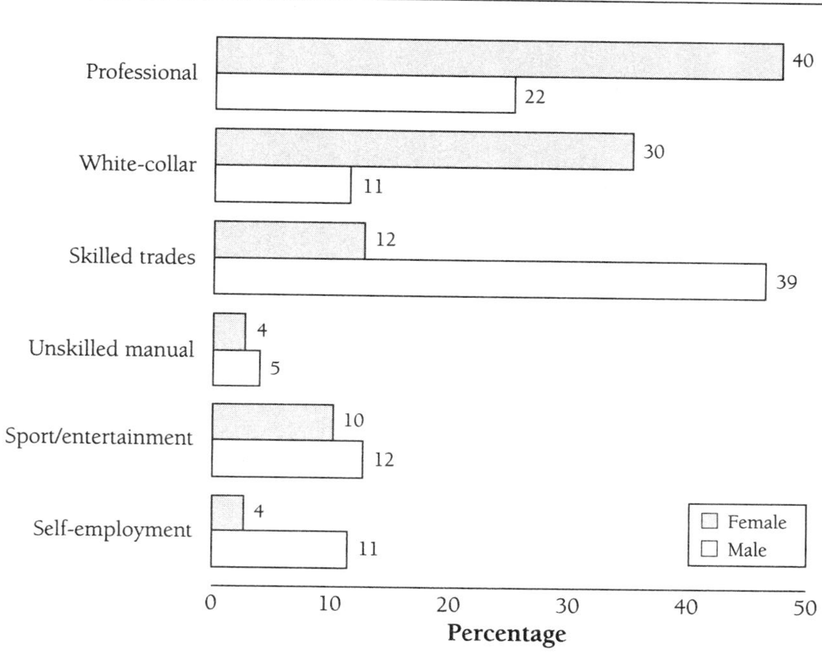

Consequently, the fairly high proportion of male dropouts in this study who mentioned a skilled trade as their occupational goal (39 per cent) is noteworthy. Their greater interest in this type of career may have resulted from contact with the skilled trades while still in school (since dropouts are more likely to have been enrolled in vocational programs) or while employed in unskilled manual jobs. Or perhaps exposure to the skilled trades occurred earlier, in their home or community, since dropouts are more likely to have parents in blue-collar occupations (Gilbert and Orok, 1993:4). Whatever the explanation, movement out of the unskilled jobs held by most members of our sample into the skilled trades would still require a significant investment in further education and training.

In general, the occupational goals of these young dropouts seem quite high: about three-quarters (82 per cent of the women and 72 per cent of the men) identified professional positions, other white-collar occupations, or skilled trades in answer to our question; only a handful mentioned unskilled jobs. However, when we compare these figures with results from a parallel 1985 survey of Edmonton high-school seniors (Krahn et al., 1985; Empson-Warner and Krahn, 1992), we observe even higher aspirations among young people about to graduate from high school. In that study, over

90 per cent of the twelfth-graders surveyed reported professional, other white-collar, or skilled-trade aspirations. In fact, over 60 per cent mentioned professional or managerial positions, demonstrating the extent to which the aspirations of Canadian youth have tended to outstrip the labour-market opportunities available to them.

Compared with the lofty aspirations of high-school seniors, then, the future occupational goals of the dropouts in our study were somewhat low. On the other hand, compared with the mostly low-skill, low-pay jobs they were currently holding (or had held in the past), their goals were relatively high, and hence quite 'normal'. Given their inadequate educational credentials and limited work histories, it is noteworthy that very few of these high-school dropouts had forsaken their ambition to do better in the labour market.

As we noted in Chapter 5, however, high and clearly-articulated occupational goals, when contrasted with menial jobs, can lead to considerable dissatisfaction. While we cannot argue with confidence that such an aspiration-reality discrepancy will also lead dropouts to reduce their aspirations,[2] the fact that unemployed dropouts were less likely than their employed counterparts to report professional career aspirations suggests that such a process might be occurring.

At the same time, unemployment encouraged some respondents to reflect on the direction their lives were taking, leading to a new realism and a more focused career strategy:

> . . . you end up thinking—you're unemployed so you've got a lot of time to figure out, 'OK, now what do I wish I could do? I wish I could do that but why?' And then you figure out what you want to do with your life. You can get a purpose, a direction [INT 078; unemployed male].

> [Unemployment] made me realize that there's a lot more to life than partying and if you want to get anywhere in your life, you've got to cut out partying for a while [INT 055; employed female].

Marginal jobs could also have a sobering effect, reminding some dropouts of the one way they knew to improve their situation—to return to school:

> When I first quit school and started working I always felt 'Oh no big deal. If I get fired from this job I can always find another one.' But now a job isn't enough, I want a trade or a skilled profession, a career. I don't just want a job and in order to get that you have to get an education [INT 051; unemployed female].

> When I was working out in the labour force, I would see people who have been in the labour force all their life and they have amounted to just a little bit more than nothing. They set an example for me. . . . I don't want to be like them. I want to be different [INT 067; male student at Alberta College].

SELF-EMPLOYMENT

The long-term goal of establishing a small business, of becoming an entrepreneur, was also reported by a minority of our respondents, most of them male (Figure 8.1). A fork-lift operator in a warehouse, describing his ambition to become an independent long-haul truck driver, clearly articulated the attractions of self-employment:

> Well, if you have the smarts, I think the thing to do is to start your own business, you know. The old capitalist method of making money. . . . Yeah, like I want to get my own truck eventually, eh? I want to be a lease-operator. I've heard that there's not much money in it but you know, I'm not really interested in making big bucks, I just—I got 'white line fever', eh. [I: You want to set your own hours, kind of thing, I guess?] Yeah, I want to be on my own, out on the road, eh? [INT 121; male].

Thus self-employment meant independence, not having a 'boss' who could tell you what to do. In fact, some of the young men (and a few women as well) aspiring to the skilled trades saw them as an avenue to potential self-employment, as well as a source of higher income, regular employment, and interesting work. Becoming a mechanic, for instance, could be seen as a preliminary step towards owning and operating a 'body shop'. Getting an electrician's 'ticket' could provide the opportunity to be an independent contractor in the future.

This belief in self-employment as a method of upward mobility has, of course, been observed in previous research on skilled male workers (e.g., Chinoy, 1955; Mackenzie, 1973). Like some of their fathers before them, a number of the young men in our sample saw in self-employment a possibility for job satisfaction, dignity, and freedom not available in other work situations. Thus, once again, the employment goals reported by our sample members were really quite conventional. While these young people had rejected society's expectations about how and when education should be acquired, they had not really forsaken the dominant value system. They continued to endorse conventional 'success' goals while, unfortunately, being in a very poor position to realize them.

MARRIAGE AND PARENTHOOD GOALS

Does dropping out of high school lead to more or less interest in getting married and having children? If parenthood, like paid employment, bestows an adult status upon the young, might it appear as an attractive option for those young people who find little satisfaction or success in formal schooling? Is this option more attractive to young women who cannot find satisfactory paid employment (Wallace, 1987)? Or do rebellious adolescents—which high-school dropouts are often assumed to be—see conventional domestic goals as part of the value system of 'adult' society that demands rejection?

These are among the questions that led us to ask, near the end of the interview, whether these high-school dropouts *might want to get married and have a family someday*. Generally speaking, our respondents had less to say about their marriage and family plans than about their employment-related ambitions. This may have been because the research was presented to them as a study of work and unemployment. Or perhaps marriage and children were still distant goals for many of these young people. Nevertheless, all but 23 of the 162 dropouts in our sample provided at least a comment on the topic,[3] and their crudely categorized answers are displayed in Table 8.2.

TABLE 8.2. MARRIAGE AND PARENTHOOD GOALS BY GENDER

	Percentage		
	Female	Male	Total
Might get married someday?			
No	9	8	9
Maybe	18	36	27
Yes	73	56	64
Total	100	100	100
N	66	73	139
Might have a family someday?			
No	6	10	8
Maybe	20	33	27
Yes	62	56	59
Already do	12	1	6
Total	100	100	100
N	69	70	139

Two-thirds of the subjects in this study said that they would get married someday (Table 8.2). Another one-quarter answered in a generally positive but still somewhat uncertain manner (e.g., 'probably, but not for a while yet'), which we have chosen to label as 'maybe'. The 18 individuals (12 women and 6 men) who were currently living with a partner were spread across these two categories. As for parenting plans, if we include in the 'yes' category the small minority who already had parental responsibilities, the distribution of answers was essentially the same: about two-thirds answered in the affirmative, and one-quarter said 'maybe' (or something to that effect).

Table 8.2 reveals some predictable gender differences. As one might expect, the young women in this sample were more receptive to the idea of marriage and children. In turn, male respondents were somewhat more likely to be in the 'maybe' category. Even so, the comments from those less certain indicated that, like their peers who answered more confidently, these young men basically took it for granted that they would eventually get married and have children—but not quite yet. The most common view was that serious thought and action about these matters should be delayed until education and career plans were on a firmer footing:

> I won't get married unless I have enough money to buy a house. That's what I told my girlfriend and she agrees. That depends on money too because I don't think I could handle the pressure of being married and wondering whether or not to have kids and not be financially stable [INT 020; male].

Another young man declared 25 to be the minimum age at which he was prepared to get married:

> I won't go any lower than that. . . . I want to get things all straightened out for me so I won't screw up both my life, her life, you know, even the family's life. So I just want to get everything settled and straightened out and just ordinary days—'Hi, honey, I'm home, what's for dinner?' sort of thing [INT 014; male].

While male sample members typically viewed domestic life positively, then, most seemed to be postponing thinking about it seriously until some time in the future. In contrast, female dropouts tended to be more immediately receptive to domestic possibilities and responsibilities, reflecting a pattern that one might perhaps observe among high-school graduates as well.

One basic pattern of female response might best be labelled as 'traditionalist'. These young women saw their adult lives as revolving more or less exclusively around marriage and children. This group, not all that large, would be typified by the respondent who clearly rejected an employment-based future: 'I don't want to be working for five years or longer, I want to be at home having kids' [INT 083]. Another example would be the young woman, living with her boyfriend and daughter, who quit school because 'I wasn't doing well at it. I thought I just wanted to get married and have kids.' Later in the interview, when discussing her future goals, she observed that 'the thing I want more than anything else out of life is to have a satisfying relationship with a man and to be married and to share my life with somebody' [INT 052]. Yet another example would be the young woman who declared that 'to have kids, that's my major goal, a family'. When asked what kind of job she would like to be doing in five or ten years' time, she replied: 'It doesn't matter as long as Mike is going to support me—he better!' [INT 123].

In contrast, there was a small but distinctive group of women in the sample who were wary of traditional 'female' roles. Some were hostile to the idea of marriage (but not necessarily parenthood):

> I don't believe in marriage, just shacking up. . . . I'm definitely never going to get married, it's too much of a hassle [INT 068].

Personal experiences—growing up in an unhappy family environment, watching parents' marriages fall apart—might have led to some of the critical assessments of marriage and/or parenthood. But other female respondents in this group were simply less sure as to whether they wanted to make men and children the focus of their lives. For example, a young woman who hoped to earn her living as a musician ('something with a little creative freedom') replied, when asked about the possibility of having children:

> I've thought about it but it's not something that I've put a lot of thought into. It's not something that I have a good opinion of in my life [INT 082].

In between the two opposing groups, the 'traditionalists' and the 'rejectors', were the majority of female respondents who hoped to balance employment and domestic goals. For some, this involved adopting the same strategy as most of the male sample members. They simply imposed a moratorium on marriage and parenthood plans until some future time when they would feel more established in a career of some sort ('Some day. . . . not right now' [INT 037]). Others, giving a little bit of thought to the question about marriage and parenthood, and to the potential future conflict between domestic and career goals, proposed the traditional female solution of part-time employment (Duffy and Pupo, 1992).

In Chapter 5 we observed that, compared with those aged 20 and older, younger sample members tended to evaluate their jobs more positively. We speculated that older dropouts might be quicker to recognize their labour-market dilemma—adult responsibilities and ambitions juxtaposed with labour-market opportunities perhaps best suited for teenagers. These kinds of contrasts led us to also examine the relationship between age and marriage/parenthood plans.

While we might have expected firmer plans about marriage and family formation among older sample members, we found the opposite. Younger dropouts were more likely to answer 'yes' to both questions, while those somewhat older (20 and over) were somewhat more inclined to answer 'maybe'. However, this pattern of answers was much more evident among the women in the sample. For example, 81 per cent of the women under 20 were in the 'yes' category for future marriage plans (9 per cent said 'maybe'), compared with 59 per cent of those 20 and older (32 per cent said 'maybe'). A similar age difference, although not quite as large, was observed for the question about having children sometime in the future.

We cannot return to these subjects to enquire about possible explanations, but we may speculate that older dropouts, beginning to recognize their precarious labour market situations, might be somewhat more ambivalent about moving into a permanent relationship and starting a family.[4] Alternatively, teenaged dropouts might see marriage and parenthood as marks of a desirable adult status, but without necessarily understanding the responsibilities attached to those roles. The much weaker pattern of age differences in domestic goals among men may simply reflect the fact that they typically move into marriage and parenting roles somewhat later in their twenties.

DISCUSSION

In this chapter we have documented the future employment and domestic aspirations of the young women and men in our sample of dropouts. In one sense, what is most noteworthy about their goals is how ordinary they really were. The majority of our respondents hoped to be financially successful and to enjoy a comfortable standard of living, to eventually obtain a professional, white-collar, or skilled blue-collar job, to get married and start a family. Most of the women aspired to traditionally 'female' types of employment, while the men were more likely to mention the skilled trades or speak wishfully about self-employment. And the women were more likely to speak positively and confidently about domestic possibilities in their future.

We did, of course, also note that the occupational aspirations of these dropouts were not quite as high as those typically expressed by high-school graduates. In addition, when compared with the 'average' Canadian male youth, the young men in this study were more likely to identify skilled blue-collar work as their occupational goal. And, in contrast to what we would expect, older dropouts, particularly women, appeared somewhat more ambivalent than younger ones about whether they would marry and have children some time in the future.

Thus, to an extent, dropouts are different in terms of their future goals. But when we compare these differences with the stereotype of dropouts as marginal, alienated, and disenchanted youth, the members of our sample seem rather ordinary.[5] The label 'high-school dropout' signals a problematic and deviant set of values and behaviours on the part of those so labelled. As we observed in Chapter 7 when discussing alcohol/drug use and criminal activities, there may be some basis for such generalizations (see also Gilbert et al., 1993:45). Even so, there is little that is deviant, or even highly distinctive, about these young people's hopes for the future. What does distinguish dropouts from graduates is their incomplete education, which in turn will significantly reduce the likelihood of reaching their employment and life-style goals.

Returning to a theme we have highlighted several times before, we might ask how dropouts handle the contradiction between their 'normal' goals and their limited labour-market opportunities. It would appear that a continuing commitment to routine goals, to the prescribed means of reaching them (through formal education), and to the dominant achievement ideology of our society (one gets ahead through individual effort) is central to the coping strategy. In short, many of the dropouts we interviewed insisted, to us and to themselves, that their situation was only temporary, that through effort and, perhaps, a return to school they would be able to overcome their labour-market disadvantage. Projecting into the future, they were sure that if they did the right things (go back to school, try harder in the job hunt), they would get the type of job they desired: 'I know what I want and I know what to do to get it' [INT 129; male].

Thus some sample members distanced themselves from their immediate predicament by confidently asserting that they could get a job if they really wanted one. In fact, past voluntary actions in quitting lousy jobs were sometimes recalled and taken as evidence that equivalent initiative might translate into new, and better, jobs in the future. When asked if her feelings about herself had changed after becoming unemployed, one young woman answered: 'I don't think so, 'cause I always knew that I would be going to another job' [INT 090].

The same kind of youthful confidence in the ability of individual effort to overcome all obstacles helped to maintain some high career aspirations. Fairly typical was the young male subject who said he wanted to become an ocean biologist. Asked if he thought it possible to attain this goal, he replied, 'Yeah, if I wanted to, if I made up my mind that's what I wanted to do, I'd go for it and I'd do it' [INT 021]. An unemployed male who wanted to become an artist answered the same question this way: 'If you want something bad enough, you go for it' [INT 057].

As we observed in Chapter 3, a large majority of the sample members continued to place great value on formal education. Their high occupational ambitions co-existed with the desire to complete high school and perhaps acquire further educational qualifications. In fact, promising themselves that they could always return to school helped many of these dropouts to maintain their belief that their current labour-market and related problems were only temporary. These paired hopes, to get more education and to get ahead (in a career and financially), were a recurring theme. One unemployed female respondent, interviewed in December, had decided to return to school after Christmas. She admitted that 'now that I'm going back to school, I feel a lot better.' Later in the interview, when asked if there was anything young people could do about high youth unemployment, she replied:

> Well, for one thing, they can get their education. That is a must. You have to have an education before you can get a good job that will make yourself feel good [INT 004].

Another female respondent had been out of school (which she hated) for two years and had been unemployed for more than two months when she was interviewed. She had quit her last job and been fired from the one before it (her only previous job). After breaking up with her boyfriend, she had moved back in with her mother, and the two of them were surviving on social assistance. She was depressed, but also felt hopeful; she had made plans to go back to school:

> I'm sort of in a rut to tell you the truth. I'm not really going anywhere. That's why I can hardly wait to get back in school. . . . four months ago I thought I was going to be working in stores for the rest of my life, you know. But it finally dawned on me that I'm young enough to go back to school [INT 034].

High aspirations can be knocked down by labour-market failures, and we have seen some evidence of this process in the present study. However, maintaining a strong belief in the value of education and promising oneself that a return to school will solve one's problems are means of coping with a marginal place in the labour market. Similarly, a strong belief in the importance of personal initiatives, in the individualistic ethic of our society, can reduce feelings of hopelessness. And as we argued in an earlier chapter, the strength of this ethic of individualism also reduces the likelihood that dropouts will develop a political interpretation of their marginal status within the labour market.

But beliefs, aspirations, and values seldom translate into real jobs. What separated most of these dropouts from the jobs, careers, incomes, and life-styles they told us they desired was their lack of a high-school diploma (and additional educational qualifications) and, to some extent, the history of personal, family, and school difficulties that had led to their dropping out. Virtually all of our respondents recognized their educational handicap, and most of them stated that they would like to return to school sometime. We don't know whether they did, but other studies (e.g., Gilbert et al., 1993) suggest that a minority of dropouts do return to complete high school and so improve their labour-market options. Those who did not return are probably still, ten years later, marginal participants in a difficult labour market.

NOTES

[1]Since interviewers could deviate from the question guide if the conversation took another useful direction, nine of the respondents were not asked this question. An additional six were asked the question about major goals, but did not answer.

[2]It remains possible that lower aspirations might lead to a higher probability of unemployment. See Empson-Warner and Krahn (1992) for an analysis of over-time data showing how experiences of unemployment can lead to reduced occupational aspirations for recent high-school graduates.

[3]Again, the semi-structured interviewing format meant that 16 sample members were

not asked the question. Another five were asked but did not answer.

[4]It is also possible that, because of our sampling strategy targeting labour-market participants (both employed and unemployed), our sample largely omitted older female dropouts who were more sympathetic to traditional female roles and who, as stay-at-home mothers, were not in the labour force.

[5]See Gilbert and Orok (1993) who make a similar argument on the basis of their analysis of data from the 1991 School Leavers Survey.

CHAPTER NINE

Summary, Conclusions, and Policy Implications

Our study of Edmonton high-school dropouts in a difficult labour market is obviously not the first analysis of the experiences, attitudes, and aspirations of early school-leavers. However, there has been relatively little Canadian research in this area, much of the (mainly US) research was conducted prior to the economic restructuring of the 1980s, and little of it focused on the post-school labour-market experiences of dropouts. Consequently, our interviews with a large sample of early school-leavers, together with the literature review that has set the context for our conclusions, offer some useful insights into the contemporary dropout phenomenon in Canada.

We begin this final chapter by briefly summarizing the central findings from our study. We then highlight a number of the more important conclusions to be drawn from these findings, as well as from the previous research on high-school dropouts. The chapter concludes with a general discussion of some of the policy implications of our findings.

A SUMMARY OF OUR FINDINGS

Becoming a dropout

Replicating findings from previous research, the young dropouts in our study mentioned school-related reasons for quitting more often than employment-related or personal reasons. Outright failure in school was typically not the main problem. Instead, for many, boredom, alienation from and rejection by the educational system, and a desire for the adult status offered by the non-school world led to class-skipping, truancy, and, eventually, dropping out. Part-time employment while attending school was typically not a direct causal factor, although young people already distancing themselves from school might use the prospect of a full-time job as a 'reason' for quitting. And, as other studies have shown, personal and family problems (e.g., non-supportive or abusive parents, psychological problems, pregnancy) also led some young people to abandon their education.

However, our study did not reveal a deep-seated antagonism towards schooling. Many of the respondents recognized, in retrospect, that the decision to quit school had been a poor one, particularly for employment reasons, and a majority stated that they would return to finish high school some day.

Looking for work

Roughly half of our respondents were not employed when interviewed, in part because of our sampling strategy. However, this high level of joblessness also reflects the difficult and unstable labour market faced by young dropouts. Although most of the unemployed claimed to be actively seeking work, their job-search methods were typically quite ad hoc and not well-organized. Looking through newspaper ads and going door-to-door enquiring about possible jobs were the most common methods. Quite a number of the currently employed also reported that they had found work in this manner, but a larger proportion noted that contacts (family and friends) had been instrumental in finding the job. Neither group made much use of Canada Employment Centres, and, compared with better-educated job-seekers, dropouts tended to rely on fewer job-search methods.

When commenting on their (frequent) job-search problems, dropouts were most likely to mention their lack of work experience as a significant handicap, along with the absence of a high-school diploma. A considerable number also felt that employers discriminated against young workers. In short, finding a job, particularly a reasonably good one, was difficult because of a lack of educational credentials, limited work experience, youth, ad hoc job-search methods, and a difficult labour market. Nevertheless, most of the unemployed dropouts still expressed a strong commitment to work and remained surprisingly optimistic about their employment prospects.

Coming to terms with marginal work

Previous research has clearly documented the difficult and disadvantaged labour-market position of high-school dropouts. The economic restructuring and recessions of the past decade have simply exacerbated this employment dilemma. Our interviews revealed very unstable work histories—for some a result of personal problems, but for most a reflection of the types of employment available at the bottom end of the secondary labour market. Sample members reported only a limited range of low-pay, low-skill, low-status jobs with few intrinsic rewards and few chances for upward career mobility.

Nevertheless, expressions of job dissatisfaction were not that common among these dropouts. They had come to terms with their marginal work in a number of different ways. Given few intrinsic and extrinsic work rewards, many focused on positive and satisfying social relationships with co-workers (and customers, depending on the job). For quite a number, limited or vaguely-defined occupational and career goals made comparisons with current jobs less problematic. Even though their jobs were near the bottom of the occupational ladder, most respondents could still identify worse jobs or compare their present job to a previous state of unemployment. Some looked forward to a (minor) promotion. And most comforted themselves with the promise that, once they returned to school and completed their education, new employment opportunities would appear.

However, in contrast to the pattern observed in the larger labour force, job satisfaction did not increase with age. Indeed, older dropouts were less positive in their job evaluations, and appeared to be more acutely aware of their limited chances for upward mobility.

Coping with unemployment

Unemployed respondents reported feeling depressed, lonely, and unmotivated somewhat more often than did dropouts with jobs. Although a cross-sectional study such as this cannot determine causality, jobless respondents attributed these feelings to unemployment (the alternative argument would be that depressed and unmotivated young people would have difficulty finding work). Many of these dropouts commented on the financial difficulties they experienced when unemployed, and the negative impacts of joblessness on their relationships with family and friends and on their life-style. Unemployment was clearly an unwelcome and unpleasant alternative to work and a pay cheque.

Nevertheless, comparisons with equivalent samples of high-school and university graduates failed to uncover widespread depression or other negative psychological states among these dropouts. As with their marginal jobs, most appeared able to cope with unemployment. Some could still rely, and did, on financial assistance and social support from family members. Most were still quite young, and so remained optimistic about their future prospects especially if, as they promised themselves, they were to return to school.

Finally, most of these dropouts, whether employed or not, did not blame society for the problem of high youth unemployment (or, by extension, their own labour-market predicament). Rather, they offered individualistic explanations, frequently suggesting that other young people had trouble finding work because they did not try hard enough, did not have the appropriate credentials, or lacked the necessary work experience. Thus, instead of reflecting a rebellious and politicized reaction against society, the work values and explanations of unemployment of these young dropouts appeared rather conventional.

Dropouts and deviance

Even so, the life-styles of these young people were less than conventional in at least one respect. Replicating previous research that has documented a positive relationship between early school-leaving and deviant behaviour, our study revealed that, compared with high-school and university graduates, dropouts reported more criminal activity and illegal substance use. While conclusions about causal direction cannot be drawn from this cross-sectional study, we did observe higher levels of criminal behaviour to be correlated with several measures of difficulty in the labour market, particularly for male dropouts.

According to their own accounts, a shortage of money (as a result of unemployment) was seldom the primary cause of criminal activity. Nor did the psychological strain resulting from the inability to obtain societal goals (material success) via conventional means (a job and pay cheque) typically lead to illegal acts. Instead, multiple causal explanations identifying the impact of boredom, free time, deviant friends, and a quest for excitement were more common.

Looking to the future

When asked about their future goals, the majority of the dropouts in this study reported fairly conventional ambitions: namely, jobs, money, independence, and material success. For the most part, these occupational goals reflected traditional gender-based occupational roles. Although, on average, these occupational goals were not as high as those of high-school graduates (and were somewhat less clearly defined), the dropouts' career ambitions extended a considerable distance above the low-level jobs they currently held (or had held). Quite clearly, additional education would be needed to obtain these goals—but then, as we have seen, most of these dropouts did state that they would return to school sometime.

TEN CONCLUSIONS

While our study has updated the research literature on high-school dropouts, particularly with respect to labour-market experiences after leaving school, the accumulated research literature still offers many important insights. The ten conclusions discussed below are drawn from the review of previous research as well as from our interview data.

1. Dropout rates are lower than past research has suggested, and continue to decline

While media commentators, along with politicians, educators, and others, have frequently asserted, with considerable confidence, that one in three young Canadians drops out of high school prior to graduation, recent research conducted by Statistics Canada suggests that the rate is considerably lower. The current best estimate of the proportion of Canadian youth who do not complete high school is about 20 per cent. Over-time comparisons of census data detailing the educational attainment of Canadians reveal that the dropout rate has been slowly declining for several decades. The unwelcoming labour market faced by young Canadians today is encouraging even more to stay in school in order to obtain marketable educational credentials.

Not all graduates finish high school without interrupting their education. A considerable number drop out and then 'drop back in' to the education system some months, or even years, later. Thus the 1991 School Leavers Survey estimated that about one in four young people drops out of high school at some point. About half of these early leavers re-enter the system, perhaps in a different type of institution, and a significant proportion stay until they obtain their high-school diploma.

2. Dropout rates vary considerably, but social class is a strong predictor
Males, individuals in lower academic streams and doing poorly in school, those reporting themselves less interested in education and more alienated from school, individuals working an excessive number of hours while still attending school, and those with single parents are more likely to drop out prior to graduation. Dropout rates are also higher in rural areas and within aboriginal communities. A number of these characteristics clearly overlap. Furthermore, it is apparent that social class may be an important underlying causal factor. For a variety of interrelated reasons, young people from lower socio-economic backgrounds are more likely to quit school. Since the absence of secondary (and post-secondary) educational credentials is a serious handicap in the labour market, higher dropout rates within disadvantaged groups can lead to the reproduction of patterns of social inequality across generations.

3. Schools matter as well
Although previous research has tended to focus on characteristics of dropouts themselves (e.g., socio-demographic characteristics, attitudes, orientations, and behaviours), an important alternative perspective has been provided by researchers asking how schools might make a difference. It has been demonstrated that the size and organization of schools, the resources available to them, and the social and educational climate fostered within them also influence dropout rates. Thus the roots of the dropout problem must be sought not only in 'problem students' but also in 'problem schools'. And, again, some of these structural factors have a social-class component, since children from wealthier families typically attend 'better' schools with more educational resources.

4. School-related reasons for quitting are mentioned most often by dropouts
The reasons that dropouts themselves provide for their decision to quit school add to our understanding of the phenomenon. School-related reasons are typically mentioned most often. In fact, such reasons may be underestimated, since, when stating other reasons (taking a full-time job, for example), dropouts may be making an implicit comparison with school as a less attractive, important, or satisfying alternative. In some cases, difficulty with school work or problems in getting along with teachers may be key factors, but more often boredom and general alienation from the school culture and the education system lead to the decision to quit.

Employment-related reasons are mentioned somewhat less often. But only a minority of dropouts quit school to take a job because of financial necessity. Instead, young students may be attracted to full-time employment because it represents adult status, money, and freedom, particularly if they feel rejected or frustrated by school. Personal reasons, the third main category, include problems in getting along with family members, emotional difficulties, poor health, and pregnancy. Problems at home, among the most frequently cited personal reasons, can upset or distract students, causing their school work to suffer, their self-esteem to drop, and their interest in school to decline.

5. Dropping out of school is a process, not an event

The accumulated previous research demonstrates that single-factor explanations of the dropout phenomenon are inadequate. It is more useful to consider a longer list of the many interrelated factors at the individual, family, school, community, labour-market, and government-policy levels. And while it is tempting to view dropping out as a single decisive act, it is probably more appropriate to see this act as only one event in a longer process of gradual disengagement from the education system. A 'process' perspective on the dropout phenomenon is more likely to uncover some of its complexities (e.g., the large number of early leavers who 'drop back in' to the education system) and to suggest useful interventions that might lead to higher graduation rates.

6. Dropouts face severe labour-market disadvantages

A number of studies over the past several decades have demonstrated that high-school dropouts earn less than graduates and are more likely to be unemployed. Our study replicates this finding and leads us to conclude that dropouts are even more handicapped in today's rapidly-changing labour market than they were a decade or two ago. Indeed, this is a major reason why dropouts have maintained their problematic status in public debates, despite declining dropout rates. The negative ramifications of early school-leaving are more acute now that they have ever been in the past.

As unemployment rates remain high and part-time work becomes more common, the occupational structure is becoming more polarized. Better-educated young people are competing for a limited number of high-skill, well-paid positions. Those unsuccessful in this competition are bumping high-school graduates from a declining number of middle-level jobs. In turn, competition for the remaining jobs at the bottom of the occupational hierarchy is more intense. High-school dropouts are at the end of the job-seekers' queue. In the past, some dropouts could hope, in time, to move into reasonably well-paying and secure jobs. But such opportunities are rare today. Thus, in our opinion, many of the dropouts we interviewed were destined to continue to work and/or seek work in the lower levels of the secondary labour market.

7. Most dropouts manage to cope with their marginal status

Most of the dropouts we interviewed were managing to cope with their marginal labour market status, with poor jobs and frequent periods of unemployment. They obviously preferred working (and a pay cheque) over unemployment, and they aspired to better jobs, but most were not overcome by unemployment or highly dissatisfied with poor jobs. In part, the support provided by family and friends helped to buffer many of these dropouts from the worst effects of unemployment and underemployment. While, for some, descriptions of interactions with family members suggested less-than-satisfactory relationships, many of these dropouts could still rely on family and friends for social (and, sometimes, financial) support. In fact, more than half still lived at home. Only a small number were truly isolated—those living in shelters, for example—and they did suffer more than the others.

It was not only the social support they received that helped these dropouts to cope. They also employed various psychological strategies to come to terms with their marginal labour-market position. This might involve making comparisons to unemployment when employed in a poor job ('it's better than no job at all') or emphasizing enjoyable social relationships with co-workers when other intrinsic and extrinsic rewards were largely absent. Although many sample members were employed in very low-status jobs, most could quickly identify an even worse job, and most continued to hope for a promotion or some improvement in their employment status, despite evidence that upward mobility was extremely limited for them.

Perhaps the most important coping strategy involved the promise that, someday, they would return to school and get a diploma, the absence of which was standing in way of their labour-market success. Ironically, the same educational system that generated the grievances that led them to quit school was also seen as the future solution to their current employment dilemma. Going back to school would get their lives back on track.

8. Most dropouts remain integrated into the dominant value system

Our interviews highlighted some of the ways in which dropouts differ from high-school graduates, perhaps the most noteworthy being the higher level of criminal activity and drug use among the former. But in some respects dropouts are not all that different from graduates. Granted, they did quit school prior to graduation. But they typically look back at this as a bad decision, remain committed to the value of education, and promise that they will return to school someday. Promises need not be kept, of course, but other research shows that almost half of those who leave school without a diploma attempt to return sometime.

Faced with marginal jobs and/or unemployment, dropouts cope by, among other means, clinging to the conventional hope that investments in further education will provide an escape out of the secondary labour market. While dropouts, as a group, report somewhat lower (and sometimes less clearly defined) occupational goals, their goals still demonstrate a strong commitment to the dominant societal value system. Female and male dropouts differ in their occupational goals, but in very conventional ways. When asked to explain why youth unemployment is high, dropouts tend to espouse the dominant ideological position that individuals are largely responsible for their own labour-market difficulties.

Thus, while the label 'dropout' often conjures up images of highly alienated, disaffected, rebellious youth, our study reveals that most dropouts are much more integrated into the dominant value system than this stereotype would suggest. Like other young people who complete high school, dropouts still believe in the value of eduction, want interesting and well-paying jobs, and would eventually like to get married and start a family. They did drop out, frequently because of negative feelings about their courses, teachers, or other aspects of school life, but they are not totally estranged from school or, for that matter, society as a whole. In fact, they remain strongly committed to the conventional value system.

9. Older dropouts are more realistic about their employment options

Our sample had a much wider age distribution than many other studies of dropouts. A number of respondents were still in their mid-teens, having only recently quit school, while a few were in their mid-twenties. These older dropouts tended to view their employment prospects and life-chances in a somewhat more realistic, hence less optimistic, manner. They had come to recognize the potentially long-term negative consequences of their earlier decision to quit school. In contrast, the teenaged dropouts appeared to be much more optimistic, sometimes naïvely so, about their employment futures. They had left school and whatever it was they disliked about it only recently, and had limited labour-market experience. They were still excited about the 'adult' status and spending money offered by a job—any job—and about the friends and fun that the job offered. Older dropouts, beginning to think about long-term employment security, having their own home and perhaps starting a family, were not nearly as positive when assessing their current jobs and future employment options.

We have already argued that, in many ways, graduates and dropouts share the same basic value system. Both groups recognize the value of higher education, have high occupational aspirations (although dropouts' career goals may not be as clearly defined), and aspire to a comfortable, affluent life-style. But while their value systems may be shared, their life-chances are not equal. Even though the labour market has become much less hospitable for high-school graduates, young people with post-secondary credentials can still expect, with some confidence, that they will find the 'good job' they aspire to, and that their income will eventually rise to the level required by their desired life-style. In contrast, the life-course prospects for dropouts are much bleaker. As they get older, the gap between their aspirations and the reality of their lives does not shrink: it merely becomes more apparent.

10. Dropouts constitute a social problem, not an economic one

We began this study when the 'dropout problem' was attracting a great deal of attention. However, when we look back a bit further we realize that dropouts have been a recurring public concern ever since the 1950s. What has changed with the passage of time is the nature of the problem that dropouts are seen to pose. In the past, they were construed as an educational problem: high dropout rates reflected badly on a publicly funded educational system committed to the ideal of equal opportunity. But over the past decade the 'dropout problem' has increasingly been couched in economic terms, the argument being that a high dropout rate is one indicator of an under-educated and under-skilled workforce, which will handicap Canada's economic performance in the increasingly-competitive global economy. As we acknowledged in Chapter 1, investments in Canada's human resources, whether via 'stay-in-school' initiatives or workplace training programs, are obviously useful. But they are unlikely, by themselves, to transform the Canadian economy. Given currently high levels of unemployment and underemployment, larger cohorts of high-school graduates (i.e., fewer dropouts) would simply encounter the same difficult labour market. Thus other interventions that would encourage investment, research and development, and job creation in expanding, globally-competitive industries are urgently required as well.

Moreover, this economistic view of the 'dropout problem' deflects attention from its social or human dimensions. But even here we need to choose our terms carefully. Dropouts are a serious social problem not because of the threat they allegedly pose to society, but because of the damage they can do to themselves. In particular, we caution against turning early school-leavers into 'folk devils' of the sort that inspire moral panics. For example, high-school dropouts are not a 'law and order' problem. Periodically, episodes of group violence by young people (e.g., the Yonge Street riots of 1992) encourage commentators to explain such anti-social behaviour with reference to the deprivation and resentment of youth encountering labour-market difficulties. However, we have argued that most dropouts lay the blame for high youth unemployment not on society or the government, but on unemployed youth themselves. There is little evidence that dropouts constitute a disadvantaged underclass that is waiting to explode. Rather, they typically share the same value system and goals as high-school graduates. As for the higher levels of deviant behaviour among dropouts, we also noted that much of this involved drug and alcohol use and minor property crime. Granted, these deviant activities are problematic for society as a whole, but in many ways the dropouts themselves are the primary victims, their deviant behaviour simply exacerbating their already marginal position in society. In the past many dropouts were able to find secure, albeit low-skill, jobs in the manufacturing industry, the agricultural sector, and the various service industries. These options are less available to young people leaving school today without qualifications. Hence the personal costs of dropping out are much greater.

It is this marginal labour-market status that constitutes the social problem of high dropout rates. Previous research has documented dropouts' low pay and frequent unemployment. In today's much more competitive and polarized labour market, opportunities for young people without credentials are even more limited, and early school-leavers are severely handicapped.

Furthermore, since children from less-advantaged families are more likely to drop out of school, a high dropout rate also reflects the reproduction, across generations, of patterns of social inequality. Thus, in our opinion, the 'dropout problem' is a serious social problem, a problem of individual disadvantage and class inequality. And if we as a society are serious about reducing disparities of wealth and opportunity, if we want to do something more than merely state this ideal, we need to concentrate on further reducing dropout rates. It is to this final issue that we now briefly turn.

SOME POLICY IMPLICATIONS

Our final few general comments regarding policy implications should not be read as a definitive list of solutions to the 'dropout problem'. They are meant simply to encourage discussion of potentially useful interventions. We recognize that others with more direct experience (e.g., teachers, school administrators, counsellors, social workers) will have equally useful and much more specific recommendations. Their experience, informed by some of our research findings, will, we hope, allow us to address the 'dropout problem' more effectively.

Reducing dropout rates

Young people quit attending school for a variety of reasons, but for the majority school-based reasons play a central role. By the time they drop out, their relations with the education system, and the various actors within it, have deteriorated. While efforts to change potential dropouts' attitudes towards schooling are obviously part of the solution, so too are attempts to change the education system itself. Recognizing the danger of diagnosing problems in others' jurisdiction ('So what are you doing about stopping university students from dropping out?'), we simply point to the research literature (see Chapter 1), stressing the importance of, among other things, (a) a school climate that encourages active participation in learning and positive personal relationships between students and teachers; (b) a curriculum that is flexible enough to provide challenges and rewarding experiences of success for a wide range of students; (c) a curriculum that students see as having relevance to their world; and (d) an administrative structure that reduces rather than constructs barriers for those students at risk of dropping out.

Over the past few years we have been encouraged to see some steps being taken towards these goals. A large-scale national study seeking to uncover some of the factors that encourage 'excellence' in high schools is currently under way. In a number of provinces, attempts to improve school-work transitions have focused on developing better linkages between employers and the work-world, on one hand, and students and school curriculum, on the other. The federal government has publicly stated its commitment to working with the provinces towards 'building better bridges to help young people move from school to the workplace' (Human Resources Development

Canada, 1994b:19). For potential dropouts who reject school as juvenile and (in their view) irrelevant, and look to the labour market as an 'adult' alternative, co-operative education and work-experience programs, school-based apprenticeships, and other programs with similar goals could appear very attractive.

At the same time, we are concerned about some other emerging trends within the educational sphere. As we noted in Chapter 1, negative evaluations of Canada's competitiveness in the global economy have led to strong criticisms of its education system. Some of these criticisms may well be justified, but we worry about an excessive push towards standardized curriculum and standardized testing, about calls to 'return to the basics' while scrapping other (presumably non-essential) courses, and about suggestions that 'streaming' be reintroduced (or extended) in high schools. Renewed emphasis on the 'basics' of reading and writing, and on standardized testing, may solve some problems, but as flexibility within the high-school system is reduced we can expect to see increased frustration on the part of students who don't quite fit the standard mould. Behaviour problems within high schools might increase, as might dropout rates. Similarly, streaming of students into academic and non-academic groups may encourage some of those labelled as less fit for school work to leave school and seek paid work instead.

Some of the negative side-effects of provincial governments' deficit-reduction agendas are also beginning to become apparent. Recently in Alberta, for example, the government decided to stop providing free high-school education to students who were taking longer than normal to complete high school. The goal was to discourage students from prolonging their time in high school by reducing their course-loads, but the policy also has the potential to discourage some students from completing high school.

Encouraging 'dropping back in'

One of the prominent findings in this study was the strong commitment among dropouts to the belief that education was important for labour-market success. A large majority stated that they would return to school some day to obtain the diploma that they recognized was needed to get ahead. The recent nation-wide survey of early school-leavers revealed that almost half of the young people who quit school prior to graduation attempt to return. A sizeable proportion of those who do drop back in eventually obtain their high-school diploma. These patterns of exit from and entry into the education system remind us, then, that dropouts are not nearly as alienated from and resentful of that system as we might expect.

Given these observations, we conclude that policies and programs to encourage dropouts to return to school should be considered at least as important as 'stay in school' initiatives. In fact, one could even argue that 'drop back in' programs might be more efficient; it is probably more difficult to motivate and teach a 16-year-old student who wants to quit school than to teach a newly-motivated (after experiencing a tough labour market) 25-year-old. Leaving that debate for future research, we would emphasize, however, that few dropouts would want to return to the same type of school they earlier rejected. Our subjects were quick to criticize the restrictive, authoritarian, juvenile environment within high schools. Some had returned to school, but typically to institutions in which they were accorded 'adult' status.

Thus alternative educational programs that can attract dropouts back into the system and keep them there until they graduate remain a high priority. Such programs, in various forms, already exist in some communities, provided by community colleges or co-ordinated by social-service agencies. But more are needed. Here too we are somewhat optimistic, given the emphasis currently being placed on education and training by Human Resources Development Canada (1994a, 1994b). Central to the challenge faced by the federal government in its social-security reform efforts will be the integration of thousands of early school-leavers into the world of decent, paid employment.[1] A first step, for many, will have to be the acquisition of a high-school diploma.

But again, there are disturbing counter-trends. For example, in 1994, as part of its deficit-reduction program, the Alberta government stopped providing social assistance to 16- and 17-year-olds. Prior to the implementation of this policy, some Edmonton dropouts were living on social assistance while attending alternative schools for high-school up-grading. Deprived of social assistance, they were instructed to apply for student loans, which, unfortunately, were restricted to regular educational programs—the kind they had left some time earlier.[2]

The provision of alternative education programs that might attract large numbers of dropouts back into the system will, no doubt, be an expensive proposition. Policy-makers at all levels of government today face extremely difficult choices between spending reduction and program provision. They may be tempted to eliminate or scale back support for 'drop back in' programs. Having concluded that the dropout problem is a serious social problem, and that bringing dropouts back into the system should be a high policy priority, we believe that spending cuts in this area would be misguided and, in the long term, socially costly.

Attacking the social roots of the dropout problem

Like other social problems, the 'dropout problem' does not exist within a social vacuum. Specifically, the research literature clearly shows that children from disadvantaged families and communities are more likely than others to quit school prior to graduation. In Canada, the extremely high dropout rates in aboriginal communities are the most obvious indicator of this statistical regularity. In the United States, higher dropout rates within the Black and Hispanic populations have the same social-class underpinning.

Stated starkly, the children of the poor are more likely to become dropouts. And, given the limited employment options that dropouts can expect in today's difficult and polarized labour market, there is a high probability that their children too will enter the education system with a handicap. In short, as we have argued at various points in this book, the 'dropout problem' is not just a matter of a poorly-performing education system, but a problem of reproduction of social inequality.

If we accept this argument, efforts aimed at reducing social inequality must be part of the public-policy response to the dropout problem. Children growing up in poverty face a severe deficit of opportunities in comparison with middle-class children. Programs that attempt to deal with this deficit (e.g., 'Head Start' programs, school-lunch programs) are part of the response to the dropout problem, as are efforts to ensure that schools in poor neighbourhoods have the same resources as those in middle-class neighbourhoods.

Finally, if we are willing to recognize the larger problem of poverty in our society as one source of the dropout problem, then efforts to reduce unemployment, to raise minimum wages, and to provide a decent standard of living for as many Canadians as possible are also part of the solution. It is unlikely that the impact on dropout rates of such initiatives would be immediate, but in the long term they might have a powerful impact.

NOTES

[1]In the *Discussion Paper Summary* released in October 1994 by Human Resources Development Canada, the commitment to education and training is clearly stated: 'more Canadians need opportunities for training and education throughout their lives—because continuous learning is key to good jobs and security' (1994b:8). However, beyond the comment that 'In the last three years . . . [j]obs for people who haven't completed high school dropped 19 per cent' (1994b:8), no mention is made of high-school dropouts. This virtual omission may well have no significance, and more detailed documents to follow may integrate concerns about dropouts into the debate about education, training, and social security reform. Alternatively, the omission may signify that in the rapidly changing world of public-policy 'issues', promoting workplace training and lifelong learning has replaced reducing dropout rates as a high priority. This would be unfortunate, in our opinion, since it would shift attention away from one of the most disadvantaged labour-market groups in Canada.

[2]'Dropouts' dreams dashed by social service cuts'. *Edmonton Journal*, 4 July 1994, p. A1.

References

Alberta Advanced Education and Career Development

1993 *The School Leavers Survey: Summary of Alberta Results.* Edmonton: Alberta Advanced Education and Career Development, Labour Market Research and Information Branch.

Alberta Education

1992 *Education in Alberta: Facts and Figures 1991*. Edmonton: Alberta Education.

Alexander, K.L., G. Natriello, and A.M. Pallas

1985 'For whom the school bell tolls: The impact of dropping out on cognitive performance'. *American Sociological Review* 50:409-20.

Anderson, G.M., and L.M. Calzavara

1986 'Networks, education and occupational success'. In K.L.P. Lundy and B. Warme, eds. *Work in the Canadian Context: Continuity Despite Change.* 2nd ed. Toronto: Butterworths.

Anisef, Paul, and Lesley A. Bellamy

1993 'The school leavers survey: What does it tell us about dropping out in Canada?' Paper presented at the conference 'Dropping In/ Dropping Out', University of British Columbia, Vancouver, BC, March 1993.

Bachman, J.G., S. Green, and I.D. Wirtanen

1971 *Youth in Transition III. Dropping Out—Problem or Symptom.* Ann Arbor, MI: Institute for Social Research.

Bachman, J.G., P.M. O'Malley, and J. Johnston

1978 *Youth in Transition VI. Adolescence to Adulthood.* Ann Arbor, MI: Institute for Social Research.

Bell-Rowbotham, B., and C.L. Boydell

1972 'Crime in Canada: A distributional analysis'. In C.L. Boydell et al., eds. *Deviant Behaviour and Societal Reaction.* Toronto: Holt, Rinehart and Winston.

Betcherman, G., K. McMullen, N. Leckie, and C. Caron

1994 *The Canadian Workplace in Transition.* Kingston: IRC Press.

Beynon, H., and R.M. Blackburn

1972 *Perceptions of Work: Variations within a Factory.* Cambridge: Cambridge University Press.

Blackburn, R.M.
1988 'Ideologies of work'. In David Rose, ed. *Social Stratification and Economic Change*. London: Hutchinson.

Blackburn, R.M., and Michael Mann
1979 *The Working Class in the Labour Market*. London: Macmillan.

Bloom, M.
1990 *Reaching for Success: Business and Education Working Together*. First National Conference on Business-Education Partnerships. Conference Report. Ottawa: Conference Board of Canada.

Boothby, Daniel
1993 'Schooling, literacy and the labour market: Towards a "literacy shortage"?' *Canadian Public Policy* 19(1):29-35.

Bourdieu, Pierre
1986 'The forms of capital'. In J.C. Richardson, ed. *Handbook of Theory and Research for the Sociology of Education*. New York: Greenwood Press.

Box, Steven
1987 *Recession, Crime and Punishment*. Basingstoke: Macmillan Education Ltd.

Box, Steven, and Chris Hale
1985 'Unemployment, imprisonment and prison overcrowding'. *Contemporary Crises* 9:209-28.

Braithwaite, J.
1979 *Inequality, Crime and Public Policy*. London: Routledge and Kegan Paul.

Breakwell, Glynis M.
1985 'Young people in and out of work'. In B. Roberts, R. Finnegan, and D. Gallie, eds. *New Approaches to Economic Life*. Manchester: Manchester University Press.
1986 *Coping With Threatened Identities*. London: Methuen.

Brenner, H.
1976 'Time-series analysis: Effects of the economy on criminal behavior and the administration of criminal justice'. In UN Social Defence Research Institute. *Economic Causes and Crime*. Rome: UN Publications no. 15.

British Columbia Royal Commission on Education (Sullivan Commission)
1988 *A Legacy for Learners: The Report of the Royal Commission on Education*. Vancouver: Province of British Columbia.

Bryk, Anthony S., and Yeow Meng Thum
1989 'The effects of high school organization on dropping out'. *American Educational Research Journal* 26: 353-83.

Bureau of the Census
1978 Current Population Reports: Series P-23, No. 66, US Dept. of Commerce. Washington, DC: Government Printing Office.

Burman, Patrick
1988 *Killing Time, Losing Ground: Experiences of Unemployment*. Toronto: Wall and Thompson.

Canadian Labour Market and Productivity Centre
1993 *Canada: Meeting the Challenge of Change*. A Statement by the Economic Restructuring Committee. Ottawa: CLMPC.

Catterall, J.S.
1985 *On the Social Costs of Dropping Out of High School*. Stanford, CA: Stanford Educational Policy Institute, Report 86-SEPI-3.

Chinoy, Ely
1955 *Automobile Workers and the American Dream*. Boston: Beacon Press.

Chubb, John E., and Terry M. Moe
1990 *Politics, Markets, and America's Schools*. Washington, DC: Brookings Institution.

Cicourel, A., and J. Kitsuse
1963 *The Education Decision-Makers*. Chicago: Rand-McNally.

Clemenson, Heather A.
1987 'Job search methods of the unemployed, 1977-1986'. *The Labour Force* (October):85-121 (cat. no. 71-001).

Cohen, Gary L.
1989 'Youth for hire'. *Perspectives on Labour and Income* (Summer): 7-14.

Cohen, Stanley
1972 *Folk Devils and Moral Panics: The Creation of the Mods and Rockers*. London: MacGibbon and Kee.

Conference Board of Canada
1992 *Dropping Out: The Cost to Canada*. Synopsis. Ottawa: Conference Board of Canada.

Corrigan, P.
1979 *Schooling the Smash Street Kids*. London: Macmillan.

Cross, Philip
1993 'The labour market: A year-end review'. *Perspectives on Labour and Income* (Spring supplement).

D'Amico, Ronald
1984 'Does working in high school impair academic progress?' *Sociology of Education* 57:157-64.

Denton, Margaret, and Alfred A. Hunter
1991 'Education and the child'. In R. Barnhorst and L.C. Johnson, eds. *The State of the Child in Ontario*. Toronto: Oxford University Press.

Denton, M.A., C.K. Davis, L. Hayward and A.A. Hunter
1987 *Employment Survey of 1985 Graduates of Ontario Universities: Report of Major Findings*. Toronto: Ontario Ministry of Colleges and Universities.

Duffy, Ann, and Norene Pupo
1992 *Part-Time Paradox: Connecting Gender, Work and Family*. Toronto: McClelland and Stewart.

Dunk, Thomas W.
1991 *It's a Working Man's Town: Male Working-Class Culture in Northwestern Ontario*. Montreal and Kingston: McGill-Queen's University Press.

Economic Council of Canada
1990 *Good Jobs, Bad Jobs: Employment in the Service Economy*. Ottawa: Supply and Services Canada.
1992a *Pulling Together: Productivity, Innovation, and Trade*. Ottawa: Supply and Services Canada.
1992 *A Lot To Learn: Education and Training in Canada*. Ottawa: Supply and Services Canada.

Ekstrom, R.B., M.E. Goertz, J.M. Pollack, and D.A. Rock
1986 'Who drops out of high school and why? Findings from a national study'. *Teachers College Record* 87(3):356-73.

Elliott, D.S.
1966 'Delinquency, school attendance and dropout'. *Social Problems* 13: 307-14.

Elliott, Delbert, and David Huisinga
1989 'Improving self-reported measures of delinquency'. In Malcolm W. Klein, ed., *Cross-National Research in Self-Reported Crime and Delinquency*. Boston: Kluwer Academic Publishers.

Elliott, D.S., and H.L. Voss
1974 *Delinquency and Dropout*. Lexington, MA: D.C. Heath.

Employment and Immigration Canada
1984 *Youth: A New Statistical Perspective on Youth in Canada*. Ottawa: Statistics Canada.
1990 *A National Stay-In-School Initiative*. Ottawa: Minister of Supply and Services.

Empson-Warner, Susan, and Harvey Krahn
1992 'Unemployment and occupational aspirations: A panel study of high school graduates'. *Canadian Review of Sociology and Anthropology* 29(1):38-54.

Environics
1986 *Youth Unemployment and Entry Level Jobs: A Survey of Ontario Employers*. Toronto: Environics Research Group Limited.

Farrington, D.P., B. Gallagher, L. Morley, R.J. St. Ledger, and D.J. West
1986 'Unemployment, school leaving, and crime'. *British Journal of Criminology* 26:335-56.

Feather, Norman T.
1990 *The Psychological Impact of Unemployment*. New York: Springer-Verlag.

Feldstein, R.B., and D.T. Ellwood
1982 'Teenage unemployment: What is the problem?' In R.B. Freeman and D.A. Wise, eds. *The Youth Labor Market*. Chicago: University of Chicago Press.

Fine, M.
1986 'Why urban adolescents drop into and out of public high school'. *Teachers College Record* 87(3):393-409.

Finn, Jeremy D.
1989 'Withdrawing from school'. *Review of Educational Research* 59:117-42.

Flude, Michael
1974 'Socioeconomic accounts of differential educational attainment'. In M. Flude and J. Ahien, eds. *Educability, Schools, and Ideology*. London: Croom Helm.

Furlong, Andy
1989 'Unemployment and labour market withdrawal among 19-year-olds in Scotland'. In A. Furlong, B. Main, and D. Raffe, *Young People's Routes into the Labour Market: Final Report*. Edinburgh: Centre for Educational Sociology, University of Edinburgh.

Furnham, Adrian, and Alan Lewis
1986 *The Economic Mind: The Social Psychology of Economic Behaviour*. Brighton: Wheatsheaf Books.

Gaskell, Jane
1987 'Education and the labour market: The logic of vocationalism'. In T. Wotherspoon, ed. *The Political Economy of Canadian Schooling*. Toronto: Methuen.

Gilbert, Sid
1993 'Labour market outcomes for high school leavers'. *Perspectives on Labour and Income* (Winter): 12-16.

Gilbert, Sid, and Bruce Orok
1993 'School leavers'. *Canadian Social Trends* (Autumn):2-7.

Gilbert, S., L. Barr, W. Clark, M. Blue, and D. Sunter
1993 *Leaving School: Results from a National Survey Comparing School Leavers and High School Graduates 18 to 20 Years of Age*. Ottawa: Minister of Supply and Services.

Grant, W.V.
1976 'Estimates of school dropouts'. *American Education* 12:34.

Greenberger, Ellen, and Laurence Steinberg
1986 *When Teen-agers Work: The Psychological and Social Costs of Adolescent Employment*. New York: Basic.

Gunderson, M., L. Muszynski, and J. Keck
1990 *Women and Labour Market Poverty*. Ottawa: Canadian Advisory Council on the Status of Women.

Hall, Richard H.
  1986 *Dimensions of Work*. Beverley Hills: Sage.

Hamilton, Richard F., and James D. Wright
  1986 *The State of the Masses*. New York: Aldine.

Hammack, F.M.
  1986 'Large school systems' dropout reports: An analysis of definitions, procedures, and findings'. *Teachers College Record* 87(3):324-41.

Hargreaves, D.
  1967 *Social Relations in a Secondary School*. London: Routledge and Kegan Paul.

Harrell, W.A. and T.F. Hartnagel
  1976 *Educational and Vocational Training Programs for Inmates in Alberta Correctional Institutions. Report to Alberta Advanced Education and Manpower*. Edmonton: Department of Sociology, University of Alberta.

Harris, C.C., and R.M. Lee
  1988 'Conceptualizing the place of redundant steelworkers in the class structure'. In David Rose, ed. *Social Stratification and Economic Change*. London: Hutchinson.

Hartnagel, T.F.
  1992 'Correlates of criminal behaviour'. In Rick Linden, ed. *Criminology: A Canadian Perspective*. 2nd ed. Toronto: Harcourt Brace Jovanovich.

Hartnagel, T.F., and H. Krahn
  1989 'High school dropouts, labour market success and criminal behaviour'. *Youth and Society* 20(4):416-44.

Hartnagel, T.F., and J. Tanner
  1982 'Class, schooling and delinquency'. *Canadian Journal of Criminology* 24:155-72.

Hartnagel, T.F., H. Krahn, G.S. Lowe, J. Tanner, and L. Walter
  1986 *Labour Market Experience and Criminal Behaviour Among Canadian Youth: A Longitudinal Study*. Research Report prepared for Solicitor General Canada.

Hayes, John, and Peter Nutman
  1981 *Understanding the Unemployed: The Psychological Effects of Unemployment*. London: Tavistock.

Hirschi, Travis
  1969 *Causes of Delinquency*. Berkeley: University of California Press.

Hogan, D.P., and N.M. Astone
  1986 'The transition to adulthood'. *Annual Review of Sociology* 12:109-30.

Holzer, Harry J
  1988 'Search method use by unemployed youth'. *Journal of Labor Economics* 7(1):1-20.

Horwitz, Allan V.

1984 'The economy and social pathology'. *Annual Review of Sociology* 10:95-119.

Human Resources Development Canada

1994a *Social Security in Canada: Background Facts*. Ottawa: Human Resources Development Canada.

1994b *Agenda: Jobs and Growth. Improving Social Security in Canada. Discussion Paper Summary*. Ottawa: Human Resources Development Canada.

Hutson, S., and R. Jenkins

1989 *Taking the Strain*. Milton Keynes: Open University Press.

Jahoda, Marie

1982 *Employment and Unemployment: A Social Psychological Analysis*. Cambridge: Cambridge University Press.

Jarjoura, G. Roger

1993 'Does dropping out of school enhance delinquent involvement?' *Criminology* 31(2):149-71.

Kalleberg, Arne

1977 'Work values and job rewards: A theory of job satisfaction'. *American Sociological Review* 42:124-43.

Kalleberg, Arne, and Larry J. Griffin

1978 'Positional sources of inequality in job satisfaction'. *Sociology of Work and Occupations* 5:371-401.

Kalleberg, Arne and Karyn A. Loscocco

1983 'Ageing, values and rewards: Explaining age differences in job satisfaction'. *American Sociological Review* 48:78-90.

Kelvin, Peter, and Joanna E. Jarrett

1985 *Unemployment: Its Social Psychological Effects*. Cambridge: Cambridge University Press.

Kirsh, Sharon

1992 *Unemployment: Its Impact on Body and Soul*. Toronto: Canadian Mental Health Association.

Kjos, Diane L.

1988 'Job search activity patterns of successful and unsuccessful job seekers'. *Journal of Employment Counselling* 25 (March):4-6.

Krahn, Harvey

1990 'Quantifying semi-structured interviews'. Edmonton: Population Research Laboratory, Department of Sociology, University of Alberta, Research Discussion Paper no. 73.

1992 *Quality of Work in the Service Sector*. Ottawa: Statistics Canada, General Social Survey Analysis Series no. 6.

Krahn, Harvey J., and Graham S. Lowe

1990 *Young Workers in the Service Economy*. Ottawa: Economic Council of Canada, Working Paper no. 14.

1991 'Transitions to work: Findings from a longitudinal study of high school and university graduates in three Canadian cities'. In D. Ashton and G.S. Lowe, eds. *Making Their Way: Education, Training and the Labour Market in Canada and Britain*. Toronto: University of Toronto Press.

1993 *Work, Industry, and Canadian Society*. 2nd ed. Scarborough, Ont.: Nelson.

Krahn, Harvey, and Julian Tanner

1989 'Bringing them back to school'. *Policy Options* 10(2):23-4.

1995 'Coming to terms with marginal work: Dropouts in a polarized labour market'. In Jane Gaskell and Deirdre Kelly, eds. *Debating Dropouts: New Policy Perspectives*. New York: Teachers College Press.

Krahn, H., T.F. Hartnagel, G.S. Lowe, J. Tanner, and L. Walter

1985 *Youth Employment, Underemployment and Unemployment: A Study of the Transition from School to Work in Edmonton*. Edmonton: Population Research Laboratory, Department of Sociology, University of Alberta.

Lawton, S.B., K.A. Leithwood, E. Batcher, E.L. Donaldson, and R. Stewart

1988 *Student Reiteration and Transition in Ontario High Schools*. Toronto: Ontario Ministry of Education, Student Retention and Transition Series.

LeBlanc, M., E. Vallieres, and P. McDuff

1993 'The prediction of males' adolescent and adult offending from school experience'. *Canadian Journal of Criminology* 35(4):459-78.

LeCompte, M.D., and A.G. Dworkin

1991 *Giving Up On School: Student Dropouts and Teacher Burnouts*. Newbury Park, CA: Corwin Press.

Levin, H.M.

1972 *The Costs to the Nation of Inadequate Education*. Washington, DC: US Government Printing Office, Report to the Select Committee on Equal Educational Opportunity.

Long, S.K. and A.D. Witte

1981 'Current economic trends: Implications for crime and criminal justice'. In K.N. Wright, ed. *Crime and Criminal Justice in a Declining Economy*. Cambridge, MA: Oelgeschlager, Gunn & Hain.

Lowe, Graham S., and Harvey Krahn

1992 'Do part-time jobs improve the labor market chances of high school graduates?' In B.D. Warme, K.L.P. Lundy, and L.A. Lundy, eds. *Working Part-time: Risks and Opportunities*. New York: Praeger.

Lowe, G.S., H. Krahn, and J. Tanner

1988 'Young people's explanations of unemployment'. *Youth and Society* 19(3): 227-49.

McDill, E.L., G. Natriello, and A.M. Pallas

1985 'Raising standards and retaining students: The impact of the reform recommendations on potential dropouts'. *Review of Educational Research* 55:415-33.

1986 'A population at risk: Potential consequences of tougher school standards for student dropouts'. *American Journal of Education* 94:135-81.

Mackenzie, Gavin

1973 *The Aristocracy of Labour*. London: Cambridge University Press.

MacLeod, Jay

1987 *Ain't No Makin' It: Leveled Aspirations in a Low-Income Neighborhood*. London: Tavistock.

Mann, D.

1986 'Can we help dropouts?: Thinking about the undoable'. *Teachers College Record* 87(3):307-23.

Marini, M.M.

1987 'Measuring the process of role change during the transition to adulthood'. *Social Science Research* 16:1-38.

Miller, Joanne

1980 'Individual and occupational determinants of job satisfaction: A focus on gender differences'. *Sociology of Work and Occupations* 7:337-66.

Mills, C. Wright

1959 *The Sociological Imagination*. London: Oxford.

Morgan, W.R.

1984 'The high school dropout in an overeducated society'. In P. Baker, S. Carpenter, J.E. Crowley, R.D. Amico, C. Kim, W. Morgan, and J. Weilgosz, eds. *Pathways to the Future, Vol. 4: A Report on the National Longitudinal Survey of Youth Labor Market Experiences in 1982*. Columbus, OH: Ohio State University, Center for Human Resource Research.

Morissette, R., J. Myles, and G. Picot

1994 'Earnings inequality and the distribution of working time in Canada'. *Canadian Business Economics* (Spring):3-16.

Mottaz, Clifford

1986 'Gender differences in work satisfaction: Work-related rewards and values, and the determinants of work satisfaction'. *Human Relations* 39:359-78.

Myles, John, G. Picot, and T. Wannell

1988 'The changing wage distribution of jobs,1981-86'. Ottawa: Statistics Canada, *The Labour Force* (October):85-138.

National Center on Education and the Economy

1990 *America's Choice: High Skills or Low Wages. Report of the Commission on the Skills of the American Workforce*. Rochester, NY: National Center on Education and the Economy.

Natriello, G., A.M. Pallas, and E.L. McDill
1986 'Taking stock: Renewing our research agenda on the causes and consequences of dropping out'. *Teachers College Record* 87(3):430-40.

New Brunswick Commission on Excellence in Education
1993 *To Live and Learn: The Challenge of Education and Training.* Fredericton: Province of New Brunswick.

Nikiforuk, Andrew
1993 *School's Out: The Catastrophe in Public Education and What We Can Do About It.* Toronto: McFarlane Walter and Ross.

Ontario Premier's Council
1990 *People and Skills in the New Global Economy.* Toronto: Queen's Printer for Ontario.

Polk, K., and W. Schafer, eds
1972 *Schools and Delinquency.* Scarborough, Ont.: Prentice-Hall.

Porter, John, Marion Porter, and Bernard R. Blishen
1982 *Stations and Callings: Making it Through the School System.* Toronto: Methuen.

Porter, Michael E., and Monitor Company
1991 *Canada at the Crossroads: The Reality of a New Competitive Environment.* Prepared for the Business Council on National Issues and the Government of Canada.

Ports, Michelle Harrison
1993 'Trends in job search methods, 1970-92'. *Monthly Labor Review* 116(10):63-6.

Pronovost, L., and M. Leblanc
1980 'Transition statutaire et délinquance'. *Canadian Journal of Criminology* 22:288-97.

Purkey, Stewart C., and Marshall S. Smith
1983 'Effective schools: A review'. *Elementary School Journal* 83:427-52.

Radwanski, George
1987 *Ontario Study of the Relevance of Education, and the Issue of Dropouts.* Toronto: Ontario Ministry of Education.

Raffe, David
1988 'The story so far: Research on education, training and the labour market from the Scottish surveys'. Pp. 40-65 in David Raffe, ed. *Education and the Youth Labour Market: Schooling and Scheming.* London: Falmer.

Rand, Alicia
1987 'Transitional life events and desistance from delinquency and crime'. In M.E. Wolfgang and T.P. Thornberry, eds. *From Boy to Man, From Delinquency to Crime.* Chicago: University of Chicago Press.

Reich, Robert B.
1991 *The Work of Nations: Preparing Ourselves for 21st-Century Capitalism*. New York: Alfred A. Knopf.

Reiter, Ester
1991 *Making Fast Food: From the Frying Pan into the Fryer*. Montreal and Kingston: McGill-Queen's University Press.

Richer, Stephen
1988 'Equality to benefit from schooling'. In Dennis Forcese and Stephen Richer, eds. *Social Issues*. Scarborough: Prentice-Hall.

Rinehart, James
1978 'Contradictions of work-related attitudes and behaviour: An interpretation'. *Canadian Review of Sociology and Anthropology* 15:1-15.

Roberts, Ken
1984 *School Leavers and Their Prospects*. Milton Keynes: Open University Press.

Rosenbaum, James
1976 *Making Inequality*. New York: John Wiley.

Rumberger, Russell W.
1983 'Dropping out of high school: The impact of race, sex, and family background'. *American Educational Research Journal* 20(2):199-220.
1987 'High school dropouts: A review of issues and evidence'. *Review of Educational Research* 57(2):101-21.

Rumberger, R.W., R. Ghatak, G. Poulos, P.L. Ritter, and S.M. Dornbusch
1990 'Family influences on dropout behavior in one California high school'. *Sociology of Education* 63:283-99.

Ryan, William
1976 *Blaming the Victim*. Rev. ed. New York: Vintage.

Samuelson, Leslie
1988 'The Out-of-School Experiences of Dropouts: Labour Market Success and Criminal Behaviour'. Unpublished Ph.D. dissertation, University of Alberta.

Samuelson, L., T.F. Hartnagel, and H. Krahn
1995 'Crime and social control among high school dropouts'. *Journal of Crime and Justice*.

Schafer, W.E., and K. Polk
1967 *Delinquency and Schools*. The President's Commission on Law Enforcement and Administration of Justice, Task Force Report: Juvenile Delinquency and Crime. Washington, DC: Government Printing Office.

Schreiber, D.
1963 'The dropout and the delinquent'. *Phi Delta Kappan* 44:215-21.

Schwartz, G.
1987 *Beyond Conformity and Rebellion: Youth and Authority in America.* Chicago: University of Chicago Press.

Shepelak, Norma
1987 'The role of self-explanations in legitimating inequality'. *American Sociological Review* 52(4):495-503.

Simpson, J.E., and M.D. Van Arsdol, Jr
1967 'Residential history and educational status of delinquents and non-delinquents'. *Social Problems* 15:25-40.

Statistics Canada
1983 *The Labour Force*, December 1983. Ottawa: Statistics Canada (cat. no. 71-001).
1984 *The Labour Force*, December 1984. Ottawa: Statistics Canada (cat. no. 71-001).
1985 *The Labour Force*, December 1985. Ottawa: Statistics Canada (cat. no. 71-001).
1989 Labour Force Annual Averages 1981-1988. Ottawa: Statistics Canada (cat. no. 71-529).
1991 'School Leavers Survey'. Ottawa: Statistics Canada, Education, Culture and Tourism Division (December).
1992 *Education in Canada: A Statistical Review for 1990-91*. Ottawa: Statistics Canada (cat. no. 81-229 annual).
1993 *Educational Attainment and School Attendance*. Ottawa: 1991 Census of Canada (cat. no. 93-328).

Stewart, A., and R.M. Blackburn
1975 'The stability of structured inequality'. *Sociological Review* 23:481-508.

Sunter, Deborah
1992 'Juggling school and work'. *Perspectives on Labour and Income* (Spring):15-21.
1993 'School, work, and dropping out'. *Perspectives on Labour and Income* (Summer):44-52.

Tanner, Julian
1990 'Reluctant rebels: A case study of Edmonton high school dropouts'. *Canadian Review of Sociology and Anthropology* 27(1):74-94.
1993 'Resilient survivors: Work and unemployment among high school dropouts'. *British Journal of Education and Work* 6(1):23-43.

Tanner, J., G.S. Lowe, and H. Krahn
1984 'Youth unemployment and moral panics'. *Perception* 7(5):27-9.

Teachman, Jay D.
1987 'Family background, educational resources, and educational attainment'. *American Sociological Review* 52:548-57.

Thornberry, T.P., and M. Farnworth
1982 'Social correlates of criminal involvement'. *American Sociological Review* 47:505-18.

Thornberry, T.P., M. Moore, and R.L. Christenson
1985 'The effect of dropping out of high school on subsequent criminal behavior'. *Criminology* 23:3-18.

Turner, R.
1960 'Sponsored and contest mobility and the school system'. *American Sociological Review* 25(6):855-67.

Wagenaar, T.C.
1987 'What do we know about dropping out of high school?' *Research in Sociology of Education and Socialization* 7:161-90.

Warr, Peter
1987 *Work, Unemployment, and Mental Health*. Oxford: Clarendon Press.

Wehlage, G.G., and R.A. Rutter
1986 'Dropping out: How much do schools contribute to the problem?' *Teachers College Record* 87(3):374-92.

Weis, Lois
1990 *Working Class Without Work: High School Students in a De-Industrializing Economy*. New York: Routledge.

West, G.
1984 *Young Offenders and the State*. Toronto: Butterworths.

Willis, Paul
1977 *Learning to Labour: How Working Class Kids Get Working Class Jobs*. London: Saxon House.

Wright, K.N.
1981 *Crime and Criminal Justice in a Declining Economy*. Cambridge, MA.: Oelgeschlager, Gunn and Hain.

Yiannis, Gabriel
1988 *Working Lives in Catering*. London: Routledge and Kegan Paul.

Interview Guide

1. REASONS FOR LEAVING SCHOOL/RELEVANCE OF SCHOOL TO WORK

Why did you leave school?

How long ago (when)?
What courses did you take? How were you doing?
How did you decide to quit school?
Any of your friends quit?
Were you skipping?
Do you think graduating would have helped you to get a job?
Would you go back to school?
So, was leaving a good/bad thing?

2. JOB SEARCH STRATEGY/WORK HISTORY

Do you have a job?

IF NO

How long have you been unemployed?

Have you been unemployed in the past? (When and for how long?)

Have you had any job(s) since you quit high school? (What were they? How long did they last?)

Are you looking for a job?

How do/have you look(ed)?

How many jobs do/have you apply(ed) for in a week? What kind(s)?

Any problems in looking for work?

Have you been given any good advice about looking for work?

What would you tell someone looking for a job?

Why do you think some kids have jobs while others don't?

Do you think school has helped you to look for work?

IF YES

What do you do at your job?

What do you like/dislike about your job? (Your work?)

How did you look for this job?

Did you have any problems looking for work?

Have you had other job(s)? What kind(s)? How long did they last?

Have you ever been unemployed? For how long?

Have you been given any good advice about looking for work?

What advice would you give to someone looking for a job?

Why do you think you have a job while some other kids don't?

Do you think school helped you look for a job?

3. LIVING ARRANGEMENTS/FINANCES

Who are you living with?

Are you supporting anyone? (boy/girlfriend, child[ren]?)
What do you live on?
Are you getting by? Are you getting any help; now or in the past? (welfare, UIC, family)
Have you had to cut back on anything? Has this caused any problems?
How would your life change if you had a job/better paying job?

4. STRUCTURE OF THE DAY

How do you spend your time when you're not looking/working?

Who do you spend your time with?
What do you do and where do you go? How much can you afford to spend per week?
How have your activities changed since you: became unemployed? found a job?
Do you belong to any groups/clubs? (sports, hobbies)
What about volunteer or community work?
Why? (reasons for leisure activities)

5. SOCIAL RELATIONSHIPS AND COPING

FAMILY	*FRIENDS (boy/girlfriend)*
How often do you get together?	How often do you get together?
What kinds of things do you do?	What kinds of things do you do?
How do they help you out?	How do they help you out?

Can you tell me how you get along with your family/friends?

When things aren't working out/when you have a real problem, is there someone you can turn to? Who?
Have any of these relationships changed since you: became unemployed? found a job?
How did your family react to your quitting school?
How far did your parents go in school?
What is your mother's/father's job? What do they do at work?
Has anyone in your family ever been unemployed? Who? When? Why? (explaining the circumstances).
Have any of your friends ever been unemployed?

6. EFFECTS OF UNEMPLOYMENT ON WELL- BEING

How have you felt lately . . . physically, mentally . . . ?

(A) How do you feel about yourself?
How do you feel about your life in general?

We would like to know how unemployment has affected you/your health/ feelings.

IF UNEMPLOYED	*IF EMPLOYED*
(B) Now that you're unemployed, how do you feel?	How did you feel when you were unemployed?
Have these feelings changed over time?	How have your feelings changed since you've been employed?

7. PERCEIVED CAUSES OF UNEMPLOYMENT

Why do you think there's so much unemployment among young people?

Whose responsibility is it?
Is there anything young people can do about unemployment? What?
Among young people, who has the best chance of getting a job?
Do you think everybody has a right to a job? Why?

8. GOALS

What are your major goals in life?

What kind of job would you like to have in 5 or 10 years?
How likely is it that you'll be able to get that type of job?
Would you get more education? What kind(s) and how would you go about it?
Think you might want to get married/have a family someday?
Do you think that your goals have changed since you've become unemployed?
Overall, what would you like to do with your life?

Is there anything I may have missed? Would you like to add anything?

9. OPTIONAL:

Would you like to talk about any trouble you might have gotten into with the law?

What sort of things were you doing?
How did you get involved in these things?
How has this changed since you've become unemployed?

Questionnaire

EDMONTON YOUTH EMPLOYMENT AND UNEMPLOYMENT STUDY

Instructions
This questionnaire should take you only a few minutes to finish. Read each question carefully and try to answer all of the questions. If the question is followed by a blank line, put in the answer that is being asked for.

For example: What school were you attending when you left school?
(name of school) ________________________________

If the answers next to a question are followed by a number, circle the number next to the answer you choose.

For example: *How many different schools did you attend?*

One	1
Two	2
Three	3

Do not sign your name on this paper. When you are finished, the interviewer will give you an envelope and you can put this in it and seal it. All of the questionnaires collected from young people being interviewed will be put together, and nobody will know who answered what.

1. *When were you born?* ____________ ____________
(month) (year)

2. *Sex:*

Female	1
Male	2

3. *Right now, do you have a full-time job, a part-time job, or no job at all?*

Full-time job	1
Part-time job	2
No job at all	3

4. *How would you describe your own financial situation?*

I usually have more money than I need	1
I usually have enough money to get by	2
I am usually short of money	3

5. *How would you describe your family's financial situation?*

Poverty level	1
Somewhat below average	2
Average	3
Somewhat above average	4
Wealthy	5

6. *What was the highest grade you finished in school?* ______________
(grade finished)

7. *What program were you in when you left school?*

Vocational/Trades and Services	1
Business	2
Academic	3

8. *Do you think you will ever get some more education (high school, Alberta College,* NAIT, *university, etc.)?*

No	1
Maybe	2
Yes	3

Here are a few more questions about how you feel about life in general. For these questions, circle one number for each.

9. *How often in the past few months have you:*	Never	Rarely	Some-times	Often	Almost always
a. felt depressed	1	2	3	4	5
b. felt lonely	1	2	3	4	5
c. felt like doing nothing at all	1	2	3	4	5
d. felt like people were unfriendly	1	2	3	4	5
e. talked less than usual	1	2	3	4	5
f. felt angry	1	2	3	4	5
g. lost your temper	1	2	3	4	5
h. yelled at people	1	2	3	4	5
i. got into fights or arguments	1	2	3	4	5

The next questions are about a part of young people's lives which we know little about—things they might have done which could get them into trouble with the law. Some of these questions may be difficult for you to answer; they may be about things you have told very few people. But if we are going to understand the lives of young people, we need each person to answer as honestly as possible. Remember, we do not want you to sign your name to this questionnaire. If you still feel you cannot answer honestly, we would prefer you leave the question blank.

10. *How many times in the last year have you:*	Number of times
a. been questioned by the police as a suspect about some crime?	______
b. been convicted of some crime (other than traffic violations) in court?	______
c. broken into a building or car?	______
d. taken something from a store without paying for it?	______
e. sold marijuana or other non-prescription drugs?	______
f. used physical force (like twisting an arm or choking) to get money or things from another person?	______
g. attacked someone with a weapon or your fists, injuring them so badly they probably needed a doctor?	______
h. got into a fight with someone just for the hell of it?	______
i. damaged or destroyed, on purpose, property that did not belong to you?	______
j. other than from a store, taken something worth less than $50 which did not belong to you?	______
k. other than from a store, taken something worth more than $50 which did not belong to you?	______

For the next few questions, again circle just one number for each.

11. *How frequently do you:*	Every day	Several times a week	Once a week	Once or twice a month	Less than once a month	Never
a. drink beer, wine or other alcohol?	5	4	3	2	1	0
b. smoke marijuana or hash?	5	4	3	2	1	0
c. use other non-prescription drugs?	5	4	3	2	1	0

The questions in this last set are about your feelings about yourself and about work and school. For each of these twelve questions, we would like to know how much you agree or disagree with it. If you Agree Strongly, circle the number '5', and if you Disagree Strongly, circle the number '1'. If you feel somewhere in between these two points, circle one of the in-between numbers which best describes your feelings.

12. How much do you disagree or agree that:	Strongly disagree				Strongly agree
a. On the whole, I am satisfied with myself	1	2	3	4	5
b. At times, I think that I am no good at all	1	2	3	4	5
c. I feel that I have a number of good qualities	1	2	3	4	5
d. I am able to do things as well as most other people	1	2	3	4	5
e. I certainly feel useless at times	1	2	3	4	5
f. All in all, I am inclined to feel that I am a failure	1	2	3	4	5
g. Overall, I have enjoyed my time in school	1	2	3	4	5
h. I'd rather collect welfare than work at a job I don't like	1	2	3	4	5
i. Most of the classes at school are a waste of time	1	2	3	4	5
j. If I could earn $15 an hour, I would take any job	1	2	3	4	5
k. When unemployment is high, men should get jobs before women do	1	2	3	4	5
l. Many younger people who get welfare are just too lazy to work	1	2	3	4	5

THANK YOU very much for helping us with this study. The interviewer will give you an envelope in which to place this set of questions. Please seal the envelope and give it back to the interviewer.

Index